The Ascent of Man

Eleanor C. Merry

The Ascent of Man

Floris Books

First published in 1944 by Rider & Co
as *I Am: The Ascent of Mankind*
Second edition published in 1963 by
New Knowledge Books, East Grinstead
Third edition published in 2008 by Floris Books
Second printing 2017

FSC
www.fsc.org
MIX
Paper from
responsible sources
FSC® C013604

British Library CIP Data available
ISBN 978-086315-642-7
Printed in Great Britain
by CPI Group (UK) Ltd, Croydon

TO THE FUTURE

"And they that shall be of thee shall build the old waste places; thou shalt raise up the foundations of many generations; and thou shalt be called, The repairer of the breach, The restorer of paths to dwell in." (Isaiah 58:12)

CONTENTS

Part II: Towards Fulfilment

INTRODUCTION

IN this book we have what may be, to some readers, a startling new view of the development of mankind. The author, Eleanor C. Merry, a life-long student of Rudolf Steiner, presents this view in a way that carries conviction.

" In truth, not the lower, but the higher, stands at the starting point of each evolution of time." The development of man displays different laws from those of natural science— and in this book the emphasis is on the word *displays*. Eleanor C. Merry does not ask us blindly to accept the above statement but shows, through many quotations revealing great erudition and wise discrimination, that at the beginning of each new development in the history of mankind there stands a personality of great spiritual stature, embodying a new impulse which gradually informs mankind. Each is portrayed, not as the product but as the originator of a phase of human history.

The aim of earthly life is here shown as the development of man's individuality, his " I am ", involving a dangerously deep descent into the realm of matter, death and evil. In this perilous adventure he is guarded and guided by the great " I AM ", the mighty Sun Spirit Who is known to Christians as the Christ. He it is Who gives men the inner power to grow in such a way that they cease to be children in leading strings to higher powers, and become conscious collaborators in bringing the divine plan for the world to a rich fulfilment in the future.

All this, and much more, is shown in Eleanor C. Merry's masterly survey, which is a challenging and powerful message of hope sent out to a world in which negation and fear are all too prevalent.

This new edition, enriched with many beautiful illustrations under the editorship of John Fletcher, is as satisfying to the eye as the contents of the book to the mind, and should bring not only joy, but an enhanced confidence in life, to a wide circle of readers.

Margaret Bennell.

Hawkwood College
  Stroud, Glos.

AUTHOR'S PREFACE

WITH the exception of the last chapter and part of the first, this book is about the past. Its beginning may seem to the critical reader to be fragmentary. It is as though we were turning over an old portfolio of sketches—scenes of long ago—not at first sight clearly connected. These pictures are not selected at random, but are grand initial letters heading the opening chapters of the story of the Ascent of Mankind, and of his ever-changing consciousness.

The chaotic conditions of our time cause the past to be forgotten, and without the past the human Ego loses a third part of its being. The present cannot stand alone; no future would ever develop its true form if the past is allowed to sink into oblivion.

Yet the future occupies all our attention. Nevertheless, to know what man *has been* can alone reveal what he shall become. The past is greater and more sublime than we imagine because of the greatness of its promise for the future.

I have quoted from the outstanding thinkers of every age, and it is really they, and not I, who have told the story of man's ascent. Hundreds of quotations have been passed in review; and all of them pointed to the " trailing clouds of glory " which form the essence of humanity. Naturally only a very few of them could be included in these pages.

At first I was tempted to call this book " The Story of the Sun ", because that is where it really begins in the thoughts of an ancient and deeply spiritual race. But the Sun, for modern mankind, has become " a scientific little luminary ". What it actually represents—the Light of the World—is forgotten.

The heart, the Sun, and the " I " of man are brothers. " I am " is the fountainhead of this trinity, and its eternal fruit.*

LONDON,
St. John's Day, 1944.

* This book was formerly published under the title " I AM: The Ascent of Mankind."

xi

ACKNOWLEDGMENTS

The Author's thanks and acknowledgments are due to the following authors and publishers for their kind permission to quote passages from the works named below:

To Messrs. Pearn, Pollinger and Higham, London; the Viking Press, New York; Mrs. Frieda Lawrence, and Messrs. W. Heinemann, for the quotation from D. H. Lawrence's *Apocalypse*. To the Oxford University Press for quotations from the *Zend Avesta* (Darmester and Mills), taken from *Yasna* 42 and *Yasht* 22; to the same for Shelley's translation of Homer's *Hymn to the Sun* in their edition of Shelley's works. And also for their permission to quote passages from *The Sacred Books of the East*, edited by F. Max Müller, namely, Vols. XI and XV, the Buddhist *Suttas* and the *Upanishads*.

To Messrs. John Grant, Edinburgh, for extracts from the *Poems of Ossian*. To the Nonesuch Press, and Messrs. C. M. Bowra and Wade-Gery for their translation of the poem from Pindar's *Pythian Odes*. To Messrs. George Allen and Unwin for the stanzas from Professor Gilbert Murray's translation of the *Eumenides* of Aeschylus. To Messrs. J. M. Dent and Sons for quoting from the *Kalevala* (Everyman's edition). To George Routledge and Sons and Messrs. Kegan, Paul, Trench, Trübner and Co. for the long extract from the *Song Celestial* (Bhagavad-Gita), translated from the Sanscrit by Sir Edwin Arnold; and for passages from the *Book of the Dead*, translated by Sir E. Wallis Budge.

To the author, Oliver St. John Gogarty, for his kind permission to quote the whole of the version of the *Lorica of St. Patrick*, as given in his book *I Follow St. Patrick*, published by Messrs. Rich and Cowan (1938).

To the Lutterworth Press (Religious Tract Society), for permission to quote from the *Book of the Cave of Treasures*, translated from the Syriac text of the British Museum MS.

To George Bell and Sons, for the extract from *Julian the Emperor*, by C. W. King. To Mr. J. M. Watkins for the extract from the *Pistis Sophia*, translated and annotated by G. R. S. Mead (1921 ed.).

To Dr. Paul Brunton and the Proprietors of " *Modern Mystic* " for the use of extracts from an article.

To J. A. Hammerton and Fleetway Publications Ltd., London for the use of some illustrations from the book " *Wonders of the Past* ".

To the Rudolf Steiner Nachlassverwaltung for use of the extracts from Rudolf Steiner's books indicated in the Bibliography.

To the Editors of " *Anthroposophical Movement* " for use of the article in the issue dated October 1932.

To the Librairie Académique Perrin, Paris, publishers of Edouard Schuré's " *The Great Initiates* ", Paul M. Allen of St. George Books, New York and Gloria Rasberry (translator) for the use of extracts from M. Schuré's book.

To Sir George Young, translator, and J. M. Dent & Sons, London and New York for the use of an extract from Sophocles' " *Oedipus Tyrannus* ".

To Maria Schindler and New Culture Publications, London for use of a passage from " *Pure Colour* " by Maria Schindler and Eleanor C. Merry.

To Gladys Mayer for use of the article " *A Call to Man* ".

To Francina van Davelaar for the use of the article " Planetary Seals ".

E. C. M.

ABOUT THE AUTHOR

Writer, poet, artist, musician, Anthroposophist with a strong Celtic impulse, and life-long, deep and active interest in esoteric wisdom, Eleanor C. Merry is well known as the author of such books as " The Flaming Door "; " Spiritual Knowledge: Its Reality and Its Shadow "; " The Year and its Festivals "; " Art; its Occult Basis and Healing Value "; " Odrun, the Rune of the Depths " (Play); " Remembered Gods " (Poems); " Easter: The Legends and the Facts "; and translator of " The Dream Song of Olaf Asteson " and " Goethe's Approach to Colour ".

Eleanor C. Merry was born at Eton, Bucks on December 17, 1873. Her father was Herbert Kynaston, D.D., descended in unbroken line from Cadwallon last King of the Britons and first King of Wales, he was a brilliant classical scholar who was Headmaster of Cheltenham College and later became Canon of Durham. Her mother was descended from a Huguenot family who came to England at the time of the massacres and bore the name Cordeaux. She married the son of Dr. Merry, Vice-Chancellor of Oxford University. Her husband died in 1922.

Eleanor Merry's early life was spent in an atmosphere of scholarship and religion, strongly influenced by the historical traditions of Durham Cathedral, probably the most neglected and certainly one of the most beautiful of English cathedrals. The many famous men she met during her youth doubtless contributed something to the spiritual questing which ended in the meeting with Rudolf Steiner (1922). Before her marriage she studied music and art, and hoped to become a professional singer. During student days in Vienna in 1895 she lost all Christian faith, falling under the influence of the intellectual agnostics.

Studies in Spiritualism preceded the discovery of H. P. Blavatsky's " Secret Doctrine ", a work for which Eleanor Merry had the highest admiration. She was introduced to the works of Rudolf Steiner in 1919 and found in his teachings the unity she had been seeking. She organised (with the late D. N. Dunlop) Summer Schools at which Rudolf Steiner gave important lecture courses, and was Secretary for the World Conference on Spiritual Science, London, 1928. Eleanor C. Merry died in 1956.

PART I
THE PREPARATION

CHAPTER I

THE NEW WORLD

RECORDS of the cultural life of mankind reveal, if we are deeply attentive to them, that the epoch marked by the beginning of the Christian era inaugurates something like a general change of consciousness. It is not a mere empty phrase to say that this change is like the end of adolescence, when to be " grown-up " means the advent of a real certainty of being *oneself*. The adult person knows that a future lies before him, and he seeks for the right pathway leading to the goal he has set himself.

Something of this kind has happened to all the civilised world. Man must step out and discover the truth of the existence of the spirit, for himself. On the other hand, he feels that the authority of faith may be set aside if he wishes to do without it. But the strength as well as the weakness of his feeling of " I am ", is determined by the fact that, since he is able to choose, he may turn towards good or towards evil. If he discards faith in the power of what is good, he denies the recognition of his own possible future perfection.

In the ancient story of the building of Solomon's Temple, the architect Hiram sought to preserve from the greed of the three evil companions a golden triangle. This was a symbol pointing to the future development in man of three higher attributes of his being: a liberated mind capable of selfless wisdom, a

3

soul transfigured by love, and a body spiritualised and no longer under the dominion of matter.

But the ascent of man is hard and difficult. He could never reach the discovery of the golden triangle of his higher Self unaided. He needs the help of One who could rebuild the Temple in three days. Three cosmic periods will be needed for the perfecting of these three higher principles.

Such a vast outline of humanity's evolution is still unrealisable and too apocalyptic for the modern mind to accept. Nevertheless, the events of the present time are certainly the forerunners, or perhaps the positive beginning, of a new epoch. In many ways the destruction of the old epoch has been foretold in the past, and characterised as the terrific struggle of the spirit of man against evil. He has to prove his newly acquired manhood. The struggle was to begin towards the end of the nineteenth century when the " coming of age " could be said to be an accomplished fact; to continue, and to reach its height in a time that still lies ahead of us.

Is there any living human being who is not roused to an intenser awareness of the significance of man's responsibility by these present years of world tension ? The very simplest person feels in his heart that what is happening in the world is not an " ordinary " tension between nations; but that the actual powers of Good and Evil are battling with one another for the future of the Earth. . . . The fearful onslaught of the Darkness against the dawning Light of a new consciousness is upon us.

If we can believe that a cosmic plan really underlies the progress of the world, then it is clear that those things may be called evil which, in any given time, work against this plan. There have been many critical

periods in history. But in our time, when every part of
the world is inescapably linked with every other part,
a spiritual crisis must arrive which dwarfs all that has
happened in the past.

At the beginning of the century the world was
already in a state of deep unrest. All serious thinkers
were convinced that great changes of some kind were
imminent; but the true spiritual causes of the changes
were not fully perceived or not perceived at all.

In the very midst of a period that was given over to
the most stubborn materialistic thought, the old way
of life was already being broken to make way for the
new life that was germinating. For thousands of years
this ending of what in the East had been called the
Kali Yuga, or dark age, had been expected to com-
mence precisely at the end of the nineteenth century.
But new life requires new forms for its expression, and
these were lacking.

One need not take exception to the announcement
of dates for great changes in human existence. For
anyone who has made a penetrating study of history
can find that its more weighty, and sometimes most
concealed, events are connected with definite rhythms;
and such dates as the above which appear perhaps
merely vaguely prophetic, are the nuclei, or else the
beginning or ending points, of these rhythms. On the
other hand, arbitrary calculations have often been
made upon incorrect adaptations of an ancient wisdom,
at a time when its esotericism was no longer understood. And these have by no means the same value.

Important changes in man's consciousness give rise
to a dim sense that the " world is coming to an end ".
And they *are* an end of the world in so far as man's
temporary conception of it is concerned, and denote
the beginning of a slow and gradual alteration of all

human and spiritual values for an ensuing period. It is, however, a quite new happening that the entire world should be involved—not only in consciously apprehending but in being shattered by—the imminence of a decisive and tremendous crisis.

The decades before the end of the nineteenth century saw the dawn of all those inventions which have physically linked continent to continent in a single and immediate bond. This was a divinely-guided preparation for the uniting of nations and individuals and races in freedom, equality, and brotherhood. But the opponents of the new era incorporated themselves in man's lust for power; and for their purpose, human individuality—the free and awakened principle of true Manhood—had to be obliterated. What is at stake to-day is the whole future evolution of humanity.

This at least is obvious enough. But what a " change of consciousness " implies is not so easily grasped. If we need a simple illustration—but on a small scale— we need only listen to the testimony of natives of a certain country in Africa—Ghana. These people have kept alive, in a remarkable state of purity and moral responsibility, a primeval reverence for the ancestors of their race. (Naturally, there may be individual exceptions.) Until recently, they still retained that utterly astonishing gift of " ancestral " memory, which was once the common property of all mankind. Their detailed history for at least a thousand years or more was taught them in childhood by word of mouth, and everything was remembered. To read a book once was still, even in our time, quite sufficient for them to remember the whole of it without effort.

With the advent of the British and the establishment of western schools and western methods of study, and note-taking, and " learning by heart ", this almost miraculous memory is now lost. Their art, once pure native art, retaining the elements of an ancient clairvoyance and steeped in the ancestral religion, has become decadent. Their consciousness is changed. Not, in this case, as a slow and natural evolution, but suddenly, and through an interpolation of something from outside.

The more enlightened ones come to the West to seek the solution of this problem in mingling with Ego-conscious people, and their power to progress towards a greater spiritual freedom. But how many of them are disillusioned! They find in the West no spirituality, but a teeming whirlpool of materialism, and a religious profession that to them is utterly insincere.

Whether this violent uprooting of the sentient soul of an older civilisation is ultimately to be accounted good or bad, need not be discussed in this book.

Over wider periods of time startling changes in general human consciousness may be traced. A poetical phrase is well known everywhere which describes the most significant of these as " the twilight of the Gods ". It means man's loss of the capacity to see spiritual beings and spiritual processes at work in all creatures and all Nature; and to lose also the vision of a spiritual world whence man has come at birth and whither he returns at death. The Mystery Schools of remote antiquity were places of Initiation where all these faculties could once be educated and raised to the level of a sublime wisdom. . . . But, as time went on, it was not the Gods who died into a twilight world, but the consciousness of man. Its inner light was darkened and its memory failed. For man had to assume responsibility and receive a new kind of consciousness which was purely earthly. Its inevitable coming was

sealed two thousand years ago by the advent of that
Being who was named in prophecy the " I am ",
because He was able to awaken the dormant Egohood
in mankind within the earthly environment. The
kingdom of Heaven " came down ".

The long twilight of the *Kali Yuga* has now run its
course. The next change is imminent. It consists in a
gradual return of spiritual insight which will reveal
the illusion of any materialistic conception of the
world. And another faculty is also to return, but as a
metamorphosis of its earlier form: the extension of the
powers of memory.

Some new kind of revelation is bound to accompany
the deepening and enlarging of all that lives in the
central point of our consciousness, the Ego. The
Founder of Christianity told His followers that the
Spirit, when It came, " will bring all things to your
remembrance, whatsoever I have said unto you ".
And He was not speaking to His disciples alone, but to
all humanity for all time.

Very slowly, through the ages that are to come, the
veil that covers these mysteries will be lifted. The kind
of remembering that must eventually dawn when the
reality of the Spirit is recognised, will not have the
character of mediumism or be produced in trance, for
it must be rooted in the self-conscious " I ", the
spiritual part of man.

Children who are born in the twentieth century,
especially in the latter half, will be—and already are—
different from those born in the nineteenth. Many
already have a faint remembrance of their former lives
on Earth, or of the spiritual world they have just left.
The idea of reincarnation will thus cease before long
to be regarded as a fantastic theory and will be

recognised as true. Memory will extend far beyond the present life.

Indeed, for many people even now, one or another past century begins to glow with a peculiar interest. Things long taken for granted as objective history waken hitherto unknown depths of feeling; there is a sense that they stand out with a new intensity and reality; one seems to *know* them. Far behind lies the original source of our former lives. Like a river it flows on and reaches our feet where we stand upon its brink to-day. . . . We, too, may have adored the " Golden Person " in the Sun; we, too, may once have shared in the great funeral rites of the Osirified dead; or listened to the sphere-harmonies when we watched the Sun rise behind the heavy shadows of the Druid stones. Some of us may even have seen, in Palestine, Him who was the " Sun wandering upon the Earth ".

The philosopher Lessing thought of reincarnation as the " education of the human race ". At any given time human beings are found at many different stages of development, of different faiths, or of no faith; gifted or not gifted; rich or poor, suffering or blessed with happiness. Nations and even races change, or decay. But the human souls pass on from one to another. The thought of reincarnation as *progress* is a thought for our own time. It is not the same as it was conceived long ago when every incarnation offered a means of ultimate escape or liberation from the trials of earthly lives by the practice of holiness. But it is to be regarded as the means of man's rising higher and higher in his will to consummate the mission of the Earth. What we have left undone, or done imperfectly, is not only our own affair, but involves countless others. So we return again and again till our debts are

paid. Not as " punishment ", but because the Earth
is something that we love eternally, and we have
assumed the responsibility for its further evolution—a
task once belonging to diviner Beings.

In addition to the extension of memory another
faculty will gradually arise—that of insight or clear-
seeing, which will reveal the interweaving of causes
and effects in our own destiny and that of others. To
remember a former life as a mere picture would have
very little importance, and probably very little truth,
but to remember the " why " of it would be the
immediate realisation of what is meant by the word
" I ".

In ordinary life we are Mr. Smith or Mrs. Jones.
This is the *person:* the complex physical body, the
sense of life, the sympathies and antipathies of the soul.
But the " I " is eternal—it is " that which was, and is,
and will be ".

Modern psychology has not this conception of the
Ego, but only grasps the personality, which is
essentially no more than a reflection of the immortal
ray of the Spirit which is the real Self.

The real Self chooses what garment of personality it
shall wear in earthly life in order to fulfil its tasks,
whether pleasant or unpleasant. We have to look into
the depths of our being to find this Ultima Thule of
freedom! It inheres in the free human spirit that
willingly, in its pre-natal life, unites itself with its
fellows and with the destiny of this planet. . . .
" Freedom is the marrow in the bone of bondage."

There is much inconsequent and foolish talk to-day
about former lives on Earth. But if the true memory
of one or more of them really wakes, the experience is
altogether too impressive to treat lightly. Silence falls
upon the soul who really knows. His illumined gaze

is turned to the future when the past is learnt, and the Ascent can then be consciously undertaken.

But this is not a book about reincarnation. It is mentioned here simply because an Ascent of Mankind has no meaning without it. Humanity could have reached a certain stage of evolution with the idea of the " I " remaining only indefinitely realised; but would not have been able to pass that point in history which has made the Ego capable of becoming a *transformer*—an ascending force—the force which can say of itself " I have overcome the world ". Not by escaping from it, but by the will to redeem it from evil. This point in history was the time of the incarnation of Christ.

If we can accept this, then it is clear that the past concerns every single human being, not only as far back as that historical moment, but far behind it. Otherwise there is no means of becoming convinced of the importance of that event by the exercise of ordinary reason alone. Moreover, we need to look not only at what is called orthodox history, but even more at those records of the past which reveal the deeper human impulses: the hidden springs of myth and legend and vision, of aspiration and prophecy and religion, and of all the arts and sciences.

Let us take a look at this twentieth century. We see that what dominates it—not only in wars but in periods of peace—is science and technology. Everything possible is done so that everybody may be educated to adopt a scientific outlook. But one thing in this connection escapes notice. It is this: In every age some particular activity or discovery is brought to birth which is able to give *power* to those who desire to have it, or, on the other hand, is able to bring greater benefit to the world at large through those by whom the acquisition of power is not desired.

An aspect of science, or of a philosophy, or a creed, may arise through some single personality who is entirely innocent of any desire for power. He may invent a formula to express his own discoveries; such as, for example, the Darwinian phrase " the survival of the fittest ". Such a formula may be used for quite other purposes than were ever dreamt of by its creator. This phrase (and the reader will be able to think of others) may be turned in two directions. The one, that all possible efforts should be made to improve the lot of the unfit so that as few as possible may be left behind in their legitimate evolution. The other, that the unfit may be left out of account, or exterminated, and that every effort should be made to produce a super-fitness of the many, who can be exploited for the advantage of the few.

In industry the principle of greater fitness is being applied with humane intentions; but also with the idea of increasing production. On the other hand, the improved conditions are at the same time a tacit acknowledgment that they are an antidote to the general and inevitable " mechanisation " of the workers themselves. All feelings of individuality or personal initiative are in danger of being dulled when scientific formulae are applied to the *human being*. He may lose the capacity to make use of his leisure in any other way than that prescribed for him either by the habits of masses, or by organised arrangements that are planned " scientifically ".

This is the hidden side of the matter. A sphere is entered where " good " and " evil " are deeply entangled with one another and hard to distinguish. For the dulling of the sense of Egohood, the holding back of the unfolding of the human spirit in any way, gives satisfaction to those retrograde elements that can at some future time reveal their mighty power to obliterate freedom. Then the old outgrown group-consciousness would return.

In war-time, life is ruled by the necessity of the moment. But if what is a virtue at such times is later carried over into the general life of mankind, into all their occupations, their homes, their education, their clothing, and everything else, then it becomes evil. It militates against the planned evolution of the human spirit. It may seem a small thing. But small things that do not " fit " are grand opportunities for the adversaries of the good, and may be stretched by them—using the pride and power inherent in human inventiveness—to unimaginable proportions.

The scientific trend, seemingly harmlessly reflected in the popular mind, emphasises—and from a certain standpoint rightly enough—the importance of physical life *to-day;* the importance of the present, and how it may influence the future. And the man in the street, told that this or that has been created by scientists and thoroughly tested in laboratories, puts all his faith in it, as a matter of course. He believes in it as something new for to-day.

Unnoticed, gradually the *past* of the world is beginning to sink into unimportance and oblivion. Men do not know that this creates an abyss; that it lames the world-process—and themselves.

The magic of modern science, while satisfying and enthralling the popular ideas of the moment, is at the same time taking gigantic and sinister strides into the future, and projects a terrible picture of man as he is to become—really a kind of machine-animal—soulless and Ego-less, " scientifically " born, sustained, and destroyed. Some recent publications by well-known scientists make the blood run cold. With such ideas, seriously put forward, science denies its own glorious inception and splendid achievements, and the long history of its heroes and martyrs.

The adversary powers would fain put this ultra-material subhuman science on the throne of religion. In their hands it could bring all humanity into a sphere where there is no immortality save a lengthening of physical life, no virtue save health and prosperity, and no God save gold.

The problem of evil! . . . Since the door is already open to it in our age, it may creep in into the most unexpected places. The remedy against it is to be *awake;* to accept no formula at its face value; to remember that this is the great testing time of the world, and the great opportunity for the rediscovery of the Spirit. Only belief in the spiritual origin and destiny of man can place itself between the exaggerated hopes of premature perfections, and the dark abyss that annihilates the power of the human spirit to choose the balanced good.

Man's being is threefold. He has body, soul, and spirit, and lives his life within a threefold experience of Time, the past, the present, and the future. This experience is to-day extremely limited—so limited that he sees himself only as a " mortal ", exhausting his being between birth and death.

A plant is unthinkable in such terms. We know it begins its life from a seed, but also that the seed is not merely the parent of a particular plant, but more than that: the whole plant is already *there*, invisibly, in the seed, which first was formed in another world—in the world of the blossom and the sunlight. Only because a seed " knows " its vanished past can it reproduce the same kind of life and flower out of itself. . . . Take away from man his past and you destroy the model upon which he has to build his future spirituality. The plant is in any case perfect " after his kind "; but man has only the picture or image of his perfection, and must strive to reach it, through many metamorphoses. He must learn to see the deeper aspects of his past history in order to foresee the future.

Whatever human plans may be made for a new world, sooner or later they will inevitably come up against what is the greatest problem of all time: whether to accept the fact that a new experience of consciousness—though still more or less latent—is here; or to reject it. A discriminating acceptance, or rejection, of anything is not possible at all if the nature of the thing itself is not known. Judgment would then be Laodicean—" neither hot nor cold ", without conviction. And where spiritual crises, as this one is, are met without conviction, it is a sowing of the empty wind, and the whirlwind is its harvest.

CHAPTER II

GENESIS

In the beginning God created the heaven and the earth.
And the earth was without form and void; and darkness was upon the face of the deep.
And the spirit of God moved upon the face of the waters.
And God said: LET THERE BE LIGHT;
And there was Light.

IN the first chapter of Genesis we find the description of how God created the Heavens and the Earth.

But in the second chapter it is said that all this creation—the generations of the Heavens and the Earth, and all the plants, and, as later verses indicate, the animals and man also—had been accomplished " *before it was in the Earth* "; before the Earth had a physical nature, such as is later suggested with the words " dust " and " rain ". Man was not yet physical, but he was there, as an image of God.

What sort of a condition could this have been?

The scientific explanation of the coming into being of our planetary system—a vast rotating nebula which " flung off " the Earth and the other heavenly bodies in the course of incalculable ages—this explanation can never be satisfying to the human mind. Because the human mind will always want to know who caused this vast whirling movement of fiery gases? Who willed the appearances from out of it of shining concentrated orbs of light? Who condensed the fire to air and gas, the air to water, and the water to solid earth—leaving the great lights for Night and Day?

In the Hebrew the word *Elohim* is used, and translated as " God ".

Those who have most deeply studied the complicated meanings of this ancient terminology understand the word *Elohim* as a plurality of Beings, who have different qualities but a single aim to create something —to begin a " movement " tending towards a goal. All this was implied in the single word *Elohim*.

A twofold creative urge lived in these Beings: to " brood " or muse about what they wanted to do (if one can use such human expressions)—and to manifest it outwardly.* If every word of the original Hebrew— a language in which meanings were not simple and limited as in modern languages—could be translated so as to give their whole pictorial content, perhaps many of the difficulties we feel about these first chapters of Genesis might be removed.

Again, " Days " of creation are not our days. For here the particular Hebrew word that is used points to other groups of Beings—not to periods of time—who work *in succession*. A limited time-period is not meant: but further stages of the creative process, carried out by Beings who are described as " days ": because, as one ends its activity, another begins. Nor are they " geological periods ". They are earlier and later Ministers of the Divine Will.

Christian esotericism has always recognised such groups of spiritual Beings; but to-day few people think of any other kind than " Angels ". All the other great names—Archangels, Virtues, Principalities, Powers, Dominions, Thrones, Cherubim, Seraphim— often seem, to modern minds, to create a kind of complicated fog between themselves and their dim conception of God. Where such mediating Beings are

* Steiner (Rudolf): *Genesis*: *Secrets of the Biblical Story of Creation*.

described in other religions, the orthodox Christian—
in spite of the testimony of St. Paul that Christianity
also speaks of them—tends to connect them with
superstition. The totality of all this power and majesty
we can perhaps dare to say issues from Him whose
Nature we try to imagine—but really cannot—and to
name, as " God the Father ".

The Genesis story of creation condenses into a few
sentences the description of a vast divine activity,
capable of so stupendous a deed as the calling into
being of a planetary system—and even of a
Universe. . . .

In the course of this process, that stage was reached
in the creation of our system where the great elemental
mass splits into two kinds—one which becomes the
Sun, and one which has the tendency to condense
towards the condition " earth ".

It is at this point, the creation of Light, that the Book
of Genesis begins its description. Then the inner
musing of the Creators establishes, before the Earth-
globe has hardened and the Moon has withdrawn
from it, the plan of physical existence—" before it
was in the Earth ".

The succession of phases of creations, the destruction
or the displacement of the earlier " generations " of
Gods, and so on, are all features of creation myths.
Four great stages are sometimes indicated, often
suggesting the process of condensation from super-
natural fire to solid matter. As for instance in the
following Indian fragment:

" Then Being, beholding, said: Let me become
great; let me give birth. Then it put forth Radiance.
Then Radiance, beholding, said: Let me become
great; let me give birth. Then it put forth the

Waters. . . . Then the Waters, beholding, said: Let
us become great; let us give birth. They put forth
the world-food. So from the Waters the world-food,
Earth, is born." (From the *Upanishads*.)

A negro myth clothes the story of creation in a
childlike picture of family life; beginning with the
primeval nebula as a huge pumpkin in which the
existence of the " children " is already latent and
concealed: the creation " before it was in the Earth ".
Then all the children come at the same time out of the
pumpkin; there are fifteen of them, all Gods. But still
they are not really manifest; they are the Ideas of the
creation, says a commentator. There has to be a
recapitulation of some kind, when all these God-
creations reappear, or become manifest, not all at
once, but in succession. This is indicated in the weaving of the story. The three most important of the God-
children, coming in the fourth generation, are Sun,
Moon, and Darkness. The latter is earthly matter. . . .
But a splinter from the staff of Darkness blinds one
of the other " heaven-born ". Sun and Moon are
driven out from the company and remain " in
heaven ". Of the rest, the most powerful one, the
representative of mankind, is left alone with Darkness.

The story shows the secret of sequence in the
creation, progressing from the invisible and spiritual
to the visible and physical.

The number of legends, fairy-tales, myths and sagas
in the world is far, far beyond computation. But if one
could for a moment imagine no other kind of history
in existence but these, and no science, but only this
gigantic and amazing tapestry of pictures, in North
and South and East and West, should we still believe
(supposing we could be spectators of it uniquely

equipped with out modern knowledge) that man had come into being on the Earth as a cellular organism devoid of consciousness and spirit? If we did, then all these pictures must be the pure " inventions " of creatures whose gift of understanding and speech was acquired through the mere automatically changing shape of his skull and brain, and nothing more.

Or has man himself created the brain as an instrument of his spirit, slowly perfecting it through the ages under the guidance of diviner creators, having been taught its mysteries " before he was in the Earth " ?

The Proverbs of Solomon have these beautiful words about the origin of man:

" The Lord possessed me in the beginning of his way, before his works of old.
I was set up from everlasting, from the beginning, or ever the earth was.
When there were no depths, I was brought forth; when there were no fountains abounding with water.
Before the mountains were settled, before the hills was I brought forth;
While as yet he had not made the earth, nor the fields, nor the highest part of the dust of the world.
When he prepared the heavens, I was there: when he set a compass upon the face of the depth:
When he established the clouds above: when he strengthened the fountains of the deep:
When he gave to the sea his decree, that the waters should not pass his commandment; when he appointed the fountains of the earth:
Then I was by him, as one brought up with him."

THE LEGEND OF THE BODY OF ADAM

" God formed Adam with His holy hands, in His own Image and Likeness, and when the Angels saw Adam's glorious appearance they were greatly moved by the beauty thereof.

For they saw the image of his face burning with glorious splendour like the orb of the Sun, and the light of his eyes was like the light of the sun, and the image of his body was like unto the sparkling of crystal.

And when he rose at full length and stood upright in the centre of the Earth, he planted his two feet on that spot whereon was set up the Cross of the Redeemer; for Adam was created in Jerusalem."

(From the *Book of the Cave of Treasures*.)

In our time which is so full of doubt about all religious questions it will become increasingly helpful to try and understand quite exactly the basis upon which the old " true " legends were composed. The earliest chroniclers were aware that the traditions with which they were largely concerned were perhaps two-thirds of them the accounts of inner experiences of the soul—of things seen with a certain clairvoyance, and clothed in pictorial and dramatic form—of the people whose lives they were writing. The remainder was history. But in former times these inner experiences were a supreme guide to the interpretation of historical happenings—though very confusing for the modern scholar.

There are several books written by early Christians which are apocryphal books about the Old Testament. And there are also the Apocryphal Gospels. The material of the former has been largely borrowed from ancient Hebrew writings, and they include what are called legends. Although, no doubt, in a great many cases these are distorted and their sources mixed, they are certainly based on hoary traditions that have been handed down for generations and have to do with the kind of experiences mentioned above.

Some of these books were written before the Christian era by professional Jewish scribes who had access to such ancient material. Sir Wallis Budge, in his Introduction to the *Book of the Cave of Treasures* describes these as " historical romances ". One of the oldest is the *Book of Jubilees* or the *Lesser Genesis*. Another is the *Book of Enoch*, better known than some, and considered authoritative up to the first centuries of our era.

Yet another is the *Book of Adam and Eve*, probably written in the sixth century A.D., much of the second part of which reappears in the famous *Book of the Cave of Treasures*,* from which we shall quote. The Cave was the burial place of Adam; and it has much to do with our whole subject.

It may be mentioned here that the Biblical accounts of the duration of the lives of the Patriarchs—many hundreds of years and in some cases nearly a thousand —do not refer to their actual physical age but to the continuation of what is called " ancestral memory ". For many generations it was possible for descendants— whose connection with ancestors was extraordinarily vital by reason of intermarriages within the tribe— really to remember the deeds and thoughts of their forefathers as clearly as if they were their own. The patriarchs " lived " so long as this memory continued —but in their descendants.

The Book of Genesis, as has been already mentioned, begins its description when the Sun separates itself from the composite cosmic mass of Sun-Moon-Earth. Before this event, the already existing spiritual man-kind possessed the light of the Sun *in themselves*. They were truly " Sun-beings ", having as yet no human form. The whole sphere, and they themselves, shone with light. But when the Sun separated it shone from *outside*, and the Moon-Earth, bereft of it, began to condense into a world of turbulent storms and mists and viscous matter.

The Bible indicates that when the creation had advanced to the subsequent separation of the Moon,†

* Translated from the Syriac text by Sir Wallis Budge (Religious Tract Society).

† Genesis, i, 16, "And God made two great lights ", etc.

the biblical Eden arose. In the apocryphal *Book of Adam and Eve* Eden is described as a mountain range, part of which was reserved as " Paradise ". After the Fall, Adam and Eve, when they were expelled from Paradise, are said to have descended on to a lower slope of the mountains of Eden. Here Cain and Abel and their twin sisters—whom they afterwards made their wives—were born.

But above, at the top of the mountain and near to the lost Paradise, Adam had created a " Cave of Treasures ", and placed therein gold and frankincense and myrrh, and consecrated it as a house of prayer. Gold: the residue of once living Sun-rays, now solidified in the Earth; frankincense, made from the viscous gums of ancient lunar plants; and myrrh, the bitter herb offered by the Earth as remembrance and aspiration: they are the symbols of Thought, Feeling and Will. Their preservation within the Cave of Treasures suggests that they were capacities which could not yet be called really human; they were still only *possibilities* for mankind, and still divine.

The volatile spiritual substances of the bodies of Adam and Eve were by now held together and en-closed within " coats of skin "—" softer than the byssus and silk of Kings' raiment ". . . . This shut them off still more from spiritual communion, which was now only possible by an ascent of the mountain to the Cave, so as to draw as near as possible to the Sun-filled consciousness once enjoyed in Paradise.

After the murder of Abel by Cain, the legend (*Book of the Cave of Treasures*) gives us the picture of the division of humanity into the " dwellers of the plains " and the " dwellers on the mountains "; that is, those who are drawn, through the deed of Cain, to the fire of earthly passion and the earthly genius of creation;

and those who are the bearers and preservers of the divine wisdom.

" Adam carried the body of Abel to the Cave of Treasures and buried him therein, and he set by the side of the body a lamp which burned day and night."

The other sons of Adam remained with their father on the mountain slopes. Cain fled down to the plains and founded his race there.

At last Adam died, and at his command was buried by his son Seth with Abel in the Cave of Treasures, and his body was embalmed. Before his death, Adam instructed Seth in the following words:

> . . . " And whosoever shall be left of your genera-
> tions in that day when your going forth from this
> country, which is round about Paradise, shall take
> place, shall carry my body with him, and shall take
> it and deposit it *in the centre of the Earth,* for in that
> place shall redemption be effected for me and for
> all my children." . . .

After this, Seth becomes the ruler of the community of the Mountain, and the purity of his people is maintained. When he dies, he, too, is buried in the Cave of Treasures. And so the succession continues, from father to son, and all regard themselves as the guardians of the body of Adam and his descendants, and as preservers of the memory of Abel. But then there comes a day when the mountain-dwellers are tempted to go down into the land of Cain; and this happens at the end of " the first thousand years ".

With the " second thousand years " the evil conse-
quent upon the descent of some of the children of Seth to the plains reaches terrible proportions. But at the same time, as a heavenly compensation, there rules in

the mountain the holy Enoch. Enoch does not die, but is translated into Heaven. The Bible says of him: " He walked with God, but was not; for God took him." Enoch was the first (according to this account) of the great Initiates—a " Friend of God ". It is said of such that they have so guarded and fostered their spirituality that neither sleep nor death blots out their consciousness. They can " go in and out and find pasture " in the spiritual world—" lay down their life and take it again "; and remain for ever in connection with humanity as its helpers.

In one of the fine works on Primeval History by Emil Bock,* he gives, partly in quotation, the following beautiful account of Enoch:

" Behind the name of Enoch we surmise the existence of a definite individual, a divine-human leader of men, who, either embodied, or as an inspirer, teaching his successors and representatives from the spiritual world, has guided mankind from long ago. Moreover, the wealth of apocryphal traditions and documents concerning him all bear a striking personal note. At the same time there are mingled with these narratives of his personal destiny, imaginative descriptions of universal destiny. Human as well as superhuman events flow together in these pictures.

" Enoch represents a new beginning. Up to the time of his father Yared we are told that Angels used to descend from Heaven to direct the ways of men. Then Enoch, who had lived for a long time in seclusion, devoted to the divine life and intercourse with God, received the call to go about among men

* Emil Bock, *Urgeschichte* (Primeval History), Vol. I, Urachhaus, Stuttgart.

and undertake the task which had formerly been that of the Angels.

. . . " With Enoch begins the mission of the Initiates who guide human progress. The legend, taking its graphic representations from much later times, nevertheless looks back into the most distant past:

" ' The Spirit of God remained over Enoch, and he instructed men in the wisdom of the Lord and showed them His ways. All men too served the Lord every day when Enoch was among them, and they came to him and listened to his words of wisdom. All Kings also, the greatest and the least, with their princes and judges, came to Enoch when they heard of his wisdom, and bowed themselves to the ground before him.'

" After the death of Adam, the sanctuary of the Mysteries recalled Enoch. The people came to know how, even as the Angels had withdrawn, so this initiated man had also gradually to withdraw himself from them. More and more insistently did the decree of the concealed Mysteries call him back. If he had been with the people, teaching them for a single day, then he would be absent from them for three days. The intervals during which he remained secluded grew longer and longer. And each time when he appeared again, the traces of his spiritual life shone like rays of light ever more and more powerfully upon his countenance.

" At first he would appear for one day during the course of a week; then for one day in the month; and at last only for one day in the whole year: ' Till all the Kings and princes and children of men began to yearn to behold the face of Enoch and to hear his words.' But the greater grew the longing to see his face, the less and less were the people able to bear the sight of its ever-increasing radiance. Many died from seeing this light. And at last, as the intervals grew ever longer and longer, men came only to listen, and kept their gaze averted.

" Now he was taken away from them to a still greater degree. An Angel called him to go and be a teacher and guide among the heavenly beings, just as he had been among men. For the last time he speaks mighty words to the people. His legacy to them is a great teaching about peace and its maintenance. . . . ' And it was so, that as the people sat and listened to Enoch as he spoke to them, they lifted up their eyes and saw the figure of a horse coming down from Heaven in a tempest.' Enoch mounted upon its back and rode away.

" The multitude followed him; but every day some of them were left behind, until at last only a very few could continue to follow:

" ' On the seventh day it happened that Enoch went up into Heaven in a storm, carried by horses of fire and a fiery chariot.' The faithful few who still remained were found on the high mountain, dead in the snow." . . .

As time went on, at the beginning of the " third thousand years ", there were none left to rule in the Mountain but Methuselah and Noah and his sons. In the *Book of the Cave of Treasures*, it is told how when Methuselah was dying he called Noah to him and told him that God would send the Flood, and what he would have to do:

" ' Hearken thou Noah, thou blessed of the Lord. I am going forth from this world, like all my

fathers, but thou and thy children shall be saved. . . .
When I die, embalm my body, and bury me in the
Cave of Treasures with my fathers. Take thy wife,
and thy sons, and the wives of thy sons, and get thee
down from this holy mountain. And take with thee
the body of our father Adam, and these three
offerings, gold, and myrrh, and frankincense; and
set the body of Adam in the middle of the Ark, and
lay these offerings upon him. . . .

" ' And when the waters of the Flood have sub-
sided from the face of the Earth . . . command thou
Shem, thy first-born, to take up with him, after thy
death, the body of our father Adam, and to carry it
and deposit it in the middle of the Earth. And let
him establish there a man from among his descendants who shall minister there. And he shall be one
who is set apart all the days of his life. . . . He shall
offer unto God Bread and Wine, for by these
redemption shall be made for Adam and all his
posterity.

" ' And the Angel of God shall go before him, and
he shall show him the place where the middle of the
Earth is situated.' . . . And when Methuselah had
commanded Noah all these things, he died with
tears in his eyes and sorrow in his heart." . . .

When the mourning for Methuselah was over, the
sorrowful procession left the holy mountain. . . .
" Noah carried the body of our father Adam . . . and
his first-born Shem carried the gold, and Ham carried
the myrrh, and Japhet the frankincense, and they went
forth from the Cave of Treasures. . . . And weeping
painfully, and wailing sorrowfully, and enveloped in
gloom, they said:

" ' Remain in peace! O holy Paradise, thou habitation of our
father Adam.

He went forth from thee alive, but stripped of glory and
naked.

And behold, at his death he was deprived of thy nearness.

He and his progeny were cast out into exile in that land of
curses, to pass their days there in pain, and sicknesses,
and in labour, and in weariness, and in trouble.

Remain in peace, O Cave of Treasures!

Remain in peace, O habitation and inheritance of our
Fathers!

Remain in peace, O our Fathers and Patriarchs!

Pray ye for us, O ye who live in the dust, ye friends and
beloved ones of the living God.

Pray ye for the remnant of your posterity which is left.

O ye who have propitiated God, make supplication unto
Him on our behalf in your prayers.

Remain in peace, O Anosh!

Remain in peace, O ye ministers of God, Kainan, and
Mahlalail, and Yared, and Methuselah, and Lamech,
and Enoch! Cry out in sorrow in our behalf.

Remain in peace, O Haven and Asylum of the Angels!

O ye Fathers, cry out in sorrow on our behalf, because ye
will be deprived of our society!

And we will cry out in sorrow, because we are cast out into
a bare land, for our habitation will be with the wild
beasts! ' "

After the Flood, and when the days of Noah were
numbered, he called his eldest son Shem to his side
and told him that after his death he was to go secretly
into the Ark (which had been preserved) and remove
the body of Adam. No one was to know. He was to
take bread and wine with him for the journey, and his
companion and helper was to be the youth Melchisedek . . . " because him hath God chosen from among
all your descendants that he may minister before Him
in respect of the body of our father Adam.

" And take the body and place it in the centre of
the Earth, and make Melchisedek to sit down there.

And the Angel of God shall go before you, and shall show you the way wherein ye shall go, and also the place wherein the body of Adam shall be deposited, which is, indeed, the centre of the Earth. There the four quarters of the Earth embrace each other, for when God made the Earth His power went before it, and the Earth, from its four quarters, ran after it, like the winds and the swift breezes, and there, in the centre of the Earth, His power stood still and was motionless. There shall redemption be made for Adam, and for all his posterity."

So Shem and Melchisedek went by night to the Ark with all secrecy, and carried away Adam's body.

" And when they arrived at Golgotha which is the centre of the Earth, the Angel of the Lord showed Shem the place for the body of Adam, and when Shem had deposited the body of our father Adam upon that place the four quarters of the Earth separated themselves from each other, and the Earth opened itself in the form of a cross, and Shem and Melchisedek deposited the body of Adam therein. And as soon as they had done so the four quarters drew quickly together, and enclosed the body of our father Adam, and the door of the created world was shut fast.

. . . " And Shem said unto Melchisedek: ' Thou shalt be the Priest of the Most High God, because thou alone hath God chosen to minister before Him in this place. And thou shalt sit here continually, and shalt not depart from this place all the days of thy life. . . . And behold the Angel of the Lord shall come down to thee and visit thee continually.' "

Long, long afterwards, about the time when Abraham offered up his son Isaac, it was rumoured that Melchisedek, " King of Salem, and Priest of the Most High God ", had appeared again before men. Twelve Kings, having heard about it, and having seen and spoken to him, decided to build a city for him to live in; and this they did.

Melchisedek called the city *Jerusalem.*

CHAPTER III

THE SUN

WE look at the sun, never able to gaze for more than a second or two at the full splendour of its light, and cannot help wondering what it really is, in its essential nature. Science gives us an overwhelming number of physical facts about it; and for the modern man, science is a kind of religion.

So vast are the dimensions of our Universe, we are told, that if the Sun were to vanish from it the effect in Space would be merely that " a tiny star had ceased its twinkling ". Though its distance from us is ninety-two millions of miles, it assumes enormous importance in our eyes. We are taught that it is a great globe of incandescent gases, in various apparently rotating layers of heat. Dark gulfs appear in it. Huge flames leap from it.

In certain moods one may get the impression from such descriptions that it is a kind of gigantic Moloch, a terrible devouring fiery vortex, compelling obedience from its attendant planets; but submitting itself nevertheless to the intelligent and patient analyses of tiny, fearless human beings.

But if we dare to look at it unflinchingly for a moment, and forget the brilliant researches of science, we have quite another impression, which assails us as a tumult of sound might assail our ears. We seem to see its centre as an endless vista—strangely blue—a gateway into infinity. Blinding whiteness surrounds this centre, and beyond it a sea of golden light streams out in all directions. The Sun fills us with the greatest awe. Something in the very core of our hearts is as though drawn irresistibly into that resounding but silent depth of light, which is pure Spirit.

We turn away and look at the familiar Earth. Everywhere is colour, life, and movement. Our hearts beat, blood courses through our veins, we breathe, have all our senses; we are alive, because of the Sun. And we have too an inner awareness of all this which is like light in the soul; and deeper still, we are able to rejoice that we are *ourselves:* the bright Sun crowns us, and the solid Earth supports us: we can know that our name is " I ". The horizons surround and embrace us, but cannot imprison our imagination. We feel our innermost self as limitless spirit.

The Sun has been adored by human beings for thousands of years. The type and the details of this worship have varied in different ages and in different parts of the world, and we can still trace the development of phases in it which point to three general tendencies. The Sun has been worshipped as the Distributor of Light, Life, and Love. But these three can only be the modes of expression of some primal divine Being. Someone—if one may use the word— must first be there, who is capable of expending this heavenly largesse—someone " behind " the Sun. St. John, in his Gospel, calls Him the *Word*, in whom was Life and Light. That he was also Love is revealed through his deeds in the Flesh.

The most ancient period of which we have definite record and which itself looks back to a still more distant past, even behind the Light, shows that the all-embracing Spirit of the Sun was looked up to as a supreme power which was the same in essence as the spirit living in every human being as his Self, or " I ". Infinite divinity enveloped this radiance—the " being of the being " of the Sun.

A few thousand years later, and under different skies, the Sun-Spirit was worshipped as the Spirit of Light, who was opposed by the Spirit of Darkness. He was not Himself the source of the Light but its receiver and reflector. Behind Him stood the still higher Divinity, the eternal One, the Ever-enduring Being of Time. Light, and the rhythms of time, taught the ancient Persians to till the soil and conquer its darkness.

Later still, in the ancient Egyptian world, the Sun was conceived as the great giver of LIFE to mankind. The Sun-Being had gathered all Life into Himself and poured it out upon the Earth in light, both directly, and reflected from the Moon. Then the Earth became important in human eyes. Heavenly Light and Life inspired men with inner wisdom and outer creative activity. To the Egyptians, the measures of the Earth were an image of the measures of the Heavens. They were the great builders.

In Grecian times, the Sun seemed a little " nearer " still. Then it was all the Sun's physical glory that was admired and loved, although still as something spiritual. The Heaven of the Greek Gods, Olympus, was the whole living Sun-filled ether, a spiritual realm that immediately touched and surrounded the Earth. The beauty and divinity of the human form was deeply experienced. Gods and men drew near to one another on the paths of beauty, and the Sun-Spirit Apollo brought healing and LOVE to man. All love upon Earth was reflected from His Light and Life. The love of Wisdom and Beauty became Philosophy.

Everything that mankind has thought about the Sun in these different ways—here only broadly outlined—has gone hand-in-hand with a corresponding sense of growing independence from divine guidance. As the Sun seemed, in progressive stages, to lose something of its original sublimity in human thought, so the feeling of selfhood with which man's consciousness was imbued became more and more connected with earthly experience and less and less like an inseparable part of the divine existence. It is almost as though humanity, in its evolution, gently draws the Sun down with it into the world of shadows; until at last, with the flowering of Greek civilisation, man found his inner strength in the awakening of a purely earthly intellect, as against the old dream-like visionary inspiration of former ages.

Compared with our life to-day, the spirituality of the ancient civilisations had not the power to make the same kind of moral distinctions that modern man possesses. To be close in consciousness to the spiritual worlds and beings could not—then—bring a clear understanding of moral values, for this can only arise and deepen when the Ego of man awakes inwardly to its human sense of responsibility. The ancient civilisations possessed a vast wisdom; but not intellect, and not compassion.

The vital change, when clairvoyant inspiration should come to an end, was foreseen and lamented by the seers of old. Many of the sacred scriptures have something about them which compels us to sense this descending arc from God-wisdom to Human-wisdom. Myths all over the world embody it in their imagery, often in connection with a darkening of the Sun, the death of the Sun-God, or the " twilight of the Gods "; and at the same time there is the promise of the ultimate dawn of something new, mythologically expressed as the Sun-God's resurrection or rebirth.

It is these intimations which have caused modern thinkers to conclude that the life, death, and resurrection of Christ, having little historical certainty, was nothing more than a repetition of this " solar myth " in another form. But it is more reasonable—and true —to see in the story of Christ's life the actual final fulfilment of something that had for ages been present as a kind of prophetic vision in the Mystery Temples of all religions.

It is hard for us to imagine how great must have been the gloom that slowly spread itself over the profound pagan knowledge of Nature when the old Gods and their Sun-like glory sank at last temporarily out of sight. Intercourse with them became dim and full of error. Nature appeared bereft of spirituality.

Nevertheless, the " solar myth "—the death and resurrection of the Sun-God—is a true image of the history of the evolution of man.

Our conception of the human Ego is to-day a very limited one. It is supposed to represent the living, co-ordinated, self-conscious *person*. But it is more than that. This spiritual and immortal part of man is indeed a " Sun-Being ", and long ago was recognised as such. This state of consciousness slowly changed, and men felt the " Sun-Being " " died " from the spiritual world, and the earthly world—the body— became its tomb.

In other words, the physical senses alone became the means whereby man gained his knowledge, and they acted as a veil between him and God.

In so far as the greater part of mankind was concerned this gradual change of consciousness was practically complete about the time of the incarnation of Christ.

The two events—the loss and the gain—belong together. Both are real, and not mythological. The Ego in man had become the " prodigal son " and must sooner or later return to the Father through the rejuvenating force of the actual Son of God—*the* Sun-Being who had come down to Earth. St. Paul expresses the truth about the intervening centuries that lie between the " twilight of the Gods " and the future full awakening of man, when he says: " Now we see through a glass darkly, but then face to face."

In the twentieth century intellectual achievements have reached the threshold of something new. The moment of the beginning of the ascent has arrived. It entails a vast struggle to disentangle the clinging hindrances and prejudices which centuries of material-ism have entwined into human thoughts. And here the adversary powers find their greatest opportunities.

Knowledge of Nature's secrets was possible in the past because man had not yet severed himself from her elemental powers or from the dominance of the tribal inherited blood; and through these two vital bonds, Nature could serve him according to his needs. Only with the fifteenth century could knowledge of Nature be gained directly through ordinary earthly intelligence, but then it arose in material form, and gradually assumed the appearance of being en-lightened through the advance of physical natural science. But science throws its light only upon matter. What is spiritual, the real source of the material creation, has become almost entirely obscured.

In order to observe Nature's *material* manifestations in the modern sense, it was necessary to separate ourselves from her, in coolness and detachment of thought. In doing so we established our human personality as " outside " her. This, of course, was progress, viewed from a certain aspect. But it has involved mankind in the many problems which must arise through this process of isolation. We have travelled a long way from that primeval oriental avowal: " *I am That.*" " That thou art " —an avowal of identity with the Divinity and with the Sun. Human thought to-day reveals how deeply it can descend. But the impulse in its descent was surely generated by a Power great enough to urge it at last heavenwards again. If not, there remains only the sunless abyss.

The more one studies the ancient writings and traditions the clearer it becomes that a kind of universal clairvoyance once existed in mankind. It was not fancy or superstition that peopled the glens and woods with fauns and dryads; not fancy that overcame the mind when the Priests in their Temples saw the " Shining Ones " and read in the smoke of the altar, or heard in the rhythms of the ether, the word of their heavenly instructors. It was a last remnant of a living connection with spiritual worlds.

In the Bible, the Old Testament is full of examples of how man was guided by his dreams and visions and intercourse with higher Beings.

But what has been lost in the course of ages can never be regained as it was. The old clairvoyance characterised a particular stage in human evolution and caused man, in a certain sense, to be unfree. The task of modern humanity is to develop a spiritual *insight* into the world, by individual and very positive activity, which can produce a new clairvoyance.

This whole sequence of ideas may really be traced in the literature and traditions of millennia. It leads us to perceive that what was once spiritually at home in the Sun has really entered the Earth as a dynamic force, able in the end to transform the nature of the planet. . . . " The Kingdom of heaven has come down. . . ." St. John of Crysostom declares that " we have seen the Sun wandering on the Earth ". He was speaking of Christ. Was it only a figure of speech?

It is entirely inconceivable that, just as man in perfecting his individuality on Earth must rise to a higher stage of being, so the Earth too might some day transcend its planetary nature, casting off its physical dross as another wandering Moon? Impregnated by the living Cosmic Spirit, Christ, could the Earth itself become a Sun? Could it shed its physical density, under which it contracts, and expand itself into radiant and dazzling light? Do there really exist the great ranks of the nine Hierarchies of Spirits, with their divine names and functions, who, together with Mankind and Christ, could bring about such a sublime metamorphosis? Is the Sun really more than Sun, the Moon more than Moon, the Earth more than Earth?

The modern writer D. H. Lawrence tried to suggest something of this in his book *Apocalypse:*

" Don't let us imagine we see the Sun as the old civilisations saw it. All we see is a scientific little luminary, dwindled to a ball of blazing gas. In the centuries before Ezekiel and John, the Sun was still a magnificent reality, men drew forth from him strength and splendour, and gave him back homage and lustre and thanks. But in us the connection is broken, the responsive centres are dead. Our Sun is a quite different thing from the cosmic Sun of the ancients, so much more trivial. We may see what we call the Sun, but we have lost Helios for ever, and the great orb of the Chaldeans still more. We have lost the Cosmos, by coming out of our responsive connections with it, and this is our chief tragedy. What is our petty little love of nature— Nature!— compared to the ancient magnificent living with the Cosmos and being honoured by the Cosmos! . . .

". . . We and the Cosmos are one. The Cosmos is a vast living body, of which we are still part. The Sun is a great heart whose tremors run through our smallest veins. The Moon is a great gleaming nerve-centre from which we quiver for ever. Who knows the power that Saturn has over us, or Venus? But it is a vital power, rippling exquisitely through us *all the time*. And if we deny Aldebaran, Aldebaran will pierce us with infinite dagger-thrusts. He who is not with me is against me!—that is a cosmic law. . . .

" Now all this is *literally* true, as men knew in the great past, and as they will know again. . . ,

" We have lost the Cosmos. The Sun strengthens us no more, neither does the Moon. In mystic language, the Moon is black to us, and the Sun is as sackcloth.

" Now we have to get back the Cosmos, and it can't be done by a trick. The great range of responses that have fallen dead in us have to come to life again. It has taken two thousand years to kill them. Who knows how long it will take to bring them to life? . . .

" Start with the Sun, and the rest will slowly, slowly happen." . . .

But all this is only half the problem. What was lost was the link with the divinity in Nature. What was *not* lost, but only transferred from cosmic heights to earthly levels, is the Divinity itself.

Nevertheless it is true that if we go back and " start with the Sun " and then follow man's thoughts about it through the ages, we shall inevitably arrive at last at the place where the Light of the World is now really shining—*in the Earth*.

CHAPTER IV

ANCIENT INDIA

WE must now pass from the more mystical and mythical to other aspects.

It is well known to-day that the primeval secret doctrine of man's beginning was imparted for thousands of years to those who were admitted into the schools of the Mysteries, where the natural clairvoyant powers became greatly enhanced through the instructions received and the rituals employed. These teachings and the experiences they evoked were handed down by word of mouth before they were ever recorded in writing, and were preserved in secret as the most sublime knowledge that man could receive; a knowledge so great, and yet so self-evident, that to the seers of those remote ages there was no possibility of doubting their truth.

The stages of creation, from the immaterial to the material and visible, were learnt; and the presence of man throughout the creative process as a spiritual being was profoundly realised. He was not the last to be created, but the first—" before the Earth was "—but was the last to appear in physical form.

To-day we speak familiarly enough of the ether and its particles and its motions. But even the ether has become " material " in comparison with that Fire-mist of spiritual ether in which primeval man existed as pure spirit—as particles of Life within the great nebula which became our solar system. Imagine what this means! The Sun itself was one with Moon and Earth and planets! and man was embraced within this totality.

The seers of old understood this well; and sought for the cosmic differentiations which took place in the primal elements, so that the separate components of the system could arise. It was not a mechanical process, but the result of the needs of different divine Beings to adapt Themselves to varying degrees of rapidity or slowness of condensation of the primal elements, suited to Their creative will. For They needed other worlds wherefrom to pour out Their influences.

But all through the æons of time these Beings had but one absorbing interest: to help in the evolution of those points of light and life which were to become Man.

To be able to look back at this was the aim of those evolved human beings who were admitted into the Temple Mysteries, wherever they had been founded in the world.

In the most ancient places of this sublime know-ledge, which were to be found in India many thou-sands of years before Christ, and whose records have descended to us in the scriptures known as the Veda (which means " Word ")—it was desired to reach a vision of that period of creation when Sun, Moon, and Earth were still a unity. The seers beheld many spiritual Beings when plunged in their meditations, and among them was One who was inconceivably exalted, and who belonged to that particular element within this " trinity in unity ", which later became the Sun of our system. And they called this manifested Being *Brahma*.

All that pervaded the Universe as Power they called

by a name which means the Word—Vishvakarman—
who was there " in the Beginning "; and what lived
in man himself, as though it were an " extract " of
the whole, this too was Brahma: man, made in the
image of that unseen Divinity who was greater than
Brahma. To feel union with Brahma was to feel
united with the Sun, which gave Life and Light
through its supreme Outpourer, Vishvakarman. This
was He whom we call Christ.

The pupils of these most ancient Mysteries were
instructed to meditate on the *archetype of the human form.*
For this, they had gradually to find themselves as it
were looking back into the cosmic Fire-mist, and to
learn to picture to themselves what this vast seed-bed
of light-forms was prepared to produce: the same as
that which the Book of Genesis describes as " Man
made in the Image of God ".

They were taught to experience through this, something which a modern writer has described in the
following words:*

" This picture (of the archetypal man) has been
willed by the most exalted spiritual Beings; this
picture is that through which unity among men is to
be achieved. In it, is revealed the meaning of earthly
evolution; in order that it might be realised, the
Sun had to withdraw from the Earth, and later the
Moon also. Thereby it has become possible for
man to become man. In this picture the ultimate
high ideal for the Earth is revealed."

The ideal is the final reunion of man with his
archtype. But he must first learn to be *man*—the
thinker and doer in the physical Earth. It was in order

* Rudolf Steiner, *Egyptian Myths and Mysteries.*

that he might not succumb to the dominion of matter, that the ancient seers kept open the way to inner illumination.

The changes that took place in this primeval conception through the following ages of civilisation will be outlined later. But first we can try to picture to ourselves something of the life and thoughts of the people of the prehistoric East.

In those days the whole world was perceived quite differently from the way in which it is perceived to-day. An inhabitant of India, living perhaps six or eight thousand years before our era, might be standing on his native soil, but would feel that nothing else except just that part of the Earth where he stood had a specific relation to him as a person. His head contained no memories because they lived as it were " outside " him, and he could find them in connection with locality only. Stones, altars, marks of some kind or another were set up where any event had taken place which the people wanted to perpetuate. The event itself, when the place was visited, was recalled in a kind of vision.

To-day we feel that we carry our memories in our heads; these ancient peoples had them in the Earth, which was to them the " head " of the solar system, while the Sun was its " heart ", and their own heart too. Such a man would feel that he carried the Earth itself on his shoulders and that his head was an image of it. And as the Earth is bathed in a Sun-filled atmosphere, so the openings in his head—nose, mouth, ears and eyes—were openings through which the " Fire-air " of the surrounding universe entered into him. All this is suggested in the old Indian writings.

North, South, East, and West, stretching far away

from the small piece of Earth he inhabited, were merged into a spiritual-cosmic world. This was important to him!—that the rest of the Earth, beyond the place on which he stood, stretched away into infinite spiritual regions. Is it any wonder that he spoke of earthly things always as *Maya*—the great illusion?

With his race, a nomadic shepherd race, he could wander; but always so that wherever he was was his own portion, and where he was not was the ALL; and from out of the bounty of this ALL he lived, and knew himself as a part of it. He could say of the universe: " I am THAT."

From this ALL the Life and Light and Heat of the Sun penetrated his heart through his breathing. The way in which he breathed could determine his true or untrue relation to the ALL. The unresting planets poured their movement-power into his limbs; the Moon bestowed upon him the moisture of birth and generation, and upon Nature the rising and falling saps, the dew, the milk of creatures. This was the " Soma-juice " of existence which permeated every living thing. The repeating rhythms that he felt pulsating in the ether entered into the rhythms of his sonorous speech.

He would teach that all beings whose existence lies upon the ocean of Time are one with Brahman, and that Brahman shines in the Sun. But more concealed than Brahman was He who was called Vishvakarman, the dweller in unapproachable Light: the greatest of the sacrificers, for He sacrificed Himself in His creations; divine, yet the representative of all mankind.

Or, turning away from this universal vision, the ancient Indian seer would look within, into himself, and find there his likeness to the Sun:

" The Self, smaller than small, greater than great, is hidden in the heart of the creature. A man who is free from desires and free from grief sees the majesty of the Self by the grace of the Creator.

" Though sitting still, he walks far; though lying down, he goes everywhere. Who, save myself, is able to know that God who rejoices and rejoices not?

" The wise who knows the Self as bodiless within the bodies, as unchanging among changing things, as great and omnipresent, does never grieve." . . .

" He who dwells in the Sun and within the Sun, whom the Sun does not know, whose body the Sun is, and who rules the Sun within—he is thy Self, the ruler within, the immortal."

" In the midst of the Sun stands the Moon, in the midst of the Moon the Fire, in the midst of the Fire, Goodness, in the midst of Goodness, the Eternal. . . .

" And he who abides in the Fire, and he who abides in the heart, and he who abides in the Sun, they are one and the same."

" This manifest Time is the great ocean of creatures. He who is called Savitri (the Sun) dwells in it, from whence the Moon, Stars, Planets, the Year, and the rest is begotten. From them comes all this, and thus, whatever of good or evil is seen in this world comes from them.

" Therefore Brahman is the Self of the Sun, and a man should worship the Sun under the name of Time. Some say the Sun is Brahman, and thus it is said:

" ' The sacrificer, the deity that enjoys the

sacrifice . . . all this is the Lord, the witness that
shines in yonder orb.'

" He was one and infinite; infinite in the East,
infinite in the South, infinite in the West, infinite in
the North, above, below, and everywhere infinite.

" East and the other regions do not exist for him,
nor across, nor below, nor above.

" The highest Self is not to be fixed, he is un-
limited, unborn, not to be reasoned about, not to be
conceived. He is like the ether, and at the destruction of the universe, he alone is awake.

" Thus from that ether he wakes all this world,
which consists of thought only, and by him alone is
all this meditated on, and in him it is dissolved.

" His is that luminous form which shines in the
Sun, and the manifold light in the smokeless fire. . . .

" Thus it is said: ' He who is in the fire, and he
who is in the heart, and he who is in the Sun,
they are one and the same.' He who knows this,
becomes one with the One."

The great stream of Eastern wisdom known as the
Vedanta is a teaching of the purest spiritual monism,
as is shown in some of the passages we have quoted:
the unity between the World-Self and the human self.
But two other streams supplement and complete—in a
certain way—the original Veda. They are known as
the Sankhya philosophy, and Yoga.

This trinity of wisdom is so great that it has flowed
like a deep undercurrent of human thought through
thousands of years, and by its very nature must continue to do so. What rises to the surface from this
three-fold wisdom takes different forms and has
different effects in accordance with the general trend
of human evolution.

As the Veda represents the idea of the profound oneness of man with God and God with man, out of which streams the interwoven unity of all souls with one another; so the Sankhya philosophy follows a contrasting idea: namely, the *differentiation* of all souls and all phenomena within the primal stream of Life. Different qualities or " coverings " clothe, in successive stages, all the souls who begin their evolution immersed in this primal essence. All tends hereby to individualisation—not only within the different human souls but also within all the elements which form the final physical world. Sankhya represents a kind of knowledge of the Laws of Life—a primeval Science.

The third, *Yoga*, is the teaching and discipline whereby every individual soul may find the path back again to its spiritual origin.

The quotations show how the Veda sees Brahman in the Sun. This conception is, however, of an abstract Unitary Being of the All, having innumerable aspects; just as we can imagine the Sun having innumerable qualities affecting all material things. But this Being, Brahman, is also represented as the World-Self—the " I " of the World—unborn, deathless, and unchanging in essence.

These three streams of primeval oriental thought, the Veda, Sankhya, and Yoga, may be compared with the three great root-elements of Christianity: the Word incarnated—the Living " Veda "—the Law of the world (Sankhya), represented through Moses and fulfilled in Christ; and Faith (Yoga), whose representative is St. Paul.

But the vital difference is that the Eastern teaching was something handed on from Master to pupil as an identical teaching for all. This was possible in an age when the individuality-principle had not yet ripened in mankind. The Christian teaching, however, takes into account the individuality—the Ego—which in each human being is different, and desires to be united with all other Egos through the universal spirituality of the world.

Christ says: " I in you, and ye in Me." This is not spoken in the sense of losing personal identity, but in the sense of supreme recognition of the principle of the Ego. This is the great difference between the ancient oriental conception and the conception of the perfected manhood of the future.

Nevertheless, the fundamental union of man with God is not thereby eliminated: the time will come when the Veda will live again, enriched by such vast experiences harvested by man, that he will gather into himself also the essence of that " Golden Person " who shines out of the dark Fatherhood of the world, and will understand the Veda as his own transfigured creative power.

CHAPTER V

ANCIENT PERSIA AND ZARATHUSTRA

ALL groups of peoples or ages of culture had their leaders who were initiated by still earlier leaders into the Mysteries. These were concerned with two main types of instruction: the spiritual was sought on the one hand—as, for instance, in India—by the contemplation of the inner nature of man; and on the other hand, particularly in the more northern countries, it was taught how spiritual laws could be applied in all fields of outer human activity: in healing, in agriculture, and so on. The foundation of all earlier civilisations was drawn directly from concrete spiritual experience.

One can hardly conceive anything more worthy to be called " great " than the life of such an early founder of culture: he would have in his hand so to say the raw stuff of all subsequent history as a seed which he could sow in the Earth.

We look back to a time which may be called the first beginnings of a great Iranian civilisation; and we find there the traditions of a tremendous war which was waged between two groups of peoples for hundreds of years—between the people of Irania and Turania. The Iranians (Persians) had a leader, a great seer, who was called Zarathustra. He, too, knew that mankind had its origin in the world of Spirit. But it was revealed to him that with the Fall of man the whole of Nature, too, had lost something of what the divine Beings had originally bestowed upon it. He believed that man was destined to apply all his energy and his spiritual knowledge to the restoration and healing of Nature; that this task was really a divine task, which could only be carried out if man immersed himself in the physical world to discover therein the spiritual laws that governed it.

Their opponents the Turanians, who lived further to the north, had no such moral feelings. They, too, had the old powers of clairvoyance, but of a degraded kind. They used these powers to help them to violence and rapine, and had no desire to labour for the improvement of the Earth.

Zarathustra, the priestly leader of the Persians— this great, compelling, noble figure, whose personal history is so obscured by innumerable later traditions, lived, as some of the more recent researches have now established, about 6,000 years before Christ. The Greeks placed him as early as 5,000 years before the Trojan war. A later Zarathustra (Zarathas) living some 600 or 700 years before Christ has been confused with the earlier.

The great scriptures which to some extent represent the original teachings of the first Zarathustra are called the Zend-Avesta. They point to the divine Light and " Word " of the Sun as the source of all spiritual wisdom.

The Zend-Avesta itself, as we now have it, is a compilation of the teachings, belonging to various dates; and only a small part of it is supposed to represent the original thoughts of Zarathustra, and even these have been estimated to be not older than perhaps 800 B.C. But a far more liberal view of it should now be taken.

It is now generally accepted that ancient scriptures —that is, what is actually written down and preserved —are invariably the latest evidences of thoughts previously handed down for generations and generations by word of mouth. Teachings may be even thousands of years older than the writings. And what is more, the ancient spoken pronouncements of great thoughts had a force of life and permanence which modern man has entirely lost from his speech. Writing was the first possible compensation for the beginning of the decline of this continuing power of the spoken word, and with it, the decline of memory.

The deeper secrets of the great religious conceptions were taught only to the chosen few within the sanctuaries of the Mysteries, and their betrayal might mean death. Only a modified form of them was made exoteric and was represented in the content of mythologies. Teachings about the Sun were especially sacred and secret.

Though it seems that the earliest part of the Zend-Avesta does not suggest Sun-worship, it by no means follows that this did not exist esoterically. The Light and Darkness which permeate the Zarathustrian teachings spring from it, and the Sun was the most holy thing imaginable to the ancient seers. They had no science to instil into them that the Sun and all the heavenly bodies were purely physical objects. They adored the majesty of their Creators whom they saw with the eyes of the spirit, and who were one with their sublime creations.

To-day, when we see the Sistine Madonna, for instance, we think of Raphael who painted it and marvel at his greatness. And if we were to think of him with sufficient intensity and love we should " see "

him in our mind's eye; and we should not be accused
of fancy or superstition.　Perhaps we might have
read his life or heard of him from others or seen his
portrait.　We know he once lived and that his
pictures are his creations and he lives on in them. . . .

In the days of the Mysteries all such powers of
enduring perception were far stronger than our
present feeble imaginings.　The unsullied blazing glory
of the Sun was not revealed only to physical sight; it
spoke to the heart.　Its rays could be seen penetrating
the Earth and returning to their source.　In this
reciprocal action lived the life and powers of its
divine Servitors; and when their light was over-
powered by the greater Light that sent them forth, this
Light revealed Itself in Sound.

We have forgotten that there is nothing in the world
that is without " speech ".　When we look at Nature—
at mountains and trees and rivers, and even the tiniest
flowers, they all tell us something, and we are able to
name them.　But if we only knew how to listen, as the
ancient founders of the Mysteries did, we too should
hear the " Cosmic Word ".

Zarathustra knew that it lived " behind the Sun "
—the Voice of Ahura-Mazdao. . . . His pupils recognised that he heard it.

So we will try to approach Zarathustra with critical
opinions on the Zend-Avesta left behind. . . . We know
that what has just been said can stand, because it is
all of it conceivable.

The ancient Indians had experienced the material
world as an illusion.　The Persians, under the guidance
of the great Zarathustra, were taught to regard it and
understand it as a reality, although as a reality
permeated by Spirit.　The Spiritual World itself was

Light; the material world offered a resistance to this Light; and the quality of resistance was Darkness.

To-day, we tend to think of Darkness as an absence of Light—a negative conception. But in ancient times it was felt to be a real entity—just as real and positive as Light itself.

Zarathustra called the Spirit of the Sun Ahura-Mazdao, the " great Aura ". His opponent, the Spirit of Darkness, he called Ahriman (or Angra-Mainyu).

The physical world, which if untended by mankind would become more and more a " dark " world, must be loved as the place where Light could be increased and become the redeemer and true brother of Darkness.

Man, as his grand field of work, had three kingdoms below him—the animals, the plants, and the minerals. Animals and plants must be his special care. Each kingdom was ruled over by a great Spiritual Being, and these were the friends of man who would teach him. As the rays of the Sun penetrate the Earth, so man could by his wise labour learn to cultivate the soil with the plough, to domesticate the animals, and to create a social order.

One must not imagine the teaching of Zarathustra as a kind of mystical dualism woven round the opposition of Light and Darkness. These Beings had behind them another and higher one, described by the Greeks long afterwards as a " Living Unity ". Zarathustra called this Being Zervane (or Zeruana) Akarene: " That which lies behind the Light."

If we think of the Sun, we know that in the course of the year—and on a vaster scale also through the

astronomical fact of the precession of the equinoxes—
it carries out an apparent movement or journey
through all the twelve constellations of fixed stars
which are called the Zodiac. These twelve describe an
infinite " line " in the heavens which meets with itself
to form a circle. The Zodiac has been called the cosmic
clock, because by its means, together with the Sun
and planets, Time is calculated.

The totality of the Zodiac is the visible picture of
" That which lies behind the Light ", the measurer
of Time. Zeruana Akarene is for Zarathustra the
divine Cause of enduring Time, the totality of the
Zodiac, the Living Unity.

The creation and sustaining of the world is not the
work of a single Being, but of hierarchies of Beings.
The twelve parts of the Zodiac are servants of Unitary
Time; and in the Zarathustrian religion they are
called the twelve Amshashpands, or Ameshas Pentas.

Of these twelve—according to the position of them
as constellations, either above or below the horizon—
seven are the servants of Light and five the servants of
Darkness. After these, came the Izods, in number
approximately twenty-four to thirty-one; and the
the Ferruhars, or Fravarshis. The two latter groups
are all those ensouling entities that pervade the whole
lesser world and its physical phenomena.

Ormuzd—also called Ahura-Mazdao—is reflected
in man's soul as his striving towards perfection; and
Ahriman, the dark power, as his imperfections. The
other Beings also imprint their influences upon man,
but in a more physical way.

The fiery energy that pervades the words of the
Zend-Avesta is in strong contrast to the contemplative
mood of the ancient Indian sayings. Both look to the
Sun. But with Zarathustra it kindles the will to outer

activity. In that sense one can feel that Ahura-Mazdao is indeed nearer to the Earth and to human existence than the Vishvakarman of the Indian sages.

As one can love a human being either for his spirituality—his real self—or for his qualities of soul, or for his body, so all these were possible in respect of the worship of the Sun.

It we love a human being for what he is as an Ego, we feel that this is expressed through his *words*, for it is out of the heart, the seat of the Ego, that " the mouth speaketh ". Words come from the innermost being of a man, and if this is pure the words that he speaks are filled with light and are creative. If we love him for his soul, we love his *thoughts*, which surround him like a calm ocean, as the " waters of Ahura ". If we love him for his body alone we ally ourselves with what is dark. But if we love him for all three, then his body will be loved as the means whereby he expresses his goodness in *deeds*.

Therefore Zarathustra, loving the Spirit, Soul, and Body of Ahura-Mazdao in the Sun, created his religion on the basis of establishing a threefold perfection in the human being—as " Good words, good thoughts, and good deeds ". All that was *not* this was Darkness, the opposition of Ahriman (Angra-mainyu), and his hosts of evil spirits.

Yet it was not the mission of Zarathustra to found a religion of morals in the sense in which we understand it, but to found a religion of deeds; and primarily of deeds which should spring from the pure desire to cultivate everything that was offered by the Earth: to till the soil, to find the healing plants, and to domesticate the animals. Man was to be a collaborator with the Sun. Purity of deeds could be learned from its pure and fiery Light.

If we compare all this with what has been described of the civilisation of ancient India we get an impression of majestic contrasts. . . . Man can do nothing with any element of which he is not first aware. To be aware of the Earth reveals the means by which it can be cultivated. But to *become aware* of something is a spiritual process. Thus the two great primeval experiences—of Heaven, and of Earth—are a tremendous step forward in the evolution of the world and of man. . . . But they are experiences which are in the beginning by no means common to all. They first arise before the souls of the great seers in the Mysteries; and they have to be taught to the people.

Imaginative pictures form themselves before the mind's eye when we think of these things:

We see the pre-Vedic and the later Indian sages plunged in inward contemplation. They are seated, their legs folded closely under them and the soles of their feet upturned. They have no desire to feel the pull of the earth-gravity upon the soles of their feet. Even in teaching they remain seated. Their sensitive hands detect and follow with delicate gestures the force of their mysterious wavelike rhythmic speech. They listen inwardly to the ripples of the ether.

Heaven is arched above them, and in it is the Sun. The air they breathe is impregnated with a holy fire. They inbreathe this divinity of the Sun, and it becomes themselves. They breathe it out, and on the outgoing breath unite themselves with the Universe.

Around them is a Nature marvellous in its tropical splendour; but it is only an image, a mirage, of the Spirit. Their peoples devote themselves to a wandering pastoral existence, and eat the fruits of Nature and drink the milk of their flocks and herds. For them the

Moon is the prolific generator of the fruitful seeds and the fertiliser of their animals.

Much sharper contours delineate the Zarathustrian age. Nature is not so full of dreams. Seasons are here more appreciable; saps visibly rise and sink; the Sun has its tenderness as well as its ardent power.

One may picture Zarathustra himself—the body is more virile; the deep, sparkling eyes can look with penetration outwardly at the world no less than inwardly into the hidden glory of the " Great Aura " of the Sun, Ahura-Mazdao.

Zarathustra shades his brow from the God's outer shining, but sees him within as the eternal Light of wisdom.

In teaching, he stands, or walks with firm tread, and his own iridescent aura wraps him round as though with fire. His pupils, too, stand upright before him. They feel under the soles of their feet the heart-beats of the Earth they have to learn to know.

Zarathustra speaks—but few words are needed. Each word and sentence is, to his pupil, as though a section of the surrounding world were made understandable to him; with the hearing of the word there is simultaneously a withdrawal in his inner vision as of some shutter or curtain that had previously concealed this picture. Step by step, the speech of Zarathustra becomes in the pupil a particle of immediate knowledge; and these particles flow together, and build themselves into capacities—and into deeds—in the outer world.

But in this outer world there are enemies. Darkness struggles against the Light. But Ahura-Mazdao, the Spirit of the Sun, provides the weapon with which to fight him: it is the human *will*.

The will manifests itself always in the action of man's limbs. To labour, to work in and for the Earth with knowledge, is possible only for the man who is able to master the forces of gravity: he is lifted upright, set upon his feet, and his ways are ordered by the all-penetrating Light.

" I will speak! " cries Zarathustra. " Hearken, ye who journey from afar, and ye that come from near at hand, with longing to hear. Mark well my words! No longer shall the Evil One, the false leader, conquer the Spirit of Good. Too long has his evil breath poured itself into human speech. I will refute him with the speech which the Highest, the Primal One, has put into my mouth. I will speak what Ahura-Mazdao says to me. And he who hears not my words nor understands their meaning as I speak them, will experience much evil ere the end of the cycles of world-time! "

Wild and barbaric were the people of the old civilisations; but among them lived the Initiates and their pupils. Even their outward appearance was not the same as that of the rest of the population, for a light seemed to shine upon their faces, and their presence was felt as something that was infinitely to be desired. What they said was remembered; what they did was venerated. They were the leaven that slowly, through the centuries, raised and tamed the lower passions of the people.

The whole character of the Zend-Avesta is a worship of purity. All its discourses are in one way and another requests for, and the reception of, instructions from Ahura-Mazdao with regard to the healing and cleansing of the Earth and all its creatures.

This primal purity, brightness, and majesty streams from Ahura-Mazdao as the most spotless wisdom for the inauguration of order in the physical world, and for the harmonising together of all the gifts of Nature.

For this sublime task Zarathustra is the appointed Priest.

We are told how on the mountain-top he receives his revelation—the Eagle sits on his shoulder; the Lion guards the centre of the mountain; and the Bull treads the plains. . . .

Zarathustra knows that inner contemplation alone, as it was to be found in the exalted spiritual wisdom of the Indian sages, must be directed, by him, into outer self-sacrificing work. He knows that some day, when the " outer shall become as the inner, and the inner as the outer ", so that the two are as one, then the Spirit of the Sun

> . . . " will descend to the Earth. He will over-come age, death, and decay. He will create freedom in decisions. Then, when the time is ripe for the resurrection of the dead, he will have won the victory of Life. He will be the victorious Saviour, surrounded by Apostles."

Could any words express more clearly than these, that the Light of the World already shines through Ahura-Mazdao?

Zarathustra's wisdom has been called the " kingly wisdom ". Knowledge that is directed towards the founding of outer civilisations has this character, and was originally identical with religion. But from ancient India had come the Priestly wisdom—that which was ultimately to develop as a preparation of the human soul to receive into itself the pure love of goodness.

Thousands of years after Zarathustra's time, three Kings, whose wisdom of the stars was drawn from the teaching of this great leader and his successors, brought their gifts of gold and frankincense and myrrh to the Child of the Sun. And three Shepherds, whose simple pastoral lives had taught them something of the peace that could rule under the stars, brought their gifts of milk and wool and a lamb. . . .

So from Persia and from India originate the two great streams that flow through the whole of human evolution: Kingly Wisdom and Priestly Devotion.

YASNA, 43. *Zend-Avesta.* (Extract.)

" That I ask Thee, tell me the right, O Ahura,
   Unto the praise of Your praise, mayest Thou,
   O Mazda, teach me, the friend.

That will I ask Thee, tell me the right, O Ahura,
How is the beginning of the best place (Paradise),
How is it to profit him who desires after both?
For Thou art through purity—the Holy over the wicked—
The Ruler over all, the Heavenly, the Friend for both
      worlds, Mazda!

That I ask Thee, tell me the right, O Ahura!
Who was the father of the pure creatures at the beginning?
Who has created the way of the Sun, of the Stars?
Who other than Thou that the Moon waxes and wanes?
That, Mazda, and other things, I desire to know.

That will I ask Thee, tell me the right, O Ahura!
Who upholds the Earth, and the unsupported?
So that they fall not—who the waters and trees?
Who has united swiftness with the winds and the clouds?
Who, O Mazda, is the creator of Vohu-mano?

That will I ask Thee, tell me the right, O Ahura!
Who, working good, has made light as well as darkness?
Who, working good, sleep and waking?
Who the morning dawns, the moons, the nights?
Who him who considers the measures of the law? "

" That will I ask Thee, tell me the right, O Ahura!
How shall I through purity get the Drujas into my power?
In order to slay them with the Manthras of Thy precept,
Bring forth a mighty overthrow among the wicked,
To the deceivers and godless that they may not come again.

That will I ask Thee, tell me the right, O Ahura!
Whether Thou rulest openly in that time with purity
When both the imperishable hosts come together?
According to those Laws which Thou, O Mazda, teachest.
Where, and to which of both, givest Thou the victory? "

YASHT, 22. *Zend-Avesta.*

" The Sun, the immortal, shining, praise we.
When the Sun shines in brightness, when the sunshine beams, then stand the heavenly Yazatas, hundreds, thousands. They bring brightness together,
they spread abroad brightness, they portion out
brightness on the Earth created by Ahura, and
advance the world of the pure, and advance the
body of the pure, and advance the Sun, the immortal, shining, having swift horses.

" When the Sun waxes, then is the Earth created
by Ahura pure, the flowing waters pure, the water
of seed pure, the waters of the seas pure, the water of
the ponds pure, the pure creatures are purified
which belong to Spenta-Mainyu.

" For if the Sun does not rise, then the Daevas
slay all which live in the seven Kareshvars. Not a
heavenly Yazata in the corporeal world would find
out defence, nor withstanding.

" Who then offers to the Sun, the immortal,
shining, with swift horses, to withstand the dark-
nesses, to withstand the Daevas which spring from
darkness, to oppose the thieves and robbers, to
oppose the Yatus and Pairikas, to oppose the
perishing destroying, he offers to Ahura-Mazda,

he offers to the Amesha-Spentas, he offers to his own soul; he gives satisfaction to all heavenly and earthly Yazatas, who offers to the Sun, the immortal, shining, with swift horses." . . .

" We draw near to Thee, Mazda-Ahura, through the
          offering of Fire.
To Thee, O holy Spirit, who repayest with sorrow him who
          inflicts it.
Happy is he to whom Thou comest in Thy might.
O Fire, Son of Ahura-Mazda.
Kindlier than the kindliest, more to be worshipped than
          the most worshipful,
Mayest thou draw near to us and help us,
At the greatest of all events (resurrection).
Fire, thou art a knower of Ahura-Mazda, a knower of the
          things celestial.
Thou, who bearest the name Vazista, thou art of Fire the
          all-holiest.

O Fire, Son of Ahura-Mazda, we draw near to thee
With good intent and with worthy purity.
With deeds and words of wise goodness we come to thee,
We praise thee. We acknowledge ourselves thy debtors
          Mazda-Ahura.
With all good thoughts, all good words, all good works, we
          come to thee.
This thy body, most glorious of all bodies,
We invoke, Mazda-Ahura,
Thou greatest of all Lights
Which is called the Sun."

                                        (Trans. by E. C. M.)

Fire is the purest of the elements.

When fire could be kindled for their ceremonies, it was to the ancient peoples like the presence of the Sun. Sacrifice by fire implied that man gave back to the Divinity of the Sun His own essence which had penetrated into the Earth.

When thousands of years later this Divinity entered a human form, as Zarathustra had prophesied, His

body was indeed the " most glorious of all bodies ",
as Fire was the " most glorious " of all the bodies, or
manifestations, of the Sun.

Fire—not the flame, but the invisible heat of it—
was that element which included in itself all the others,
just as the great fiery cosmic nebula had included in
itself the power to condense to gas, or air, and to water
and earth.

Spiritual Fire is the enveloper, the inspirer, the
baptiser, of men—the Pentecostal Spirit—born from
the Sun.

CHAPTER VI

ANCIENT EGYPT

SOME of the Egyptian Gods were the offspring of time and were associated with Darkness, Matter, and Death; and some were the offspring of Space, Light, and Eternity.

One day the Gods made a feast, and one of their number, Typhon (or Set), a son of Time and Darkness, had prepared a coffin, and whoever among the company would fit perfectly in this coffin would possess a wealth of gold. No one fitted it but Osiris, the son of the Sun. So soon as he lay down in it Typhon and his giants covered it with lead and sealed it up, and then cast it out of the window into the Nile. Thus the divine " son of Space " passed under the dominion of the Titans of Time. The world was filled with the lamentations of Isis, spouse and sister of Osiris.

This death is a symbol of birth.

When a human being is born, his spirit, child of the Heavens, enters into an earthly body.

At the moment of birth, the first action of the child is to breathe. He draws in the stormy wind of darkness, Typhon. With this first breath he becomes human, and dies to the spiritual world of his origin. Seized by Typhon, the spirit is enclosed in the heart and cast out into the bloodstream, where it is divided—dismembered—as Typhon afterwards dismembered Osiris. The spirit lives on then, like Osiris in the Underworld, in the human body in the world of matter. But in the soul, Isis, is the longing for the spirit, and this longing is the son—Horus—who alone is able to conquer the darkness. . . . After death, the spirit of man is released from the body, and must confront the divine Osiris and be judged. If he is worthy, he becomes himself once more an " Osiris ".

The great civilisation of Egypt was founded upon this profound spiritual conception.

We have seen that every genuine myth is based upon the actual vision of super-sensible facts. Divine laws, higher than the laws of Nature, revealed themselves to the seers of old, and their souls grasped their content and understood it, not in the form of thoughts but in the form of pictures.

When great spiritual truths were discovered in this way it was not possible to find expressions or ideas in which to clothe them which might be taken only from the earthly surroundings. But the heavenly events, and the Beings who belonged to the stars, the wandering planets, the Sun and Moon—these sublime creations could best be the living foundations for expressing the mysteries of Man.

Spirit, soul, and Body: these make up the threefold nature of the human being. Sun, Moon, and Earth— these were their cosmic counterparts.

As the old Indians had sought to experience Unity in the world, by looking back to the original wholeness of the solar system; and the Persians, sensing deeply the importance of the Earth, had looked to a primeval time when the Sun and the greater planets had withdrawn and left behind them a Moon-and-Earth totality, and out of this had created their conception of the Beings of Light and Darkness; so now, in this age, the Egyptians looked to the established Trinity of

Sun, Moon, and Earth, and discovered the tremendous fact of the Equilibrium that arises between opposites.

Everything in the Universe was to them living Being. What the Sun or the Moon was doing in the Heavens was done by spiritual Beings in relation to the life of man; and so it was also with all other celestial manifestations.

" As above, so below " is the great axiom of the Egyptian Hermetic wisdom.

The hieroglyphs that stand for the name of Osiris mean " throne " and " eye "; because Osiris, Spirit of the Sun and prototype of the human spirit, was also the ruler of the power of vision.

As the Moon reflects the Sun, so Isis, the soul, carries in herself the reflected shining of the spirit. Osiris, though he is the Spirit of the Sun, nevertheless sends out his power to mankind also from the Moon. In the myth, Osiris and Isis are brother and sister, husband and wife. For without the power of vision the spirit cannot be known by the soul of man, and the vision in the soul cannot be true that is not ruled by the spirit.

The old Indians looked up into the Infinity behind the Sun for the Creative Word; Zarathustra found it in the Sun itself; Egypt found it in the sunlight of the Moon, and thus brought nearer to the Earth. But the death of Osiris from the Moon and the widowhood of Isis prophesies something deeper still.

Egypt has no great epic story of living heroes, only the myth of Osiris and Isis. But there is the epic of all the immortal dead, their journeys and trials in the Underworld and their quest for reunion with the divine Osiris.

It is the *Book of the Dead* which is the principle means

of our knowledge of this great period of culture, and it is from this that our quotations are taken.

In a certain sense the wisdom of Egypt is shadowed by a mood of tragedy. It is centred round the inner experiences of the human soul, represented by Isis, which feels already the forewarning of the approach of a darkening of spiritual vision—the death of Osiris.

Vast, divine, heroic, utterly pure, these Three— Osiris, Isis and Horus, were for the Egyptians the prototypes of all human experience.

The Egyptian initiation into the Mysteries was preceded by a training which led the aspirant first of all to understand how his " Osiris-nature "—his spiritual Ego—had been overwhelmed in the dense matter of his physical body. Cosmic pictures of the evolution of the planetary system accompanied this teaching. The human counterpart of the forsaking of the Earth by the Sun had to be experienced by his passing through a " mystical death "—a deep, death-like trance—induced by the initiating Priests.

In the stages of the approach to this death, he had to become intensely conscious of his whole bodily organism; until at last he could be aware of those portals in the four chambers of his physical heart where the Typhon-slain Osiris had been cast at the moment of his own birth.

In mystic language, the wanderings through his bodily organism, through blood, and nerves, and organs, were like wanderings through the primeval elements—through Fire and Air and Water. All these must be known, and the darkness and density of their ultimate material and fallen nature be understood and vanquished. This accomplished, he met, in his death-like trance, with his own soul, with Isis. She revealed to him the Osiris-Sun, his immortal Spirit, shining in the midnight of his earthly existence.

The vision of Osiris—or of Ra—was at the same time the vision of all other celestial beings—the spiritual world. Having been once experienced in the rites of initiation, it was never forgotten. It became, for the rest of the initiate's life, his key of knowledge.

" I am that God Ra who shineth in the night. Every being who followeth in his train shall have life in the following of the God Thoth, and he shall give unto him the risings of Horus in the darkness. . . .

" I am a Khu (soul), and I have come to the divine prince at the bounds of the horizon.

" I have met, and I have received the mighty Goddess Isis. . . . Homage to thee O great God in the east of Heaven, let me embark in thy boat, O Ra, let me open myself out in the form of a divine hawk. . . .

" Let me embark in thy boat, O Ra, in peace, and let me sail in peace to the beautiful Amentet. . . .

" And I say, on every road and among these millions of years is Ra the Lord, and his path is in the fire.

" And they go round about behind him, and they go round about behind him." . . .

Hymns to the *setting* Sun have a special significance.

Our waking senses, seeing, hearing, and so on, bind us to the objects of the physical world. But when the senses are dimmed—it may be in sleep, or in death, or in the mystical death of initiation as it was experienced long ago—then the spiritual senses awake.

Ra-Osiris, when he was adored as the setting Sun,

when he sank below the edge of the world, was no longer visible in his physical splendour. But he was visible, in the conditions described, as the Spirit of the Sun. The darker the physical world, the brighter grew the radiance of the spiritual world and its inhabitants.

Ra was adored in the day-time as the power that moved the Sun from horizon to horizon. In the night-time he assumed all the divinity which by day was hidden in his external beauty.

The very heart of all that is esoteric in religion is the great secret of " Light *in* Darkness ". Only in the distant future will the active power hinted at in the words " Light in Darkness " be understood by humanity as a whole. . . . The climax of the old Egyptian rites of initiation was called " seeing the Sun at Midnight ".

Osiris and Ra can be regarded in a certain sense as the same, but the names apply to different aspects of the " threefold Sun ", Ra, Osiris, Horus. The *Book of the Dead* calls Ra the soul of Osiris, and Osiris the soul of Ra. This does not make them identical; but indicates rather a diversity of function or attribute, in the same Being.

(A HYMN TO THE SETTING SUN.)　(Extracts.)

" A Hymn of praise to Ra at eventide, when he setteth as a living being. . . . The great God who dwelleth in his Disk riseth in his Two Eyes (Sun and Moon) and all the *Khus** of the underworld receive him in his horizon of Amentet. . . .
And they sing hymns of joy to Ra when they have received him at the head of his beautiful path of Amentet.
. . . Praise be unto thee, O Ra, praise be unto thee, O Tem, in thy splendid progress.
Thou hast risen and thou hast put on strength, and thou settest like a living being amid thy glories in the

* Souls.

horizon of Amentet, in thy domain which is in Manu. . . .*

Thou sailest forth over heaven, and thou makest the Earth to be stablished; thou joinest thyself unto the upper heaven, O luminary.

The two regions of the East and West make adoration unto thee, bowing low and paying homage unto thee, and they praise thee day by day; the gods of Amentet rejoice in thy splendid beauties.

The hidden places adore thee, the aged ones make offerings unto thee, and they create for thee protecting powers.

The divine beings who dwell in the eastern and western horizons transport thee, and those who are in the Sektet boat convey thee round and about.

The Souls of Amentet cry out unto thee and say unto thee when they meet thy majesty ' All hail, all hail! '

When thou comest forth in peace there arise shouts of delight in thee, O thou Lord of heaven, thou Prince of Amentet.

The mother Isis embraceth thee, and in thee she recogniseth her son, the lord of fear, the mighty one of terror.

Thou settest as a living being within the dark portal.

Thy father Tatunen lifteth thee up and he stretcheth out his two hands behind thee;

Thou becomest a divine being in the Earth.

Thou wakest as thou settest, and thy habitation is in Manu. . . ."

" Thou becomest a divine being in the Earth. . . ."

" Thou wakest as thou settest. . . ."

These are most strange words. How can the Sun become a divine being *in the Earth?* How is it that he wakes when apparently all his activity vanishes in the night? It is just in such words as these that the greatest secrets are laid.

The true nature of the Sun is concealed from physical sight. When the Sun is not visible, its spiritual forces are perceived most clearly by the inner eyes of the soul.

* Mountain of the Sunset.

As the soul " wakes in sleep " in order to perceive the spirit, or wakes after death and knows it and unites with it, so Ra " wakes " to divine activity when he does not manifest physically.

When he appears to sink into the Earth in setting, his divinity shines into the eyes of the soul of the man whose physical eyes can no longer see him. When the living man found the divine Ra-Osiris in the trance-sleep of initiation, he found him truly as " Light in Darkness "—the rising Sun of the spiritual world.

" Homage to thee O Ra when thou risest!*
    Thou art adored by me when thy beauties are before mine
        eyes and when thy radiance falleth upon my body. . . .
    Thou stridest over the heavens in peace, and all thy foes
        are cast down.
    The never-resting stars sing hymns of praise to thee, and the
        stars which rest, and the stars which never fail glorify
        thee as thou sinkest to rest in the horizon of Manu,
    O thou who art beautiful at morn and at eve,
    O thou Lord who livest and art established, O my Lord! "

" Thou sendest forth the word, and the earth is flooded with
        silence, O thou only One,
    Who didst dwell in heaven before ever the earth and the
        mountains came into existence.
    O Runner, O Lord, O only One,
    Thou maker of things which are!
    Thou hast fashioned the tongue of the company of the gods,
    Thou hast produced whatsoever cometh forth from the
        waters,
    And thou springest up from them over the flooded land of
        the lake of Horus." . . .

" Thou turnest thy face upon Amentet, and thou makest the
        earth to shine as with refined copper.
    Those who have lain down (the dead) rise up to see thee,
    They breathe the air and they look upon thy face
    When thy Disk riseth on its horizon;
    Their hearts are at peace inasmuch as they behold thee;
    O thou who art Eternity and Everlastingness! "

    * *Litany to the Sun-God* (Extract from the *Book of the Dead*).

" Those who are in the Underworld come forth to meet thee,
And they bow in homage as they come towards thee
To behold thy beautiful Image.
And I have come before thee that I may be with thee
To behold thy Disk every day.
May I not be shut up in the tomb!
May I not be turned back!
May the limbs of my body be made new again
When I view thy beauties, even as all thy favoured ones,
Because I am one of those who worshipped thee upon
    earth.
May I come into the land of eternity,
May I even come into the everlasting land,
For behold, O my Lord, this hast thou ordained for me."

" Grant thou that I may come into the heaven which is
    everlasting
And unto the mountain where dwell thy favoured ones.
May I be joined unto those shining beings
Holy and perfect
Who are in the underworld.
And may I come forth with them to behold thy beauties
When thou shinest at eventide." . . .

(" *And the god saith*:)

Thou shalt come forth into heaven,
Thou shalt pass over the sky,
Thou shalt be joined unto the starry deities.
Praises shall be offered unto thee in thy boat,
Thou shalt be hymned in the *Atet* boat,
Thou shalt behold Ra within his shrine,
Thou shalt set together with his Disk
Day by Day." . . .

There is a tremendous rugged grandeur in all these
words from the *Book of the Dead*. They thrust themselves deep into our hearts. We feel at once that it is
not the physical Sun that is portrayed under the
various God-names, but something infinite and
terrible in its relentless livingness and majesty. When

the great Disk, at the moment of rising or setting, touched the edge of the horizon, leaving a tiny spark of fire, it flamed into the soul of every watcher, and kindled in him the conviction:

" *I am* Ra, who rose in the Beginning—the Ruler of what he made." . . .

But there are many problems when we consider the Egyptian culture as a whole—so far, that is, as we are able to judge of it from its remains. But we can be sure that whatever strikes us as grotesque, or rankly superstitious and primitve, does not belong to the great period of its spiritual maturity, but is already decadent. " We must not ", says Rudolf Steiner, " ascribe primitive and simple conditions to the early stages of civilisations. On the contrary, *primitive conditions belong to periods of decadence* which have set in after the original spiritual treasures have been lost."

The peculiar kind of animal worship, for instance, which seems to have prevailed, is actually the remains of an original and profound reverence for the stages of creation. Form after form, planned " before they were in the Earth ", whether of mineral, plant, or animal, were revered as showing the great waves of primordial evolution, coming to rest in the visible world; until at last a form arose that was able to receive the spiritual imprint of man himself, who had been there from the beginning, in the light of the Sun.

The Egyptian " remembered " the animal forms as Gods;   that is, as spiritual forms assumed during primeval evolution by the human archetypes.   As the forms were discarded, they became " fixed " in matter as the animal kingdom;   but the spiritual *qualities* which had governed the different forms could become human qualities.

The eagle form, for example, leaves behind it in man the penetrating power of vision and the aspiring thought that rises to Heaven. The lion form, a fiery courage and the strength of enthusiasm . . . and so on. The predatory nature that still lives on in these forms as purely animal characteristics is that which man, in his ascending evolution, overcomes.

It was not superstition therefore which caused the Egyptians to depict their gods with animal-like heads, but a deep insight into the creative process.

All the ancient wisdom could regard the three kingdoms of Nature as the sacrifices of the creatures; they had built the foundations so that Man could rise above them.*

Through all flowed the great stream of Life from the Sun—the " ever-living One " who is " Yesterday ", and " To-day ", the " Lord of millions of Years "— who shone in the soul of the enlightened man as the " Sun of Midnight ". And after death, the Sun was Life immortal, carrying the human soul into his realm of spiritual Light.

The deeper study of the Egyptian myths and mysteries discloses that a whole science of man as an earthly and as a heavenly being was taught by means of them. The extraordinary rituals of the *Book of the Dead* pay minute attention to the anatomy and physiology of the body, and link its every detail with some detail of the experiences of the soul after death. Everywhere it is stressed that the dead person must find his way back to Osiris, his spiritual archetype.

All links in the chain of the bodily life that is over must be in some way mentioned in the funeral rites;

* Rudolf Steiner. Egyptian Myths and Mysteries. (*Lecture* XI).

for everything that is earthly man was once, before his birth, heavenly man, and no part of the earthly body is unimportant. Osiris was waiting in the world of after-death for the return of his " image ", man, who had finished his earthly life. He was the *Light of the World of the Dead*.

The initiated seers of old Egypt were well aware that the necessity of man's becoming more at home on the Earth, more densely physical, as time went on, would inevitably darken his consciousness in the spiritual world after death. They knew that in order to prevent this darkening, or mitigate it, they must keep alive, in the living human beings, the spark of knowledge which alone would lead them, after death, to the Light of Osiris.

In their wisdom they were preparers for that which could only be there is full strength after this Being had descended into a human body, and died, and entered the " Underworld " to " give light to them that sit in darkness and in the shadow of death ". Osiris was Christ.

" That which is called Christianity to-day ", said St. Augustine, " has always existed, even at the beginning of the human race; only, until Christ came in the flesh, the true religion was not called Christianity ".

The imperial power of Egypt rose to great grandeur with the beginning of the eighteenth dynasty, but its spirituality had by then become decadent.

The worship of Amun-Ra, under the decline of the old clairvoyant wisdom, became the means towards wordly power and personal ambition in the hands of the priesthood of the Temples. The true progress of mankind was destined to be dependent upon the loss of seership; not because seership itself was wrong, but because man had to come to the point of feeling himself responsible for his own progress, and had not to feel that he was for ever to be under the guidance of higher Powers who in a certain sense took the responsibility upon themselves. The decline of vision was the beginning of the " twilight of the Gods ", and the rise of earthly knowledge.*

About 1500 B.C. Egypt stood at the height of its temporal power and in the decadence of its religion. In 1375 B.C. Amenophis IV, the young Pharaoh known to us as Akhenaton, ascended the throne.

Excavations in Egypt have shed a romantic light on his brief life. The tragic aspect of his reign was that he was destined to experience more or less consciously what was really already taking place in a more hidden way in the evolution of civilised humanity—the advance towards self-conscious individuality.

The now decadent cult of Amun had become the begetter and nurturer of power—the power to create a tremendous civilisation and empire. But Akhenaton wanted to change power into love; and so incurred the deadly hatred of the priesthood of Amen. There had dawned in his heart a warmth of love for the world; it was as though he felt the approach of the spirituality of the Sun itself as divine love streaming to the Earth.

He could no longer feel himself bound, like his immediate predecessors, in the thrall of a majestic ceremonial system, for the light of his own Ego had kindled his self-knowledge, and his eyes beheld *mankind*.

The symbol of the new Aton worship which he instituted was a solar disk from which descended many rays of light terminating in human hands, some

* See Rudolf Steiner. " Four Mystery Plays " (Egyptian Scene).

of them holding the emblem of life, and all of them seeming to bless the worshippers with love.

It was not, as some believe, that Akhenaton had any thought of instituting a materialistic Sun-worship; but it was an attempt to point to the increasing nearness of the spiritual powers of the Sun to earthly life. His actions were prophetic, conceived out of the premonition of the Sun-Being's approach. He found His life-giving influence in Nature; and His rays as love. Under Akhenaton's short rule there dawned a more naturalistic art, and a gentler beauty.

The new religion was a step towards the establishment of human freedom. The older religion had been an acknowledgment of the dependence of man upon the divine worlds and the inspiration bestowed by them. But the Aton—the Sun of Life and Love—was a foreshadowing of the beginning of individual freedom in the life of the soul: the gaining of conciousness of self in order to spend it freely in love.

But a more arduous way was first needed for mankind.

Akhenaton died very young; and the priests of the dethroned and decadent cult of Amun, and all those whom they influenced, covered his memory with curses. Most terrible must have been their words and deeds of hatred!

Part of a hymn to Amun, written at the downfall of Akhenaton's Aton worship, is quoted in James Blaikie's book *The Amarna Age*:

" Thou (Amun) findest him who transgresses against thee,
Woe to him who assails thee!
Thy city endures;
But he who assails thee falls. . . .
The Sun of him who knows thee not goes down, O Amun!

ANCIENT EGYPT

But as for him who knows thee, he shines.
The forecourt of him who assailed thee is in darkness,
But the whole Earth is in light.
Whoever puts thee in his heart, O Amun,
Lo, his Sun dawns.

Akhenaton's two great Hymns to the Sun are known
all over the world. Here are some extracts from one of
them:

Thy dawning is beautiful in the horizon of the sky
O living Aton, beginning of life!
When thou risest in the eastern horizon,
Thou fillest every land with thy beauty.
Thou art beautiful, great, glittering, high above every land,
Thy rays, they encompass the lands, even all that thou hast
    made.
Thou art Ra, and thou carriest them all away captive;
Thou bindest them by thy love.
Though thou art far away, thy rays are upon the earth;
Though thou art on high, thy footprints are the day.

When thou settest in the western horizon of the sky,
The earth is in darkness like the dead;
They sleep in their chambers,
Their heads are wrapped up,
Their nostrils are stopped,
And none seeth the other,
While all other things are stolen
Which are under their heads,
And they know it not.*
Every lion cometh forth from his den,
All serpents they sting.
The world is in silence,
He that made them resteth in his horizon.

Bright is the earth when thou risest in the horizon,
When thou shinest as Aton by day,
Thou drivest away the darkness.
When thou sendest forth thy rays,
The Two Lands are in daily festivity,
Awake and standing upon their feet
When thou hast raised them up.

* Perhaps a reference to the loss of consciousness in sleep.

Their limbs are bathed, they take their clothing,
Their arms uplifted in adoration to thy dawning.
Then in all the world they do their work.

All cattle rest upon their pasturage,
The trees and the plants flourish,
The birds flutter in their marshes,
Their wings uplifted in adoration to thee.
All the sheep dance upon their feet,
All winged things fly,
They live when thou hast shone upon them.
The barques sail up stream and down stream alike.
Every highway is open because thou dawnest.
The fish in the river leap up before thee.
Thy rays are in the midst of the great green sea.

How manifold are thy works!
They are hidden from before us,
O Sole God, whose powers no other possesseth.
Thou didst create the world according to thy heart
While thou wast alone:
Men, all cattle large and small,
All that are upon the earth,
That go about upon their feet;
All that are on high,
That fly with their wings,
The foreign countries, Syria and Kush,
The land of Egypt;
Thou settest every man into his place,
Thou suppliest their necessities,
Everyone has his possessions,
And his days are reckoned.
The tongues are diverse in speech,
Their forms likewise, and their skins are distinguished.
For thou makest different the strangers.

Thy rays nourish every garden;
When thou risest they live,
They grow by thee.
Thou makest the seasons
In order to create all thy work;
Winter to bring them coolness,
And heat that they may taste thee.
Thou didst make the distant sky to rise therein,

In order to behold all that thou hast made,
Thou alone, shining in thy form as living Aton,
Dawning, glittering, going afar and returning.
Thou makest millions of forms
Through thyself alone;
Cities, towns and tribes, highways and rivers
All eyes see thee before them,
For thou art Aton of the day over the earth. . . .

Thou art in my heart,
There is no other that knoweth thee
Save thy son Akhenaton.
Thou hast made him wise
In thy designs and thy might.
The world is in thy hand,
Even as thou hast made them.
When thou risest they live,
When thou settest they die;
For thou art length of life of thyself,
Men live through thee,
While their eyes are upon thy beauty,
Until thou settest.
All labour is put away
When thou settest in the west. . . ."

Contrast this hymn with one which is said to be the oldest Egyptian hymn that is known:

He permits thee not to hearken to the Westerners,
He permits thee not to hearken to the Easterners,
He permits thee not to hearken to the Southerners,
He permits thee not to hearken to the Northerners,
He permits thee not to hearken to the dwellers in the midst
    of the earth.
But thou hearkenest to Horus.

The doors that are on thee stand fast like Inmutef,
They open not to the Westerners,
They open not to the Easterners,
They open not to the Southerners,
They open not to the Northerners,
They open not to the dwellers in the midst of the earth,
    They open to Horus.
It was he who made them,
It was he who set them up.*

* From *The Armarna Age*, Blaikie.

Here an impenetrable curtain is drawn over the Temple Mysteries. It is thought that this hymn represents a jealous possessiveness on the part of the Egyptians for their religion. It may be so. But the Hymn may also be a fragment of some ritual carried out in the performance of secret Temple ceremonies.

One might imagine the four cardinal directions as symbols for the stations of the watchers, whose task it was, by secret gestures and recitations, to cleanse the Temple from the Intrusion of lesser super-sensible beings. It is *Horus* for whom the ceremonial is prepared; and for his presence, the sanctuary must be isolated and consecrated, and be his alone.

How different is Akhenaton's joy in the universal beneficence of the Sun-God!—he gives his God Aton to all countries and all peoples and all languages, and is glad that he can do this. Even his great Temple is built open to the sky. . . . No wonder the Priests of Amun hated him!

But, too early though it was, the first step had been taken on the path of freedom.

The outer imperial splendour of Egypt, in spite of temporary revival, was at an end.

CHAPTER VII

ANCIENT GREECE

Offspring of Jove, Calliope, once more
To the bright Sun, thy hymn of music pour;
Whom to the child of star-clad Heaven and Earth
Euryphaessa, large-eyed nymph, brought forth;
Euryphaessa, the famed sister fair
Of great Hyperion, who to him did bear
A race of loveliest children; the young Morn,
Whose arms are like twin roses newly born,
The fair-haired Moon, and the immortal Sun,
Who borne by heavenly steeds his race doth run
Unconquerably, illumining the abodes
Of mortal men and the eternal Gods.
Fiercely look forth his awe-inspiring eyes,
Beneath his golden helmet, whence arise
And are shot forth afar, clear beams of light;
His countenance, with radiant glory bright,
Beneath his graceful locks far shines around,
And the light vest with which his limbs are bound,
Of woof ethereal delicately twined,
Glows in the stream of the uplifting wind.
His rapid steeds soon bear him to the West;
Where their steep flight his hands divine arrest,
And the fleet car with yoke of gold, which he
Sends from bright Heaven beneath the shadowy sea.

HOMER'S HYMN TO THE SUN (900 B.C.)
(Shelley's translation.)

APOLLO

O Lyre of gold, Apollo's
Treasure, shared with the violet-wreathèd Muses,
The light foot hears you, and the brightness begins:
Your notes compel the singer
When to lead out the dance,

85

The prelude is sounded on your trembling strings.
You quench the warrior Thunderbolt's everlasting flame:
On God's sceptre the Eagle sleeps,
Drooping his swift wings on either side.
The King of Birds!
You have poured a cloud on his beak and head and dar-
    kened his face:
His eyelids are shut with a sweet seal.
He sleeps, his lithe back heaves:
Your quivering song has conquered him.
Even Ares the violent
Leaving aside his harsh and pointed spears
Comforts his heart in drowsiness.
Your shafts enchant the souls even of the Gods
Through the wisdom of Lato's son and the deep-bosomed
    Muses. . . .

(PINDAR, 522-448 B.C.)

THE GOLDEN FLEECE

PHRIXUS and Helle were the son and daughter of
Athama and Nephele the Cloud Goddess. The
children were to be sacrificed to Zeus, but Hermes
gave them a golden ram, and on its back they were to
be carried to safety through the air.

Between Sigeum and Chersonesus, Helle fell into the
sea, now called the Hellespont. Phrixus arrived safely
in Colchis and sacrificed the ram to Zeus. Its golden
fleece was given to Ætes and became the object of the
quest of the Argonauts.

It seemed to the pre-Grecian Heroes the most
desirable thing imaginable—this effulgent, eternal,
golden covering, that flowed round about them in their
visions in eddies and streams and wavelets like a
peaceful ocean of Sunbeams. . . . " He that hath this,
hath all." . . . For the Golden Fleece is the utterly
spotless Soul of the Being of the Sun.

Apollo is bathed in this light. But the Golden Ram
itself has been sacrificed. All that can be found on the

quest for it is its fleece and horns of gold. But he who finds these, knows, in the Mysteries, the secret of the Sun.

The sacrifice of the Ram means the loss of the ancient powers of seership. If the Ego was to develop itself in man and bring about in him the attainment of intellectual independence, which was the primary task of the coming age of Greek culture, then this sacrifice must be made, and the fact must be accepted that in the Mysteries of that period the former heights of spiritual wisdom would not be able to be reached.

The clairvoyant faculty has its physical focus in the brain. Those who in past times could actually see this faculty in action, likened it to two horns of light, resembling the horns of a ram. This has often been depicted in old Egyptian drawings, and was accepted as a fact of common knowledge. The horns, springing from the upper part of the head, revolved, and their roots were interlocked. Their rays, invisible to ordinary physical sight, illumined for the seer the realms of the spirit. In the Mystery Temples, all seership, if it was pure, was an offering which the Gods repaid with wisdom. But the killing of seership, or its loss as a sign of the newer development of the intellect, was a killing of the offering itself—of the golden Light itself.

If it was to be re-created, or re-found, the " waters under the Earth " must be traversed; the dark depths of the soul must be explored; suffering and sadness must be endured. Only in this transition age, from the old clairvoyant faculty to intellectual clarity, could the story of the Golden Fleece and the sacrifice of the Golden Ram, and the Heroes' quest for it through the hidden subterranean waters, have arisen.

The main period of every great epoch of civilisation falls within 2,160 years, which is the duration of the

Sun's passage through each single sign of the Zodiac. In the year 747 B.C. the Sun entered the sign of the Ram; and it is this sign which ruled the time during which the Greek culture continued to shed its greatest influence.

So much tragedy and conflict and courage enter into the Greek legends because the age is the great battlefield of the soul. It is Herculean. It stands at a turning-point in man's evolution. And the nature of this turning-point is revealed prophetically in the two great legends which herald the dawn of this Græco-Roman epoch of civilisation. This singular epoch, standing alone in the midst between the past and the future development of the civilised world, announces itself in the Quest of the Golden Fleece and the Siege of Troy.

In that age legend and actual history meet. Troy is a legend; but it really existed. The quest of the Golden Fleece is a legend but it really happened; actual dangerous journeys were undertaken to Mystery centres where particular teachings were given. And the preservation of the supreme treasure of Troy, the Palladium, points to the continual but hidden preservation of all the sublime and ancient wisdom.

APOLLO

How strange is the impression one has of Greek culture after contemplating the Egyptian! We feel somehow as though the free intermingling of Gods and Heroes and men in all the magnificent heroic stories; the perfection of thought; the whole sunlit world of Grecian art; were like a dream poised on the edge of a dark awakening. How near is Hades and its grey realm of Shades; how heavy the fate of Persephone and the sorrows of Demeter; how cruel the grim tragedies of the great kings' houses!

It is as though Light and Darkness, each of them living, real, cosmic entities, draw close together; and we see the human beings through a veil woven of this shimmering half-light which is so drenched in beauty, and so full of sadness.

And dominating this world were the great Greek Schools of the Mysteries: the Ephesian, the Samothracian, the Eleusinian, the Orphic—each, when in the prime of its unsullied wisdom, offering to show to men the difficult and painful way back to the golden Light of the Sun.

In the Greek age of culture the last glimmer of the ancient clairvoyant wisdom was battling with the tremendous awakening of intellectual thought, in its most pure and perfect form. And so the solemn warning was given to those who wished to enter the Schools of the Greek Mysteries: " O Man, know thyself! "

What Zarathustra had prophesied more than five thousand years before, saying that a Saviour would come and make it possible for man to create out of himself his free decisions in all events of life, developed, in Greece, a step further towards its fulfilment. In the Oracle Sanctuaries the Sibils were prophetesses who would foretell events to those who were faced with momentous decisions; but their utterances placed the inquirer into the position of having to decide for himself what he would do.

The old way of acting out of visions, dreams, and inspirations had no longer any certainty. The question: *What shall I do?* is one which, in any case, throws the human being upon his own resources, no matter what answer he may get. He has to choose. And that is true even to-day. The Sibils could impart no really divine authority; and the fact that they were consulted shows that man had no intuitive certainty in himself.

The Greek age typifies the approaching solitariness of man, who is not yet certain of his inner ruler, the Ego; and quite uncertain of divine guidance, unless he is initiated in the Mysteries.

If we seek for direct links between Greece and the Egyptian civilisation we shall find many that have an external reality and justification.   But if we look deeper we shall discover outstanding differences. It is a curious fact that each of the past ages of civilisation should take its secret spiritual character from looking back at some special world-condition that has passed away, and out of this should gain a certain vision of what must come. The Greeks could look back, and with a certain " realism ", only a comparatively short distance—to a time when order was first becoming possible in the confused soul-life of humanity. This order they felt reflected into their own time by Apollo. He brought them music, which helps to regulate the powers of thought; he brought them healing, and inspired the Heroes to superhuman courage.   Order among the planets is reflected as order in the human soul; the Greek Gods were called by the names of the planets, and Apollo's heavenly brightness ruled among them as the Sun. Yet all these celestial activities were at a lower level than of old. Zeus, the father of the Gods, flamed in the lightning, rolled as the thunder through the clouds, called the rainbow around his throne, and filled all the ether with his power. Apollo, as the Healer, radiated love through warmth and air and water and earth. *The Sun-Spirit was drawing ever nearer to the Earth.*

The Greek age is saturated with everything that has to do with the natural elements, and their creative and destructive working. The Greek really felt himself bound up with the whole of Nature. At night, he could still become " awake in sleep ", and feel himself poured out into the Universe—into stars, and clouds, moisture and cold, heat and dryness; into rivers and seas and mountains, and into every flower of the field. All his Gods and Goddesses shaped and clothed themselves and their deeds in clouds and fire and water and earth. Natural phenomena were directly intermingled with human destiny.

In this epoch one could say a certain balance existed between the human and the divine. Inward experiences were often externalised—for instance, in the pursuit of the evil-doer by the Furies, who were like Conscience made visible to the clairvoyant sight. And outer events were mirrored inwardly as psychic experience.

Then, in the Mystery Schools of Greece, this natural kinship with the elements could be used as the basis upon which the teachers could build up an intimate knowledge of the physical nature of man. The art of healing gradually emerges from the old methods which had prevailed in the Egyptian Temples. The love of wisdom is now grasped by the loftiest levels of intellectual thinking; it is called " philosophy ". The divine and the human touch each other—less in supersensible experience than in earthly beauty. In Greek sculpture and architecture it is stamped even upon marble and stone, in the image of the perfect physical human form.

In Greece, all former ages of culture live on, but as memories which are transformed by the growing sense of human personality. Since they live on in this way,

the Greek mythology stresses the importance of the
" generations " of Gods. As the three earlier ages of
culture had remembered in their Mysteries three
stages of *cosmic* evolution, so the Greeks experience
these three as the history of their Gods, descending
through the ages.

Something new had therefore to arise in the fourth
age of civilisation; and this was the gradual realisation
of Man, as a bearer of Ego-consciousness.

It was through Apollo that what was new in the
Grecian age took root. It was in effect a transformation of the old laws of punishment for evil into the
capacity to see the beauty in what was not evil. What
the Gods *do* is in reality what man himself *learns* by
experience; he sees his experience—with truth—as
due to the deeds of the Gods: all is reciprocal: such a
thing as remorse, for instance, must in the end reveal
that it can be redeemed by positive attachment to the
good. But the revelation would never come if man
were not divinely guided.

Even " good " and " evil " go through their stages
of evolution: that man finds the choice between them
a problem is new in our *own* age. That may seem
strange. But not if we see that it is the very development of the human Ego—only quite at its beginning
in the Greek age—which helps good and evil to mask
themselves in a whole multitude of *pros* and *cons*, so
that they are now hardly to be distinguished from one
another.

It was decreed in the primeval world-creation that
the violent deeds of men should arouse the vengeance
of the Furies, called by the Greeks the Erinyes. They
pursued and haunted the evil-doer till his death—
plainly visible to his clairvoyant sight—and after death
too they gave him no peace. These terrible Goddesses

were like Gorgons, with hair of snakes, bloodshot eyes and grinding teeth, and cloud-black garments that whirled and whispered about them giving warning of their deadly presence. They punished only those who sinned with violence against a guest, a parent, or a God. Once roused from the depths, there was no way of escape from them.

At the instigation of Apollo, acting under the command of Zeus, the hero Orestes kills his mother Clytemnestra for her diabolical treachery and for her murder of Orestes' father.

Orestes, knowing that Apollo will never fail him, since it was he who had inspired the murderous deed, flees to the Temple of Delphi. The Furies follow him. In the Temple they lie—a heaving darkness—in deep sleep beside him. Then the dead Clytemnestra appears, and taunts them till they wake.

Apollo, aware of the desecration of his Temple by their presence, reveals himself. The Furies accuse him of having inspired the deed; but he defends Orestes because in killing his mother he was avenging the murder of his father. He decrees that Pallas Athena shall be the judge, and she is to be summoned to the Temple. Orestes in the meantime is left alone, prostrate before the alter, while the Furies begin their fearful spell-binding dance. . . .

" Not Lord Apollo's, not Athena's power
  Shall reach thee any more. Forgot, forgot,
  Thou reelest back to darkness, knowing not
  Where in man's heart joy dwelleth; without blood,
  A shadow—flung to devils for their food!
  Wilt answer not my word? Wilt spurn thereat,
  Thou that art mine, born, doomed and consecrate
  My living feast, at no high altar slain?
  Hark thou this song to bind thee like a chain!"

The Furies cluster round their leader and proclaim
their utter righteousness and their skill in apportioning
to man his " fated burdens ".   Their songs weave
powerlessness and despair into Orestes' soul:

" But our sacrifice to bind,
   Lo the music that we wind,
   How it dazeth and amazeth
      And the will it maketh blind,
   As it moves without a lyre
   To the throb of my desire;
      'Tis a chain about the brain,
      'Tis a wasting of mankind." . . .

Deeper and stronger and darker grows the spell:

" The glories of Man that were proud where the Sunlight
         came,
   Below in the dark are wasted and cast to shame;
      For he trembles at the hearing
      Of the Black Garments nearing,
   And the beating of the feet, like flame——

   He falls and knows not; the blow hath made blind his eyes;
   And above hangs Sin, as a darkening of the skies,
      And a great voice swelling
      Like a mist about his dwelling,
   And sobbing in the mist and cries.

   For so it abideth: subtle are we to plan,
      Sure to fulfil, and forget not any Sin;
      And Venerable they call us, but none can win
         Our pardon for child of man.
   Unhonoured and undesired though our kingdom be,
      Where the Sun is dead and no God in all the skies,
   Great crags and trackless, alike for them that see,
      And them of the wasted eyes;

   What mortal man but quaketh before my power,
      And boweth in worship to hear my rule of doom,
   God-given of old, fate-woven on the ageless loom
      And ripe to the perfect hour?

To the end of all abideth mine ancient Right,
  Whose word shall never be broke nor its deed undone,
Though my seat is below in the Grave, in the place where
    sight
  Fails, and there is no Sun."

Following the story as Æschylus tells it in his great
drama *The Eumenides* (from which these extracts are
taken),* Pallas Athena now arrives in her Temple in
Athens and soon the Council of the Areopagus is summoned. The scene is set for the wondrous trial which
changes for ever the destinies of men.

At the last moment, Apollo himself enters the
assembly. Orestes admits the killing; and there
follows the great argument between Apollo and the
Furies: Apollo was obeying the law of Zeus: they
were obeying the ancient law of Chronos.

Apollo exclaims:

" Ye worms of hate, O ye that Gods abhor,
  Bonds can be loosened; there is cure therefor,
  And many and many a plan in God's great mind
  To free the prisoners whom he erst did bind.
  But once the dust hath drunk the blood of men
  Murdered, there is no gathering it again.
  For that no magic doth my Father know,
  Thou all things else he changeth high and low
  Or fixeth, and no toil is in his breath." . . .

Thus Apollo points to the law of change: Time is
not unalterable and its laws are not fixed for ever.
Even Zeus himself had touched without pollution, and
forgiven, the first murderer Ixion, because he pleaded
to be cleansed. Even Zeus " learns and heals ". . . .
Orestes had cast himself at the feet of the Sun-God
Apollo: he would protect him. What he had done was
not sin, but was the fulfilment of a fearful destiny.

When at last the lots are drawn, they are equal in
number and Orestes is free.

* After a considerable interval of time.

But now the whole weight of the tragedy falls upon the Furies. Their rule is overwhelmed; their law is broken, their mission ended. They are despised by the younger Gods. Their leader cries:

" Woe on you, woe, ye younger Gods!
   Ye have trampled the great Laws of old
Beneath your chariots! Ye have broke the rods
   Of justice, yea and torn them from my hold!
Mine office gone, unhappy and angered sore,
I rage alone. What have I any more
   To do? Or be? Shall not mine injury turn
   And crush this people? Shall not poison rain
Upon them, even the poison of this pain
   Wherewith my heart doth burn?
And up therefrom shall a lichen creep,
   A lifeless, childless blight,
A stain in the earth, man-slaying. . . . O just Throne of
   Right!
   Have ye not suffered deep,
Deep, ye unhappy children of old Night,
   Born to be scorned and weep! "

Athena, moved to pity, but with reverence for the great foundations of things that have trembled at the touch of Apollo, leads the Erinyes gently towards a new hope. They will no longer be the wild, demoniac fulfillers of an ancient doom, but will become the mild upholders of the right, in peace and wisdom; and from the veil of Earth will

" Hold down the evil that shall die
   Send up the good that shall prevail."

Apollo, even though obeying the law of Zeus in communicating his command to Orestes, has nevertheless opened the door to freedom. Things that had been rooted in and born from the destinies of the high Gods in the beginning—who created the race of men— could be changed by the *Law of Love*.

The Erinyes are the Avengers that come out of man's own heart, out of his blind obedience to the law of the blood. This is a destiny which from that moment the Gods take on their own shoulders, because Apollo shows that there exists a way of peace. Man can choose. He can be free.

The fierce Erinyes become gentle. They lose their old name, and are called from henceforth *Eumenides*, the kindly ones. The law of the Forgiveness of Sin is born, through the intervention of Apollo, the God of Light and Love.

Through all the great Mystery Schools of Greece there runs the wonderful thread which is slowly weaving the pattern of understanding, of nearer understanding, between the divine and the earthly worlds.

If all the visible and invisible things of the God's creation are sought for—as they were in Greece—in their elemental substance: in Sun and fire, in wind and weather, in seas and rivers, and in the darkness of rock and cave, they are very near. All surrounding things are themselves the ethical and moral foundations of life; they are living spiritual substance of Eros—creative Love—itself. They are both dark and gloomy, bright and effulgent.

And above all they are filled with expectancy; they transpose their expectancy—this unwritten and unspoken urge to eager service—to men: into the human thoughts themselves.

All men look for something more than that which is. They listen, spiritually, to the Word, which sounds as though from the Sun, but is in the air, and in the fire, and in the water, and in the earth. They can even feel themselves wedded to the nymphs, the river-Gods, the fauns. . . .

One wonders—is it a childhood that has come back to mankind? And then one listens to the Grecian sages: one ponders on the strange words of a Heraclitus; delights in the wisdom of a Socrates; and feels pride in the brilliance of an Aristotle. . . .

No; it is not a childhood, nor is it an old age, nor a middle age of mankind. It is in no way relative. It is, somehow pure, MAN . . . a being, resting in the balance. A being *ready* for the grand ascent.

To what? To more Light?

TROY

Two things made the possession of the city of Troy into a beacon of longing. One was the beauty of Helen; the other was the wooden image of Pallas Athena, the goddess of the highest wisdom.

If the Golden Fleece was an image of the purified human soul and of the Soul of the Sun, this figure of Athena, called the Palladium, was the symbol of the Gnosis of the Spirit.

The ancient Gnosis was a system of knowledge that was an echo of all the Mystery wisdom of the past. It recognised the essence of all things as threefold, including the Sun. The Palladium was its symbol. The Gnosis was destined to disappear within the intellectual life of the Grecian people. In order that this should happen many human destinies had to become involved.

Paris, son of King Priam of Troy, is offered the choice between the favour of one of three Goddesses: one is Wisdom, Athena; one is Strength, Hera; and

one is Beauty, Aphrodite. They are the three foundations of human Ego-hood, the power to think, to will,
and to feel.

Paris chose the Goddess of Beauty, Aphrodite, and
she bestowed Helen upon him. The desire for Beauty
is the opposite of the desire for transcendent knowledge, but it is also one of the ways by which it can be
found. Paris had already a wife, Œnone, who was a
nymph and therefore not quite a mortal. Through
Œnone, Paris the Trojan was still united with the
higher worlds and with the old clairvoyance; but he
forsook her for Helen the Greek, and in doing so turned
away from the vision of his spiritual self—Œnone.
Such a decision must always bring strife in its train.
The historic event of the Trojan war is the struggle for
human progress.

A whole age goes down in the flames of Troy. But
the Palladium, sacred symbol of the ancient wisdom,
has to be preserved. It is stolen, and finds its way into
Greece; and because the Greek age has to be entwined
with the Roman, it comes later into the possession of
the Roman King Numa Pompilius.

Then, only a few knew the secret meaning of the
Palladium; but Rome, by virtue of its presence there,
becomes the " Eternal City ". Rome awakens in men
a longing which they cannot understand. The
Apostles are said to have known that the Palladium
was there; and they knew it was the symbol of the
Mysteries of Incarnation and of the three-fold nature
of God and Man. Rome drew them to her; and they
laid in her the foundations of Christianity.

In the year A.D. 330 Constantine removed the
Palladium to Constantinople, and made that city the
capital of the Empire. He buried the Treasure under

the pillar of his statue, which he had made in the likeness of Apollo. The narrow strip of sea on whose bank stands the city of Constantinople is called the Golden Horn, the golden horn of the Lamb of Gold. And near the buried Palladium was the Temple of the Holy Wisdom, Santa Sophia.

Tradition is strong on these points. Many will dismiss it as a fable. But there is more truth in it than in much that is accepted as history.

Even if this were only legend, one could be amazed at its profound significance. For it would point to the truth that nothing but renewed and purified seership, reborn out of the waters of the past, and regenerated, could ever bring light to the buried treasures of the divine and holy wisdom.

So the whole age of Grecian culture stands in history like a moment of pregnant silence between the old divine guidance and the entrance of earthly intelligence into the human Ego. It holds fast to its own peculiar conception of the threefold order of the world: steadfast belief in an equilibrium which places mankind in balance between Heaven and Earth.

We shall turn now to another part of the world and see how this same Trinity appears when we trade it to its primal and eternal source: the dynamic equilibrium between the " inner " and the " outer " of all existence.

CHAPTER VIII

HIBERNIA

A GREAT many old writings and traditions, going far back into pre-Christian times, have pointed to the West as the original home of all the secret wisdom of the world. The earliest historical records repeat these traditions. We find again and again, in Egypt, in Greece, in the far East, mention of the West as that part of the world where the secret of immortality was to be found; and it is said too that the " divine Fathers " of the human race used to be met with in Angelic forms, in ancient western sanctuaries, and that they were the primeval teachers of mankind. That it was through their influence that the first Mystery Schools were founded and the first Initiates created.

This may perhaps be called " mythological history "; but in our own time a great deal has been discovered which may some day cause us to call it rather " spiritual history ". . . . Much has been established too about the actual existence of the great continent of Atlantis now vanished under the Atlantic Ocean.* And we can trace how strongly there remained, and still remain, last faint remnants in Ireland and the Western coasts of Northern Europe, of the old clairvoyant powers, whose possessors still hint at the former existence of a once vast insight into the

* During the International Geophysical Year (1957–1958) and between 1959–1963 the Great Atlantic Ridge has been charted, with mountains 6,000 feet high. (" I.G.Y. The Year of the New Moons " by J. Tuzo Wilson.)

spiritual sources of the world and of the creation of
man; and that much of this wisdom is engraved in
strange forms upon the ancient stones, but is still uncomprehended.

Among modern investigators none have been able
to discover the hidden meanings of these ɩraditions and
documents relating to the West, and of their excavated
relics, to the same extent as has been done by Rudolf
Steiner. We shall do no more here than touch very
lightly upon one or two conclusions that can be
drawn from the results of his, and others', investiga-
tions.

It is a fact that neither ancient India, Persia,
Egypt, nor Greece can be said to have represented,
from their different standpoints, the whole content of
pre-Christian wisdom. Each taught a part of it, and
that part which was most profoundly connected with
the particular stage of the evolution of human consciousness existing at the time.

In a certain sense all these majestic phases and
aspects of the Mysteries can be said to arise and pass,
even though at the root of them there is that which is
immortal. For behind them all lies something that is
unchangeable and complete, the very essence of
human life on Earth, which is present still in our own
day although more or less unnoticed.

Actually, there is a basic and original conception
of Religion. It is, that man lives in two worlds, in the
sense that he recognises the world *outside* himself on the
one hand, and on the other hand an *inner* world—his
own reactions to the outer. No matter what form his
inner reactions may take, and no matter what kind of
Nature surrounds him, he himself must endeavour to
create a harmony between them. If they do not meet

in him, like a perfected complement of question and answer, his life will not be free from confusion.

Religion is, so to say, the Answerer of the questions aroused by both worlds in man. His inner life went astray from the sublime and original Nature, and how to reunite them was the content of what once were called the Great Mysteries. They are based upon a Triad—Two, and One.

The ages of civilisation which we have already mentioned approached, in the main, but one side or the other: the whole world of Nature was the primal concern of the Persian wisdom for example; the whole world of the spiritual inwardness of man was the concern of ancient India. In Hibernia they were united.

In view of the great researches that have been made into the Atlantean question,* one can really assume that the great early civilisations arose from a very slow and gradual development of pressure-points caused by the movement of large masses of the original wanderers from Atlantis back again from their settlements in Asia, westward towards the lost continent of Atlantis. An end of this movement, with its intervening pauses and settlements, was reached at the borders of the Atlantic Ocean. It is at this point that we are usually accustomed to speak definitely of the Celtic peoples. But some say that this is where, and when, the Celtic race comes, not to its cultural beginning, but to its end; that they end where they began, perhaps eight or nine thousand years before, where the feet of some of their Atlantean ancestors had been stayed— in Ireland, and the Western coasts of Europe; and old traditions say that those who had settled there

* Guenther Wachsmuth. " The Evolution of Mankind."

after the Deluge were " gods " who kept themselves secluded, and knew everything.

But one can perhaps apply the epithet " Celt " not so much to an ancient race, as to a certain state of consciousness existing long ago among groups of the original eastward-wandering Atlanteans: something that was like a persistent longing, a kind of dim dreamlike ancestral memory, to seek for the vanished world that had gone down under the waters, and to turn once more to the West.

The West has always been a place of longing. It is where the Sun goes down; but in going down reveals itself spiritually. Thus arose the universal tradition that the secret of immortality would be discovered fully only in the " mountain of the West ".

For those lands whose Mysteries we have already mentioned, the general direction was North-west, rather than due West. The " birthplace " of the world was thought to be in the North. The West was the place of death—and immortality. In the North-west the Earth would surely offer all of her secrets to the soul who could go in memory, by the " path of his ancestors " through the desolation of the deluge to the spiritual Atlantis. There he would find his questions answered.

We have an example of this search for the West in the Babylonian epic of Gilgamesh, engraved on tablets which are preserved in the British Museum. He journeyed—it was an inner mystical journey as well as an actual one—to a central European offshoot of the old *Hibernian* Mysteries; for it was in Ireland (Hibernia)—the meeting-place of the remnants of Atlantean wisdom with that of the post-diluvian world—that the original Great Mysteries had taken root.

Strange things still remain in existence there, whose origins must have been older than the Druid Temples —underground chambers, single pairs of rough, pillar-like stones, mysterious references to the " Twins ". . . .

One of the most ancient of all traditions is that knowledge of all the Sciences and all the Arts was once inscribed upon two twin pillars of stone. It touches the fundamental principle of man's two-fold mode of existence: looking outwards at the world and all its creatures, connecting himself with everything that is outside him by means of his senses; and looking inwardly—seeing that everything in his inner life of soul consists of all possible impressions and experiences, feelings, passions, imaginations, and impulses. Through the one pole he is " awake " to the outer world; through the other he " dreams " his own creations.

These archaic Mystery centres in Ireland were schools for " Science " and " Art ", culminating in a religious revelation.* But the final object of the teaching was only attained by first of all training the neophyte to perceive the illusory nature of both worlds. For this, each pole of life had to be approached separately, to begin with, during years of both practical study and application, and intense and solitary meditation.

The peculiar nature of the training made it possible for the pupil to feel as though he lost his own identity when all remembrance of his inner life was excluded,

* Science and Art cannot in this connection be interpreted in the strictly modern sense. "Art ", for instance, denotes what man creates from within himself, which in a certain sense is always representative of a mere transient portion of his being, and as such cannot be wholly true. " Science " is all outer knowledge which, since the created world itself is impermanent, subject to continue metamorphosis. Thus both these spheres can be experienced as illusions; the latter having no real " being " and the former no truth.

so that he felt himself as though drawn out and absorbed into the whole outer Universe. He discovered then that however great his knowledge of the outer world might be it was nothing but the pursuit of an endless expansion and scattering of himself into an infinite past—into " what has been made ". Nothing that he could learn had any reality if there were no human response to it, in his own, or others', inner world. So the outer world was an illusion.

And on the other hand, when in his training the outer world was excluded from him, and only the inner remained, then all creative fantasy, all experiences of the soul, all self-born impulses to live and to do, were seen to have no truth in themselves and were vain. For if the inner life finds no touchstone in any outer world there is nothing that enables one to say " that is true ". So the inner world was also an illusion.

Two mysterious statues standing in the gloom of the Temple were the two " stones " upon which, spiritually, all this was engraved. They stood there, presenting a vast enigma—the seeming denial of the very meaning and sense of all human existence. To face this apparent nothingness was the great and incredible trial of that ancient form of initiation. Revelation and victory came only when the terrible experience seemed to threaten the annihilation of life itself.

The solution arose as a vision. It was a vision of the God who was able to hold these two " pillars " of existence in equilibrium, and able to give each of them their true meaning and significance. It was the same Being whom all peoples have revered under various names as the divine Sun-Spirit, and whom we revere as Christ.

The Hibernian initiate knew then that in a certain

sense this Being was like unto himself, the cosmic archetype of his own Ego; and that it is only by virtue of his own *self* that man can find his way between the two extremes of his human nature. He himself, seen in the " Light of the World ", is Religion.

The " way between the two extremes " is the supreme law of life wherever and whenever human souls are capable of comprehending it. Moreover the riddle of death was answered by this Being who is deathless; and the riddle of fruitless creation was answered by the same Being; for whatever is created through the true wisdom of the " I am " is never without fruit, but builds the future world.

So the whole event was the experiencing of a Triad: first the Two—" Science " and " Art ", the Outer and the Inner. They are united by the Third, which is Religion.

That was the real secret of the ancient West, which drew men's souls like a magnet for hundreds and hundreds of years.

One of these Mystery sanctuaries was at Tara in County Meath; and not far away is another site which bore the name of *Emain Macha* which means the Twins of Macha.

The " long green hill " of Tara, riddled deep with undisclosed subterranean chambers, was, as a writer says, " the nursery and heart of Ireland's heroic past. It dates from dateless neolithic ages. It is as old as the Tiber's Town of the Twins. . . . Was Tara, like Rome, a Twin Town? . . . From Murrisk on the edge of the Western ocean to Tara of the Kings, there are twin stones in many a field. Was Tara a Twin Town like the Rome of Romulus and Remus? Did the ancient Irish worship the Twins? "*

* *I Follow St. Patrick*, Gogarty (Rich and Cowan).

Indeed they did. And we have seen in what manner. We can imagine them best on Ireland's Western shores, where the voice of the Atlantic, murmuring over a buried continent, echoes like far-off thunder in some secret cavity of the cliffs, sheltering the two inscrutable Figures—the dread Twin Pillars of the world.

But the supreme importance of these oldest Mysteries is crowned by the fact of the preservation, in Ireland, of a pure and powerful seership up to, and beyond, the beginning of our era. This made it possible for the unique vision of the Sun-Being, Christ, as the One between the Two, to be carried over into the new age. The physical events of Christ's life in Palestine were seen by the Hibernian Priests at the moment of their occurrence!

The Death and Resurrection of Christ took place far away from these remote and hidden sanctuaries. The Saviour prophesied by Zarathustra, and who had appeared as the Revealer in the ancient Temples, had at last descended to the physical plane. When He had formerly appeared in the vision of the Irish Initiates, He was not yet on Earth—He was still a heavenly Being. But now He was in His human Form, and had to pass through death, and this they saw. And were there not three Crosses on Golgotha? The One between the Two?—Christ united in Himself the two poles of existence and fulfilled the ancient saying: " When the Two shall become One, the Outer as the Inner."

We cannot here mention the many spiritual and historical undercurrents which could substantiate this statement about the Hibernian vision. That would take us too far away from our present subject. But there is a legend that the Irish poet, W. B. Yeats, has touched upon in his lovely poem *The Secret Rose*, of the King

" whose eyes
Saw the Pierced Hands and Rood of elder, rise
In Druid vapour and make the torches dim "... .

The King who saw the vision in the smoke of the altar incense was Conchubar of Ireland. He did not see the Crucifixion, but on the first Good Friday he saw " unusual changes of the Creation, and the eclipse of the Sun, and the Moon at the full; and he asked of Bucrach, the Leinster Druid, who was along with him, what it was that brought that unusual change upon the Planets of Heaven, and upon the Earth. . . . ' Jesus Christ, the Son of God ', said the Druid, ' who is now being crucified by the Jews '."...

The remarkable thing about this legend is that Conchubar realised that a change had come over the whole planetary system. The event that caused it could have been no ordinary happening, but something affecting worlds beyond the Earth to a tremendous degree. Yet the answer given by the Druid to his question pointed to an earthly event. Therefore this earthly event must have been in direct connection with the whole Cosmos.

The Druids were not Christian in our sense of the word, even the greatest of them were but pre-Christian recorders of the Sun-Being's transcendental way to the Earth. They had to wait; until the great arc of light which flashed upon their vision from Palestine to Ireland could at last focus itself in the teachings of a Patrick or a Columba, and disperse what was left of the old Temple shadows.

It was this " Sun of the West ", shining between its

Pillars, that finally lit the flame of love and sacrifice and kindled the true understanding of the Trinity, enabling the Irish Christian missionaries to preserve Christianity in its purest form for centuries, and to be the means for the conversion of nearly all Europe. They knew Christ as a Cosmic Being:

> Son of the dawn
> Son of the clouds
> Son of the planets
> Son of the stars
> Son of the elements
> Son of the Heavens
> Son of the Moon
> Son of the SUN.

This oldest source of Science and Art and Religion is, so to say, super-historical. Its beginnings are rooted beyond the dawn of the civilisations of the Eastern hemisphere; and its end is not yet. To-day we find its traces most plainly in all early Celtic literature and art, and reflected in the " Triads " of the Bards.

Its influences reveal themselves too in the sphere of history. They can be traced right into the seventeenth and eighteenth centuries, and even now; not as mere tradition, but as *forces* working into historical events and into individual deeds, and even into the chaos between modern Science, Art, and Religion.

Yet the only " literary " remains of Hibernia's original Mysteries are the signs and patterns graven into grey and ancient stones. The teachings live on, even though unknown—because they must. They are written daily afresh in every heart and are stamped upon every momentous decision.

The " Triads " of the Welsh Bards are a clear echo of the old Irish Mysteries. And again and again it is

the Sun which appears in them or in other writings as
the source or centre of the Trinity:

". . . The Trinity (Deity) in the course of the Sun
Having His habitation in the bright Sun ". . . .

A commentator (1760) says: " I have not yet noticed
in any place which I have read, that they themselves
worshipped the Sun, but only Him who dwelt in it.
Therefore, in the act of worshipping, as well as in the
performance of every other solemn rite, they did all in
the face of the Sun and the eye of light, that is, in the
face, or before the face, of Him whom they regarded as
living and existing in the Sun and the light."

In the *Barddas*, a pupil is asked by the Teacher:
" Why is the face turned towards the Sun in every
asseveration and prayer? "

Answer: " Because God is in every light, and the
chief of every light is the Sun. It is through fire that
God brings back to Himself all things that emanated
from Him; and therefore it is not right to ally oneself
to God but in the light.

" There are three kinds of light, namely: that which
is obtained in the sciences of the Teachers; and that
which is possessed in the understanding of the head
and heart, that is, in the soul. On that account, every
vow is made in the face of the three lights, that is, in
the light of the Sun is seen the light of a Teacher, or
demonstration; and from both of these is the light of
the intellect, or that of the soul.". . .

The three lights are here pure " Hibernian ": the
science of the Teacher; the Sun, in whom he is; and
the light of the inner life, or soul.

. . . " There are three primeval Unities, and more
than one of each cannot exist: one God; one Truth;

and one point of liberty, and this is where all opposites equiponderate.

"Three things proceed from the three primeval Unities: all life; all goodness; all power."

In this Triad God, from whom proceeds all life, is the equivalent of all knowledge—" science "; Truth is the positive aspect of that which is " untrue " in human creations that proceed from the still unknowing human soul; when clarified, it produces goodness. This comes from within man, and is " art ", in the Hibernian sense. And finally, " one point of liberty " —this is the *I am;* and from its balance between the two proceeds power.

And from another aspect:

" Three things united will produce power: I, Thou, and It; that is to say the I willing, the Thou performing what the I wills, and the It becoming that which is decided by the I, willing in union with the Thou. And they are called the Three fundamentals, because from them in one are produced might and existence.". . .

" Three things will prevail at last: fire, truth, and life.". . .

The old wisdom of the Bards became Christianised in later centuries, and there are many beautiful Christian " Triads ". But these fragments point unquestionably, if rather intellectually, back to those great Mysteries of the past which we have tried to describe. They overshadow us powerfully to-day. Who does not know the sorrow that comes from the inability to unite what the heart knows as truth, with what it sees in the outer world as man has made it?*

---

* For more detailed study of Hibernia read *The Flaming Door*, Eleanor C. Merry (New Knowledge Books).

CHAPTER IX

THE SUN OF THE NORTH

SEEN from the West, a certain wholeness is given to all we have so far considered; everything becomes Form; beginning and end mould themselves into a totality; a whole Cosmos shapes itself in the light of the westering Sun; and we found in Hibernia the original substance of a vast section of the coming evolution of human consciousness, based on what is most ancient.

The reflection of Hibernian wisdom gleams in a thousand facets of history and mythology; in King Arthur and his Queen and the Round Table, in the Eddas, in the Finnish Kalevala, in the legend of Floris and Blanchefleur; and hidden behind the history of the making of Europe and its nations; in revolutions and wars no less than in arts and sciences. Far back, its secrets were echoed beneath the towers of Troy, and in the Temples of Eleusis and Samothrace; it hovered over Hiram and Solomon in the building in the Temple; it was in the three crosses on the hill of Golgotha.

And none of these are isolated things in their origins and effects; they form a whole—a single scroll—like the " little book " that the Angel gave to St. John to eat.

In the space of this volume it is, of course, impossible to cover more than a fraction of the ground. So we must confine ourselves to the main trends which arise

113

from the cultural epochs we have already alluded to. From Hibernia and the West, we are drawn first to look towards the North.

But here we are faced with a certain difficulty in apportioning the right place in this narrative to all that was born out of the Scandinavian and North-Germanic peoples. We cannot quite fit this into any precise sequence. Because, in the evolution of different peoples through the ages, their psychological development is often a question of what is *remembered* in the ancestral stream and what is *present* in the consciousness, and what is *forgotten*, and how these are combined.

Different kinds of Gods or different ranks of spiritual beings are remembered or forgotten in the passage of the ages, and the world-picture differs accordingly.

The Northern peoples developed certain faculties later than others, and have livingly combined what was actually developing and present in them at the beginning of our era, with things of a far-distant past. Even in post-Christian times they could feel the creative world-processes in Nature as Powers still forging their own humanness, still working in the pulsation of their blood and the rhythmic flow of their breathing—as the Gods Thor and Odin—still shaping their souls to think, to feel, and to will. And they embodied this past-in-present of the world-creation in their myths.

Since they kept longest the living consciousness of a Nature that was saturated with spiritual activity, they felt the more deeply the fading away of clairvoyant vision.

The Sun, in the far northern countries, is something other than the Sun known in more temperate zones. The colours of Heaven are not the same. The Midnight Sun shows itself in physical reality; and the long nights of winter are aflame with the Aurora Borealis. Spring, when the snows have gone, is a thing of incredible wonder. . . . Nature is a continual miracle; and the intensity of light that was kindled by the vision of her illimitable power was in truth like an inner and utterly magical sunlight for the soul.

Only such a people could experience to the full the tragedy of the darkening of this light. The epics and myths of the North are born of the approaching twilight: a twilight wherein the Gods of all the distant past live on as though still active in the midst of a soul-consciousness that in some ways is already beyond them.

When other peoples were establishing themselves in the awareness of their Ego, the Spirit of the North stayed a little longer in its twilight; and the people could experience together both loss, and joy, in the certainty of the ultimate return of the Sun-God, Baldur the Beautiful, who had been killed by the blind Hödur.

Christianity did not begin to spread in the far North till the ninth century after Christ, and reached it as a new dawn, shining into souls that were filled with longing.

For all these reasons it is perhaps inevitable that we should quote some fragments from their Sun-stories here, at this point, though strictly speaking they survived until much later.

The Scandinavian mythology sees the Fall of man as resulting in three things: selfishness, lying, and illness leading to death; and these they called the Midgard Snake, the Fenris Wolf, and Hel, or Hela. These three were instrumental in causing the power of spiritual vision to grow dim. A " seeing " and a " not-seeing " then alternated with one another; and these two states were perceived—even in later centuries—as beings—the not-seeing or blind Hödur and the seeing Sun-like Baldur. Then Hödur killed Baldur.

Vision of the dwelling-place of the Gods, Asgard, slowly vanished. This is expressed as *Ragnarok*, the " twilight of the Gods ". Odin and Thor, Baldur and Hödur and Freya are no longer seen. But what they have been and done in the building up of the spirit and soul and life of the people remains. The Gods themselves sink out of sight—Odin wrestling with the Fenris Wolf; Thor has killed the Midgard Snake, and Freya is slain by the flaming sword of Surtur who rises out of the Earth.

The teacher-seers of the Scandinavian people warn their pupils that the twilight would one day give place to a new dawn, and that later the old capacities of vision would return, but would then, if they were alone depended on, reveal what was *untrue*. For in the meantime the vanished Gods would have undergone an evolution themselves, and a new light would be accessible to the human soul; while the old vision, turned into untruth by the Fenris Wolf, would have to be finally overcome, not by Odin, but by the grace of the God Vidar—the " silent Vidar "—who would break his long silence and appear as the Saviour.

Vidar is none other than He who is the creator even of Odin. Odin is the God of the power of speech. Vidar will fight with the God of untrue speech, the Fenris Wolf. The new inner self-awareness will in the end produce a regenerated way of vision—a clearer-seeing Baldur. But the Fenris Wolf continually struggles to seize hold of the *old* way and to use it for deceit and delusion. He " swallows the Sun ".

The Fenris Wolf can only be vanquished by Vidar,

because Vidar (Veda) is the WORD itself, is Christ—
the Restorer of true vision.

The Edda tells the story of Baldur's death. This
Son of the Sun had a premonition that he was about to
die, and told the assembled Gods.

The Goddess Freya exacted an oath from fire and
water, from iron and all the other metals, as well as
from stones, earths, diseases, beasts, birds, poisons, and
creeping things, that none of them would harm him.
But one thing was omitted, because Freya thought it
was entirely harmless; and this was the mistletoe.

All the Gods, in sport, began to throw their weapons
at Baldur, who, of course, received no hurt from them.
But the evil Loki determined that he should die; and
having heard that the mistletoe had not been asked to
take the oath, he put a branch of it into the hand of
the blind Hödur, and directed his aim. . . .

" So on the floor lay Baldur dead; and round
  Lay thickly strewn swords, axes, darts, and spears,
  Which all the Gods in sport had idly thrown
  At Baldur, whom no weapon pierced or clove;
  But in his breast stood fixed the fatal bough
  Of mistletoe, which Lok the Accuser gave
  To Hödur, and unwitting Hödur threw—
  'Gainst that alone had Baldur's life no charm."

(The spirit of Baldur speaks) :

" Far to the south, beyond the blue, there spreads
  Another Heaven, the boundless—no one yet
  Hath reached it; there hereafter shall arise
  The second Asgard, with another name.
  Thither, when o'er this present Earth and Heavens
  The tempest of the latter days hath swept,
  And they from sight have disappeared, and sunk,
  Shall a small remnant of the Gods repair;
  Hödur and I shall join them from the grave.
  There reassembling we shall see emerge

From the bright Ocean at our feet an Earth
More fresh, more verdant than the last, with fruits
Self-springing, and a seed of man preserved,
Who then shall live in peace as now in war.
But we in Heaven shall find again with joy
The ruin'd palaces of Odin, seats
Familiar, halls where we have supp'd of old;
Re-enter them with wonder, never fill
Our eyes with gazing, and rebuild with tears.
And we shall tread once more the well-known plain
Of Ida, and among the grass shall find
The golden dice wherewith we played of yore;
And that will bring to mind the former life
And pastimes of the Gods, the wise discourse
Of Odin, the delights of other days,
O Hermod, pray that thou may'st join us then!
Such for the future is my hope; meanwhile,
I rest the thrall of Hela, and endure
Death, and the gloom which round me even now
Thickens, and to its inner gulph recalls.
Farewell, for longer speech is not allow'd."

MATTHEW ARNOLD. From *Baldur Dead.*

Every nation has taken its rise out of some special psychological characteristic, conditioned by physical geography, which is subject to modification by other influences reaching it from other peoples.

In Finland, long ago, the feeling of identity with certain forces of the surrounding Nature was peculiarly strong; and in a dreamlike way made the people feel that their souls were influenced and moulded by three great tendencies. These three became, for their imaginative vision, three Heroes—Vainamoinen, Ilmarinen, and Lemminkainen. Vainamoinen was the inspiring force, and the creator of music; Ilmarinen was the cunning smith and builder—the source of the powers of the mind; Lemminkainen was more connected with what was physical corporeal power.

A crisis occurs and is described in the Epic *Kalevala,*

when the Sun and Moon are stolen away from Heaven and hidden in the Earth. The Heroes are unable to release them from their earthly prison. This can only come about through a gradual evolution which tends to merge the three aspects of the soul into one; and this is a step towards the dawning realisation of Egohood.

(The old witch of Pohjola has imprisoned the Sun and Moon in a mountain. Vainamoinen discovers by divination where they are. Meanwhile his brother the smith, Ilmarinen, forges a new Moon and Sun, and puts them in the sky, but they will not shine. Vainamoinen tries to deliver the imprisoned Sun and Moon, but cannot succeed in spite of all his sorcery. He vows vengence on Louhi, the old witch. She is alarmed, and lets the Sun and Moon go free.

The following are some fragments from Runo 49.)

Still the Sun was never shining,
Neither gleamed the golden moonlight,
Not in Vainola's dark dwellings,
Not on Kalevala's broad heathlands.
Frost upon the crops descended,
And the cattle suffered greatly,
And the birds of air felt strangely,
All mankind felt ever mournful,
For the sunlight shone no longer,
Neither did there shine the moonlight. . . .

From the hearth arose the craftsman
From beneath the wall the craftsman,
That a new moon he might forge them,
And a new sun he might make them,
And a moon of gold constructed,
And a sun he made of silver. . . .

" Out of gold a moon I'm shaping,
And a sun of silver making,

In the sky I then will place them,
Over six of starry heavens."
   Then the aged Vainamoinen
Answered in the words that follow:
" O thou smith, O Ilmarinen,
What you make is wholly useless,
Gold will never shine like moonlight,
Silver will not shine like sunlight."
   Thus the smith a moon constructed,
And a sun completely finished,
Eagerly he raised them upward,
Raised them to the best position,
Raised the moon to fir-tree's summit,
Set the sun upon a pine-tree. . . .
   But the moon shed forth no lustre,
And the sun was likewise rayless. . . .

(Vainamoinen journeys to Pohjola and the sons of
Pohja come out to meet him, determined that he shall
not find the Sun and Moon's prison-house. He
questions them):

Vainamoinen, old and steadfast,
Answered in the words which follow:
" Of the moon are curious tidings,
Of the sun are wondrous tidings,
Where is now the sun imprisoned,
Whither has the moon been taken? "
   Answered then the sons of Pohja,
And the evil army answered:
" Thus it is the sun is hidden,
Sun is hidden, moon imprisoned,
In the stones of many colours,
In the rocks as hard as iron,
And from this escape they cannot,
And release shall never reach them."
   Then the aged Vainamoinen
Answered in the words that follow:
" If the sun from rock ascends not,
   Nor the moon from rocky mountain,
Let us join in closest conflict,
Let us grasp our trusty sword-blades." . . .

Out into the yard they hastened,
On the grass to meet in conflict,
And the aged Vainamoinen
Struck a blow with lightning swiftness,
Struck a blow and struck a second,
And he sheared, like roots of turnips,
Off he shore, like heads of flax-plant,
Heads of all the sons of Pohja.
  Then the aged Vainamoinen
Sought for where the moon was hidden,
Likewise would release the sunlight
From the rocks of varied colour,
From the depths of steely mountain,
From the rocks as hard as iron.
  Then he walked a little distance,
But a very little distance,
When he saw a copse all verdant,
In the copse a lovely birch-tree,
And a large stone block beneath it,
And a rock beneath the stone-block,
And there were nine doors before it,
In the doors were bolts a hundred. . . .

  " Unto spells the bolts will yield not,
And the locks my magic breaks not;
Strength of hands will never move them,
And no strength of arm will force them."

  To the smith's forge then he wandered,
And he spoke the words which follow:
" O thou smith, O Ilmarinen,
Forge me now a mighty trident,
And a dozen hatchets forge me,
And a bunch of keys enormous,
From the stone the moon to rescue,
From the rock the sun deliver.". . .

(The old witch, Louhi, sensing her danger, disguises
herself as a hawk and flies to Ilmarinen to ask him what
he is doing. He tells the bird that he is forging a ring for
the neck of Louhi in order to fetter her to a mountain.
The witch flies away and soon comes back in the form
of a dove. Then she tells Ilmarinen that she has

released the sun and moon from their prison. Ilmarinen sees
that she has spoken the truth, and hurries to Vainamoinen to tell him the good news.)

> And he gazed aloft to heaven;
> Moon was risen, sun was loosened,
> In the sky the sun was beaming.
>   Then the aged Vainamoinen
> Made a speech without delaying,
> And he spoke the words which follow,
> And in words like this expressed him:
> " Hail O Moon who beamest yonder,
> Thus thy fair cheek well displaying,
> Golden Sun who risest yonder,
> Sun who once again arisest!
> Golden Moon from stone delivered,
> Fairest Sun from rock arisen,
> Like the golden cuckoo rise you,
> Lead the life ye led afore-time,
> And resume your former journeys,
> Rise for ever in the morning,
> From this present day hereafter.
> Bring us always happy greetings,
> That our wealth increases ever,
> Game for ever in our fingers,
> Fortune at the points of fish-hooks.
>   Go ye on your path with blessings,
> Go ye on your charming journey,
> Let your crescent now be beauteous,
> Rest ye joyful in the evening."

The Rune that follows is the last one of the Epic. It
describes the miraculous virgin birth of a child from
the maiden Marjatta. Her parents drive her from
their home, and the child is born in a stable. Neither
an old man, nor Vainamoinen, whom she asks to
baptise her son, will do so. Then the child himself
rebukes them, and the old man finally signs him with
the cross and baptises him King of Karelia. Vainamoinen, angry that the child should be greater than
he, " sings himself " a new boat of copper and voyages

away in it, leaving behind him the gift of Music for the people, but knowing that he will some day return.

Soon after, the child disappears. Marjatta looks for him everywhere. She asks a star, and then the Moon and the Sun, where he is; and first the Star and then the Moon reply that they know him because he created them, but they will not tell where he is. Then the Sun, confessing that the child was his creator also, says he will be found half-sunk in the marshland. . . .

Some commentators think that this last Rune is an addition to the Epic, made to give it a Christian character. But it is in fact an inseparable part of the whole.

The " old " Sun and Moon have been imprisoned by the witch, Louhi, who represents the beginning of mere intellectual and arid reasoning and its consequent doubt. Ilmarinen, who is a worker in metals and knows much sorcery, tries to create substitutes for the lost light by making another Sun and Moon. He makes the mistake of creating the Moon out of gold and the Sun out of silver, instead of the other way about; and so they will not shine. Then Louhi sets the real Sun and Moon free. This is prophetic, for she shows herself for a moment in the form of a dove, symbol of the Spirit that is to create the redeemed and spiritualised Thinking of mankind.* Then a " risen " Sun and Moon give their light to the world.

Vainamoinen, " old and steadfast ", must depart. He belongs to a vanished age. But he leaves behind him Music, the Heavenly archetype of Speech, which can lift human souls once more to the divine.

The birth of the Child is part and parcel of all such

* The awakening of intellectual thought to spiritual thought occurs in other myths and legends too.

mythological representations of the great World-Mysteries. It belongs to all time. Every individual can experience it, when in his own soul the old witch, Louhi, is vanquished.

The whole Creation knows this Child of the virgin birth. But he is to be found only when the word of the Sun points to him " sunk in the marshland "—for he is the Spirit of the Sun, come down from Heaven to be the Spirit of the Earth.

CHAPTER X

KRISHNA AND BUDDHA

KRISHNA

IN endeavouring to follow the ancient records connected with the gradual approach of Christ to the Earth we find that everything that has to do with it must be sought, so far as the more ancient civilisations are concerned, in a wandering through geographical Space.

A regular time-sequence cannot easily be followed. We go from the ancient Asiatic wisdom to Persia; then to Egypt and on to Greece and Rome. Then the trail takes us to the North. In Hibernia we must touch upon things whose real origins are infinitely remote, but which reveal their closeness to the main theme only when we trace their later manifestations. In Scandinavia it is the same. Its vast depths of wisdom come to the surface so late that they seem to be quite out of place as historical sequence. The Druid wisdom of Britain had risen to its heights long before the Scandinavian epics appeared, and must be linked on the other hand to the age-old Hibernian mysteries of the Trinity. All the wisdoms themselves, in their geographical positions, are employed in the service of the secrets of Space—Stars, Moon, Planets, Elements. . . . What we find about it all is " here " or " there ", rather than " when ".

But as we come nearer to the time of Christ, this changes. Men begin to feel more clearly their " I-am-ness ", and that it is involved in *history*. It is only after Christ that Time really begins to dominate this epic of the Sun. . . . Yet Time itself, urging mankind into a realisation of progress, then reveals a new secret of Space: *the world is discovered*.

Through this, men slowly come to perceive the value, not only of themselves, but of others. They have to learn the secret of individuals that live side by side with one another in Space. The " I " comes more and more to apprehend the " Thou "—of whatever tribe or race, or nation. Dimly it is perceived that the lesson which has ultimately to be learnt is that the Ego, if it lives in itself alone, remains nothing but a shadow of the reality. It must learn to know itself through others. In every other soul lives that which reflects our own self back to us. In all humanity we have to see— innumerably multiplied—the One. . . .

Taking all this into consideration we find our attention turned once more to the East which presents us with a particular aspect of the dawn of individual responsibility. When speaking of India we might have quoted a fragment from the great poem of the *Bhagavad Gita*, placing it there in advance of its historical time because we know that it is rooted in the depths of a much more ancient and sublime wisdom. But the vision of Arjuna described in the *Gita*, and the teaching given to him by Krishna, actually belong very near to the period of seven hundred years before Christ, which we shall now try to picture.

In this fragment of the great epic, the *Mahabarata*, the three paths of oriental wisdom* are brought together. When it became known in Europe in the

* Page 227.

nineteenth century it was acclaimed as the greatest philosophical poem in the world. It must be introduced here because it touches the heart of the problems that arise through the gradual weakening in mankind of the ties of blood, and thereby the furthering of the evolution of free Egohood.

We have already seen how deep is the connection between this development of the " I " and the age-long changes in thought and consciousness, especially in respect of the Sun. In the *Gita* we see more than a hint of this. The three philosophical trends upon which the poem is built—from the Veda, through Sankhya, to Yoga, lead the human soul to the recognition of its independence. The World-Self, appearing as Krishna, is here appreciable as the " inner teacher " leading man towards freedom through taking the responsibility of goodness upon himself. Krishna points forward to Christ.

Arjuna, the hero Prince, is compelled by duty to fight to the death against members of his own family. The anguish he feels gives him vision before the battle begins. The Lord Krishna appears before him and teaches him. Leading him step by step, he first shows Arjuna how he need have no fear, for he is only the instrument of the great Self in whom all lives are hidden, created and destroyed. Even if a man turns away from duty altogether, his destiny would lead him to his fulfilment in the end.

In this sense, those whom Arjuna will kill have already been slain by Krishna. Yet none perish, for all are part of that Self of Worlds who is unborn, ever-existent, and imperishable. He is Krishna, Krishna is mankind. He lives in every human being and all are at the same time in him. This is the teaching of the Veda.

Once in a cosmic age the great Self can appear before men as their teacher. Arjuna is to be granted this unique experience.

All deeds which are necessary and lawful in life must be done. But there is no pain in doing them if a man can lift himself above them, if in every action he renounces all desire for its fruits. This is the first step.

Krishna says:

> ... *Therefore thy task prescribed
> With spirit unattached gladly perform,
> Since in performance of plain duty man
> Mounts to his highest bliss. By works alone,
> Janak and ancient saints reached blessedness.
> Moreover for the upholding of thy kind,
> Action thou shouldst embrace. What the wise choose
> The unwise people take; what best men do
> The multitude will follow. Look on me,
> Thou Son of Pritha! In the three wide worlds
> I am not bound to any toil, no height
> Awaits to scale, no gift remains to gain,
> Yet I act here! and, if I acted not—
> Earnest and watchful—those that look to me
> For guidance, sinking back to sloth again
> Because I slumbered, would decline from good,
> And I should break Earth's order and commit
> Her offspring unto ruin, Bharata!
> Even as the unknowing toil, wedded to sense,
> So let the enlightened toil, sense-freed, but set
> To bring the world deliverance, and its bliss;
> Not sowing in those simple, busy hearts
> Seeds of despair. Yea! Let each play his part
> In all he finds to do, with unyoked soul.
> All things are everywhere by Nature wrought
> In interaction of the qualities.
> The fool, cheated by self, thinks, " This I did "
> And " That I wrought "; but—ah, thou strong-armed
>   Prince!—
> A better-lessoned mind, knowing the play
> Of visible things within the world of sense,

* Translation by Matthew Arnold, *The Song Celestial*. Kegan Paul, Trench & Co.

And how the qualities must qualify,
Standeth aloof even from his acts. Th'untaught
Live mixed with them, knowing not Nature's way,
Of highest aims unwitting, slow and dull.
Those make thou not to stumble, having the light;
But all thy dues discharging, for my sake,
With meditation centred inwardly,
Seeking no profit, satisfied, serene,
Heedless of issue—fight! . . .

Here is a hint of the qualifying, individualising force working in the world—the Sankhya philosophy.

Then, Krishna leads Arjuna along the way of Yoga, teaching the overcoming of the hindrances in which the soul is immersed in the stream of life. As each is overcome, man rises nearer and nearer to the vision of that which is pure and above all things, though permeating all.

He learns to hold fast to himself, and to the divine prototype of himself, which as yet he cannot see. Only the highest spiritual achievement can reveal Krishna as he is in his divine nature, which includes within its purity every created being. Then Krishna, in special grace, bestows upon Arjuna the " divine eye ", and he sees the vision:

Arjuna's vision.

Yea! I have seen! I see!
Lord! all is wrapped in Thee!
The gods are in Thy glorious frame! the creatures
Of earth, and heaven, and hell
In Thy Divine form dwell,
And in Thy countenance shine all the features

Of Brahma, sitting lone
Upon his lotus-throne;
Of saints and sages, and the serpent races
Ananta, Vasuki;
Yea! mightiest Lord! I see
Thy thousand thousand arms, and breasts, and faces.

And eyes—on every side
Perfect, diversified;
And nowhere end of Thee, nowhere beginning,
Nowhere a centre! Shifts—
Wherever soul's gaze lifts—
Thy central Self, all-wielding, and all-winning!

Infinite King! I see
The anadem on Thee,
The club, the shell, the discus; see Thee burning
In beams insufferable,
Lighting earth, heaven, and hell
With brilliance blazing, glowing, flashing; turning

Darkness to dazzling day,
Look I whichever way;
Ah, Lord! I worship Thee, the Undivided,
The Uttermost of thought,
The Treasure-Palace wrought
To hold the wealth of the worlds; the Shield provided

To shelter Virtue's laws;
The Fount whence Life's stream draws
All waters of all rivers of all being;
The One Unborn, Unending;
Unchanging and Unblending!
With might and majesty, past thought, past seeing!

Silver of moon, and gold
Or sun, are glories rolled
From Thy great eyes; Thy visage, beaming tender
Throughout the stars and skies,
Doth to warm life surprise
Thy Universe. The worlds are filled with wonder

Of Thy perfections! Space
Star-sprinkled, and void place
From Pole to Pole of the Blue, from bound to bound,
Hath Thee in every spot,
Thee, Thee!—Where Thou art not,
O Holy, Marvellous Form! is nowhere found!

O Mystic, Awful One!
At sight of Thee, made known,
The Three Worlds quake; the lower gods draw nigh Thee;
They fold their palms, and bow
Body and breast, and brow,
And, whispering worship, laud and magnify Thee!

Rishis and Siddhas cry
" Hail! Highest Majesty! "
From sage and singer breaks the hymn of glory
In dulcet harmony,
Sounding the praise of Thee;
While countless companies take up the story,

Rudras, who ride the storms,
Th'Adityas' shining forms,
Vasus and Sadhyas, Viswas, Ushampas;
Maruts, and those great Twins
The heavenly, fair, Aswins,
Gandharvas, Rakshasas, Siddhas, and Asuras—

These see Thee, and revere
In sudden-stricken fear;
Yea! the Worlds—seeing Thee with form stupendous,
With faces manifold,
With eyes which all behold,
Unnumbered eyes, vast arms, members tremendous,

Flanks, lit with sun and star,
Feet planted near and far,
Tushes of terror, mouths wrathful and tender;
The Three wide Worlds before Thee
Adore, as I adore Thee,
Quake, as I quake, to witness so much splendour!

I mark Thee strike the skies
With front, in wondrous wise
Huge, rainbow-painted, glittering; and Thy mouth
Opened, and orbs which see
All things, whatever be
In all Thy worlds, east, west, and north and south.

O Eyes of God! O Head!
My strength of soul is fled,
Gone is my heart's force, rebuked is mind's desire!
When I behold Thee so,
With awful brows aglow,
With burning glance, and lips lighted by fire

Fierce as those flames which shall
Consume, at close of all,
Earth, Heaven! Ah me! I see no Earth and Heaven!
Thee, Lord of Lords! I see
Thee only—only Thee!
Now let Thy mercy unto me be given,

Thou Refuge of the World! . . .

The hymn continues; and at last Krishna in compassion reveals himself once more in his human form, and teaches Arjuna further. He explains to him the three " qualities " through which the soul has to find its way. He tells him what makes the distinction between ordinary egoism which is swayed by desires, and that higher egoism which, " free from attachment " and resting on the knowledge of the Eternal, is *selfless*.

The old attachments to the ties of blood and the duties arising out of them, which are temporal, are nevertheless as much a part of Krishna as the Timeless. But only if such deeds are done in the perfect freedom of being done *in him*, are they also part of the Eternal.

This is the true freedom of Egohood. And it is the way of Love. Krishna tells him of this:

. . . " his soul,
Equally loving all that lives, loves well
Me, Who have made them, and attains to Me.
By this same love and worship doth he know
Me as I am, how high and wonderful,
And knowing, straightway enters into Me.

And whatsoever deeds he doeth—fixed
In Me, as in his refuge—he hath won
For ever and for ever by My grace
Th'Eternal Rest! So win thou! In thy thoughts
Do all thou dost for Me! Renounce for Me!
Sacrifice heart and mind and will to Me!
Live in the faith of Me! " ...

None other of the ancient Gods ever spoke to their devotees as Krishna spoke to Arjuna. It was in part a divine discourse, uttered from a realm of supremest spiritual splendours; and in part an intimate and exquisite human teaching, Krishna revealing himself as a man like other men. It ended with words of such great love and tenderness as have only been surpassed by the words of Christ Himself. And all this is addressed, not to many, but to a single individual—at the moment when that individual has to find the initiative in himself to accomplish a deed hitherto unheard of.

We see that all this points to an enormous change imminent for the world. The old clairvoyant spiritual knowledge was inherited through intermarriages; it lived in the blood; it made men entirely dependent upon spiritual guidance which they were aware of coming to them from " outside "—that is, from beings other than themselves—spiritual beings whose spheres were Sun and Moon and Stars.

But now the ties of blood are to be loosened, and the way to God will have to be found in the solitude of each individual soul. Nevertheless:

" There lives a Master in the hearts of men
Maketh their deeds, by subtle pulling-strings,
Dance to what tune He will. With all thy soul
Trust Him, and take Him for thy succour, Prince!
So—only so, Arjuna!—shalt thou gain—
By grace of Him—the uttermost repose,

The Eternal Place!
    Thus hath been opened thee
This Truth of Truths, the Mystery more hid
Than any secret Mystery. Meditate!
And as thou wilt—then act!

        Nay! but once more
Take my last word, my utmost meaning have!
Precious thou art to me; right well-beloved!
Listen! I tell thee for thy comfort this.
Give me thy heart! adore me! serve me! cling
In faith and love and reverence to me!
So shalt thou come to me! I promise true,
For thou art sweet to me!
        And let go those—
Rites and writ duties! Fly to me alone!
Make me thy single refuge! I will free
Thy soul from all its sins! Be of good cheer! "

It is not, however, intended to suggest that in
Krishna the climax of Christian ethic is represented.
For that is something more. If there were one who
could be deeply initiated into the Mysteries of Christ,
he would have to touch a still greater degree of
independence; he would have to be a " brother " of
Christ rather than a " child " of Krishna; able to
face, as Christ does, the great *Cosmic* Powers of
spiritual darkness, clothed in the strength of His
Light.

BUDDHA

About six hundred years before Christ, India sees the birth of Gautama Buddha. What does he teach? He teaches the " way between the two extremes ", and embodies it in the pure Gospel of the " Noble Eightfold Path ". Through his influence two things are brought to birth in humanity: the quality of *compassion* and the realisation of the meaning of *peace*.

Buddha steps forward on the stage of history in front of the overwhelming revelation of Krishna, as one who has himself walked beside Krishna in another world. Now he appears clothed physically in all the splendours of a royalty that Krishna had revealed spiritually: he is a King's son—guarded from every kind of contact with the outside world, entirely ignorant of the existence of poverty and suffering.

But because in the depths of his soul he knows already what he has to do for mankind, he leaves the palace and all his possessions and goes forth to become acquainted with the word's sorrow. All know the immortal story of how Buddha found the answers to his three great questions: What is suffering? What is the origin of it? How may it be destroyed? And how out of the answers, he created the precepts of the Eightfold Path.

Sorrow, according to Buddha, is the fruit of what is still unredeemed in man in his lives on earth. Liberation from sorrow is liberation from the call of these results, or fruits, of earlier lives that urge the soul to return to Earth. When a life is entirely free from desire and from the sorrowful effects of earlier desires, there is no longer any need to reincarnate.

In a certain sense therefore the teaching of Buddha

appears the opposite of the teaching of Krishna. The latter points to the *individual* and his ability to achieve the highest by union with Krishna; he has to understand this, dedicate himself to this " best ", which is in him, and act out of his own enlightened initiative: this suggests a tremendous impulsive force for the future development of mankind.

Buddha apparently teaches something like an abandonment of earthly life; true, he also points to the need for individual effort, but it is for the purpose of achieving a spirituality which is set free from the destiny of the Earth.

This, however, is only apparent. In reality, if the precepts of the Eightfold Path are studied as deeply as possible, it will be realised that the goal they set before man is one which can only be reached in a distant future; and the spirituality which would have to be developed in following this path would bear such fruits that the whole Earth would become sanctified. The moving fundamental urge would of itself—by practice and realisation—become *compassion* in the truest sense of the word; a suffering *with* others. And therefore there would be peace.

Buddha gives the wisdom that transforms itself into Love. Christ at last bestows Love itself, as a child of the Ego.

In these pre-Christian centuries the two streams of enlightenment flowing from Krishna and Buddha may be said to complement each other though they appear in some degree contradictory. And the two together form an element in that part of the evolution of mankind which belongs to his *inner* life; and is one of those elements, or streams, of spirituality which, with others, point already towards the Christian ideal.

Buddha is speaking to five of his special disciples:*

" There are two extremes, O Bikkhus, which the man who has given up the world ought not to follow—the habitual practice, on the one hand, of those things whose attraction depends upon the passions, and especially of sensuality—a low and pagan way, unworthy, unprofitable, and fit only for the worldly-minded—and the habitual practice, on the other hand, of ascetism (or self-mortification), which is painful, unworthy, and unprofitable.

" There is a middle path, O Bikkhus, avoiding these two extremes, discovered by the Tathagata†— a path which opens the eyes, and bestows understanding, which leads to peace of mind, to the higher wisdom, to full enlightenment, to Nirvana!

" What is the middle path, O Bikkhus, avoiding these two extremes, discovered by the Tathagata— that path which opens the eyes, and bestows understanding, which leads to peace of mind, to the higher wisdom, to full enlightenment, to Nirvana? Verily! it is this noble eightfold path; that is to say:

Right views,
Right aspirations,
Right speech,
Right conduct,
Right livelihood,
Right effort,
Right mindfulness; and
Right contemplation.

" This, O Bikkhus, is that middle path, avoiding these two extremes, discovered by the Tathagata—

* *Sacred Books of the East.* Vol. XI. Edited by Max Muller.
† Buddha.

that path which opens the eyes, and bestows understanding, which leads to peace of mind, to the higher
wisdom, to full enlightenment, to Nirvana! "

" Now this, O Bikkhus, is the noble truth concerning suffering:
Birth is attended with pain, decay is painful,
disease is painful, death is painful. Union with the
unpleasant is painful, painful is separation from the
pleasant; and any craving that is unsatisfied, that
too is painful. In brief, the five aggregates which
spring from attachment are painful.
" This then, O Bikkhus, is the noble truth concerning suffering." . . .
Buddha goes on to describe the cravings which are
the originators of suffering, and finally the destruction,
" in which no passion remains ", of this " thirst ".
He explains that these three Truths concerning
suffering and sorrow each entered into his comprehension in four stages, and until these twelve stages of
enlightenment had been accomplished by him, he
could not yet be certain.
" And now ", he concludes, " this knowledge and
this insight have arisen within me. Immovable is the
emancipation of my heart. This is my last existence.
There will now be no rebirth for me! "

It is difficult for us to realise that such a thing as
Compassion, as it was taught, or rather *lived*, by
Buddha, represented something new in human psychology; and it is perhaps only when this is understood—and when we remember how in leaving the
palace Buddha saw human suffering for the first time,
and that all his teaching was based upon compassion—
it is only then that we see the enormous future that his

vision really embraces. It is this which makes it, like the teaching of Krishna, something that can flow into the whole evolution of man; and in so doing, flow also into the cosmic stream of Christianity, and make Christianity itself more fruitful thereby.

CHAPTER XI

HERACLITUS AND ARISTOTLE

HERACLITUS

ALMOST contemporary with the inauguration of Buddhism, but a little later, we find in Greece the great philosopher Heraclitus of Ephesus, called the " dark " on account of the seeming obscurity of many of his utterances.

If we take this date, about five centuries before Christ, and recall some of the things that have already been described—namely the peculiar character of the Hibernian Mysteries and their continuation in the teachings of the Druids and Bards; and think then of the far East and the teachings of Buddha concerning the " way between the two extremes "; and turn to Greece and read the words of Heraclitus (and many other things will occur to us)—we may get a strange impression.

It is as though we could be aware of something like a heavenly dome stretched over the world from West to East; and from the cloudy heights of this dome we hear the echoes of a celestial teaching which is making itself dimly heard in the hearts of men. We hear the far-off thunder of Cosmic thoughts that have divided human existence into the " contraries ", so that the Son of the Sun might appear between them; and how the Temples of the world responded with their

" Baptism by Fire and Water ". We hear the ancient
sages tell how all things began and will end in Fire.
We listen to the Druids greet the Midsummer Sun and
worship its rising between the shadows of the pillars of
their trilithons. We hear the Buddha tell his pupils of
the extremes in human conduct—the passionate and
the falsely ascetic—outer world and inner world—and
the way between. We hear Heraclitus: " the world
is an eternally living Fire ", and in it is " the flowing
stream of life " wherein all that happens is the
" result of the operation of contraries ".

Listening once more, we hear the prophet Isaiah,
who lived near to the time of Heraclitus, crying:
" Every valley shall be filled, and every mountain and
hill brought low, the crooked shall be made straight,
and the rough places plain! " What is to come—the
Messiah—levels all contraries. And, still unborn, but
coming towards us from the future: " I baptise you
with water. He shall baptise you with the Holy Ghost
and with Fire." . . .

These last centuries before Christ are terrible in
their spiritual grandeur, heralding the birth of the
human Ego!—The coming of age of Man!

Heraclitus sees all things in a state of perpetual flux
and change; but within this eternal flow, the co-
existence of contrary properties and forces which are
for ever equalising one another, since they are in
constant opposition and interchange. These conflicting principles he says are to be discovered everywhere
—in every occurrence both in Nature and in the
Heavens.

But this seeming chaos, and the apparently senseless
interplay of a thousand dissonances, reveal themselves
to the listening spiritual ear of the philosopher as a

mighty harmony, a profound and basic Reason. . . .
From this conception of the world Heraclitus reaches
at last the central truth of his philosophy, the idea of
the Logos; which is identical with the supersensible
all-pervading cosmic Reason; while the visible
universe is nothing else than the " living garment of
the Godhead "—as Goethe also conceived it. Man
holds his appointed place in the world, as a *spiritual
being,* and is one with the Logos who created him.

One sees therefore that on the one hand Heraclitus
touches the fringe of the Sankhya philosophy of India
in his idea of the primal stream of Life in which all
souls and all creatures reach their differentiation
according to the Law of this Life; and together with
this individualising process, conceived by him as
arising through conflict, he also draws something from
the undying source of the Veda philosophy, which
creates unity between man and the Divine.

But on the other hand, his conception of the
" opposites ", their conflicts, interchangeability, and
even " Sun " and " Moon " characteristics, is connected with the pure Hibernian Mystery wisdom.

It seems that East and West really meet in the
philosophy of Heraclitus; but in such a way that Man
himself emerges—more real, more individual, more
clear-cut, than would have been possible in earlier
times. For in Man is the " word "—the true harmonising principle—which, as part of the divine Logos,
makes it possible for the ever-moving contraries not
only to be at rest, but also to create the *new,* through
their own inherent law of Metamorphosis.

The aphoristic sentences of Heraclitus seem to read
more like a proclamation than a philosophy; and his
passionate sense of separateness from the people of his
surroundings drove him literally into the desert, to

seek in Nature herself, and in a spiritual sense, for the
" waters of Life ".   His contemporaries could not
understand him.

". . . This cosmic Law, the Logos, which is
nevertheless eternal, is not understood by men,
either before they have heard of it, nor even when
they have heard of it.   For, although everything
takes place through this Law, yet they seem to have
no idea of its existence, even in striving with such
words and works of mine wherein I announce it;
and wherein I make clear how it works in every
entity of Nature. . . ."

". . . Though a man may step again into the same
stream, it is always another and another water that
flows therein. . . .   In this stream of all things, to
which man himself is also subject, every phase of its
flowing is ruled by the same unitary principle. . . ."

". . . One and the same thing is revealed in the
living and the dead, in sleeping and waking, in
young and old.   For the one, when it is transformed,
becomes the other, and the other, transformed
again, becomes the first. . . ."

". . . Everything that happens, happens as the
result of the operation of contraries. . . .

" Fire lives the death of Earth, and Air lives the
death of Fire; the Water lives the death of Air, and
the Earth the death of Water. . . ."

" Conflicting opposites unite, and out of contrary
tones there arises the most perfect harmony, and all
things come into being by way of opposition. . . ."

- ". . . God is Day and Night, Winter and Summer,
War and Peace, Satiety and Hunger; but He transforms Himself even as Fire takes another name from
the smoke of every different incense. . . ."

". . . This world, with all things that belong to it, have been made neither by the Godhead nor even one of them by Man, but the world always was, and is, and ever will be, an eternally living Fire, according to one or another degree enkindling or extinguishing itself. . . ."

In the Mysteries of Ephesus, where Heraclitus had been initiated, the secrets of the Logos, of the Divine Word in relation to human speech, had been taught.

The human word was conceived as arising and becoming operative through the elements; in the " fire " of thought, the " water " of feeling, and the " air " of speech. These are its creative essences, just as the elements themselves are the essence out of which the Divine Logos has created the world.

In these centuries before Christ, the Ego of man was seeking for itself in the sphere below that of the fire and air and water of the world—in the *earth*, in the physical body.

The fire-philosophers, like Heraclitus, looked back to the beginning of the creation of the world out of a spiritual Fire—and forward to its end also in a great spiritual conflagration. The first was the " need " of Fire to manifest in creation—it is the same as *Will;* and the second is its satiety, its fulfilment, and return to God.

In this ever-flowing stream, wherein the Word as it were sank and rose in the perpetual creation of harmonies and opposites, the self-conscious Ego in man could not as yet find its firm foothold—though it was very near.

We see here the great difference between the older quests—such as the seeking for the Golden Fleece— for a super-sensible Light, and this later seeking;

where the soul isolates itself in a wilderness, and tries
to learn from Nature herself the way to the Divine; to
grasp the meaning of growth and wisdom through the
laws of metamorphosis, which are everywhere to be
discerned.

And again, an echo of this metamorphosis sounds
towards us from the age that is approaching: " Change
your hearts!—for the Kingdom of Heaven is at
hand! . . ."

Judged by our present-day ideas it may seem
improbable that an influence from Ireland would be
likely to colour the thoughts of the Greek philosopher
Heraclitus. Yet we have evidence that the so-called
Hibernian Mysteries had spread far from their
original ancient home; and some of these influences
have already been referred to. But to the reader who
has some feeling for the possibilities arising through
reincarnation, many such problems will be clarified
from yet another aspect.

Apart from that, all over the world there are clear
traces of the fundamental idea of the opposition of
contraries in human life, which resolve themselves
through a third and harmonising principle. For the
most part, however, people are content just to recognise these contraries—for they make themselves known
in every moment of our existence; but few realise the
fact that when, in a moment of decision, one or other
of the contraries is accepted, it is due solely to the
choice made by our own enlightened or unenlightened
self.

This is the " third ". To Greek philosophers it was
Nous, the highest Reason; to the ancient Orientals, the
supreme Self; to the Western sages, the same—but
more clearly seen as that which was attainable by man

through his perfected individuality, not yet " incarnated " for all. In Ephesus, this divine principle was
recognised as the Word, the Logos.

ARISTOTLE

As we survey all these long-past human experiences
we begin gradually to be aware how, out of their
totality, there emerges something which tends to
crystallise them into a kind of formula, as a preparation for another stage of consciousness. An example
lies before us, just in these immediate pre-Christian
centuries.

Aristotle, the great inaugurator of logical thinking,
lived, and also his pupil Alexander the Great, in the
fourth century before Christ.   By that time the
Mystery Schools had become actually decadent, but
great things could still be learnt and experienced in
them, especially in the School of Samothrace. Alexander and Aristotle both participated in the teachings
of this School;   and the ancient truths that were
recalled there awakened in Aristotle the power to re-
create them in a new way, which could, and did,
work as a kind of illumination of human thinking, for
centuries to come.

One great historical event made it possible for this
new light to be kindled; this was the burning to the
ground of the great Temple of Diana at Ephesus—the
Temple of the Logos.

It seems like a fulfilment of the thoughts of Heraclitus: the spiritual Fire comes down into manifestation, and when its manifestation is complete, it returns
to Fire, and writes the script of its achievements in the
Heavens whence it came.

As though in a celestial writing of flame Aristotle

read the Mysteries of the Logos. But the time had
come when they must be given in a new form to the
world; a form that could be grasped by the conscious
intellectual soul of man.

What he had learned in Samothrace about the ranks
of the spiritual Hierarchies, the grand synthesis of the
Cosmic Word, with its infinite in-dwelling verity,
must be transformed so that it could become the
foundation and framework for an age of intellectual
thinking. Aristotle embodied the ten Hierarchies in
the Ten Categories of his philosophy. The divine
Names of the spiritual Beings remained written only in
Heaven. The Ten Categories were written on Earth,
Logic was born.

With this, one more step has been taken by the Ego
from supersensible to physical relationships.

POLARITY

The characteristic differences between the religious
impulses of those peoples who had looked up to
the Sun through all the varied world of Nature, and
the others who had looked towards it as the highest
prototype of the human Self, are now becoming
merged in a general sense of loss. The latter type turn
more and more towards understanding the inner life
and its possibilities, and even in a certain isolation of
soul; and the former experience, dimly and in distress,
a kind of abyss widening between themselves and the
spiritual heart of Nature, which external knowledge is
not able to bridge.

The whole world of evolving mankind stands, as it
were, full of questions, before the two Pillars. The
goal is still to discover, as the single initiates in
Hibernia had had to discover, through what Power

they can be woven together in perfect equilibrium. . . .
" When the Two shall become One, the Inner as the
Outer."

Looking back from our own time, we can see that no
problem in the whole world has been subject to so
many misinterpretations and abuses as this one,
because the knowledge of its spiritual origin has been
lost for so long.

When in the ordinary course of life—not as formerly
in the " Great Mysteries "—man comes to realise his
Ego in himself, it is his grand opportunity for learning
that, if unrighteously conceived, it can become the
" blunted weapon of Cain "—self-assertion and ego-
ism. Rightly understood, it can be the Giver, the
self-sacrificer.

" I " and " Thou "! The " I " is within; the
" Thou " is outside. They are rightly united only
through a loftier conception of what the " I " really is
—a projection of the heavenly Self. This alone makes
the " inner ", the human personality, identify itself
with all the " Thou's " in the world. Then it becomes
selfless. " *Thou shalt love thy neighbour as thyself.*"

In the old Hibernian Mysteries the polarity
between the Inner and the Outer was seen so to say
from *above*—from the divine standpoint.

This, in a certain sense, reversed the view—as one
might see something in a mirror. . . . For from this
divine standpoint, which had to be painfully attained
by the pupil in the Mysteries, then, and in later times,
he came to see that the Outer—everything that was
" not I "—was nevertheless *himself* because he was a
part of it all; and everything that was " I " in the
ordinary sense of selfhood—his inner world—belonged
to all others. It could be Itself, and yet so wide, so
selfless, that the Outer could have the same value for

him as the Inner. In other words, the gift of the Ego to man was to enable him to be as much interested in everything outside him as he was in himself.

These two pillars, or statues—these two world-polarities—are also representative of the eternally interchangeable Masculine and Feminine principles of earth existence: the Kingly and the Priestly; Man and Woman.

All the Mysteries fell into decadence when these principles could no longer be seen from the " divine standpoint ". Their ultimate downfall was when the union of the Inner and the Outer was finally cast out from spiritual experience into sexual misinterpretation and passion. . . .

There is another aspect. . . .

Near the Roman Forum there stood the Temple of Janus, the god with two faces, looking different ways.

What is the Janus Temple, whose gates were sometimes open and sometimes closed? . . . " It is a threshold between one world and another. When the doors are open, there is war, but successive wars built up the Empire: the Janus-power leaves the Temple and goes out into the world. What is the world?—the Roman Empire! When the doors are closed there is peace. Then this Janus-power goes *in* to the Temple, and builds up the opposite of war—the inner structure of the Roman state."*

Before the Christian era the building up of culture was a priestly function. War is a function of external power.

Only three times in Roman history were the doors of the Temple of Janus closed. And one of these was when Augustus was Emperor and Christ was born. . . .

War and Peace are the same problems of the Outer

* Dr. E. Kolisko, *Between War and Peace* (The Modern Mystic, 1939).

and the Inner, the Male and the Female, the King and the Priest.

The answer can come only from the Being who has always been the Answerer—the Light of the World.

We have looked into ancient history to discover this Light. From twelve directions the rays have been gathered: from Hibernia, Finland, Scandinavia; from the Rishis of ancient India; from Persia and Egypt and Babylon; from Troy; from Krishna and Buddha, and from all the Greek Mysteries; and from Rome— from the Rome that was the guardian of the darkly-shining Palladium, symbol of all ancient Gnosis.

But the rays of this Light seem to grow more faint as they draw near to the time of their focusing. They sink lower. The Twilight of the old Gods deepens; it receives into its dim heart the waters of a new birth. The rays of the divine Sun lie like the dew on Hermon and wait for the morning.

In this expectancy, Space turns to its brother Time. Far off in time, somewhere the preparation must have been made, and still, in these last centuries, be in the making, which will have appointed the physical race and its succession of generations to provide the physical body for the Christ.

Time has its own journey to make in order to meet with this gathering together of spiritual light from many world-directions.

It is not only Space that is focused at the " centre of the Earth ", but all history, all Time.

The Prophets in the Old Testament are all concerned with Time—with *When?* All the old Mysteries were concerned with Space—with *Whence?* . . . Soon they must meet; quite soon.

So we must take one glance at this preparation in Time; a very brief glance at the history of a people.

CHAPTER XII

MELCHISEDEK

SCARCELY anyone who has read the book of Genesis will have failed to notice the first and unexplained appearance of Melchisedek to the still childless Abraham, after the slaughter of the Kings (Gen. xiv, 17). His coming seems outwardly to have no actual connection with the events. This wonderful and mysterious figure is suddenly there; he gives Abraham bread and wine, blesses him, and is gone.

He is called there the Priest of the Most High God. He is not the Priest of Jehovah, but of One greater than Jehovah. He makes no blood-sacrifice, offers up no lamb or any other sacrificial beast, for these things belong to the Moon-ritual of Jehovah worship. But he brings the gift of the Sun and the fruit of the Earth —Bread and Wine.

This is an intimation that the way of mankind must go from " Moon " to " Sun ". The blood-sacrifices helped to induce the old ecstatic visions. The blood-less offering wakened the inner light of self-ruled devotion to a higher spirituality. The old rituals would still continue for a long time; but the Bread and Wine would remain a secret of the inner Sanctuary. Meanwhile the seed of the change had to be laid in Abraham, the father of the chosen race.

He and his descendants have to become different from other men and nations, and, for a time, ahead of them in evolution. They are to become able to know and experience in the course of their history, how the spiritual essence of Egohood is capable of *focusing* the Divinity that had revealed Itself in the spiritual world, so that It could work within them. This is the human sense of " I "-hood. It feels itself at first severed from the divine worlds; and each man learns to know himself distinct from all others, and from all Nature. It enables intelligence to awake as *intellect*.

Such a change of consciousness brings about a physical change in the body—and actually in the brain.

In ancient times the body was more plastic. The vital forces could extrude themselves from the brain and receive impressions—as though by invisible " feelers "—from the plastic, mobile, vital force of the surrounding world, without the effort of thought. This was to cease. The power of *reason* was to grow.

It is a spiritual law that what has to happen to humanity as a whole must first be implanted in the life of a single human being.

Not long after the meeting with Melchisedek, Abraham fell into a deep sleep, and knew a " horror of great darkness ". Immediately before, when the Sun had set, the " word of the Lord " had given him the promise of his mission—to be the father of a great multitude which would be numbered in the twelvefold order of the Zodiac. He gazed in spirit on the stars. Centuries of coming history were unfolded before him. He understood all; but now not alone as some illumination coming to him from without, and stirring in him the old dream-power of visions reflected from another world, but as grand and majestic *thoughts*, that seemed to be born of his own body.

He knew that he was changed. The hands of

Melchisedek, blessing him, seemed already to have wrought the miracle.

So that he could ask—*how shall I know?* . . . " Whereby shall I know that I shall inherit this land ? "

A whole step nearer to the Earth has come the power of thinking through the Ego! The power of self-conscious intellectual thought.

But the weight of the communications he had received plunged the soul of Abraham into the " horror of great darkness ", which is a part of all self-knowledge. The animals he had laid ready for sacrifice at the word of the Lord, as a test of the truth of what he had been told, were surrounded in the deep night by a " smoking furnace " and a moving, burning lamp, not made by man. For the visions had still for a time to mingle with the thoughts. . . . But the old way of ritual must have appeared before Abraham's soul as the very antithesis of that which had sealed, beforehand, through the bread and wine offered by Melchisedek the way of the future.

But for the outer conduct of life, the old forms must continue. The secret of Melchisedek, which was a secret of the Sun, must grow silently to maturity in Abraham's heart and brain. He must sacrifice the old clairvoyance.

Melchisedek!*. . . The name sounds in our ears like a mysterious call to the dark fountains of our memory.

Melchisedek! . . . Who is he? We read the words of St. Paul about him, and feel them as though they wished to tell us something, but may not. St. Paul *knows:* but he leaves the riddle before us still—like a challenge to the profoundest depths of our being.

* See plate 73.

Melchisedek! . . . " without father, without mother, without descent, having neither beginning of days nor end of life; *but made like unto the Son of God;* abiding a Priest continually."

St. Paul goes on to say that he is not counted as one who belongs to the sons of Levi (the Priests of Israel). Nor is he Christ; for it was said of Christ Himself that He was a High Priest " after the order of Melchisedek ".*

No other answer is possible than that Melchisedek is the greatest of all those Initiate Leaders of humanity who guide it, through countless ages, along the path of its true evolution. They are those who, like Enoch, like Elijah, like Zarathustra, like others who have risen to a superhuman nature, or else have retained their primal angelic or even archangelic nature and are freemen of all worlds; able to " go in and out " through the Door of the Sun—which is Christ.

The barriers of birth and death do not exist for them; they may be in the body, or out of the body; but they never forsake us. Hard is the way they have to tread; but they make it easier for the rest of mankind because they have trodden it first.

And they know with precision the tasks they have to perform. No sooner, for instance, had the mission of Noah come to an end, than Melchisedek is ready to continue the guidance of man.† It is almost as though Noah himself would live on in Melchisedek's youthful purity, desirous of sharing in the founding of a world newly risen from the waters. And again, long after, the moment that Abraham is ripe for the creation of a new race, Melchisedek appears with the bread and wine; and then, going on as it were ahead, returns to

* Epistle to the Hebrews, vii.
† Legend of the Body of Adam, page 23.

Jerusalem and waits for the dawn of yet another world-age, when the Bread and Wine will be offered by the hand of One who is also of the Order of Melchisedek.

Now we begin to understand why the legend tells that the body of Adam was placed in the centre of the Earth at the very place where the blood of Christ was to be shed.*

It is the place of utmost spiritual equilibrium. The archetype of man's physical body—the " body of Adam "—is brought together there, at the turning-point of time, with the descent of the spiritual power of the " I am ", in Christ. The new Adam unites with, and redeems, the old Adam. . . . Does this even fore-shadow the æonic time when the Sun itself will once more be united with the Earth? Is this why the sound of that other name for Jerusalem—Zion (which means " sunny ")—can fill us with an indescribable tender-ness of longing? It is the Jerusalem of Light, the goal of the Earth, achieved!

* Legend of the Body of Adam, page 23.

CHAPTER XIII

ZION AND THE PROPHETS

ABOUT fourteen hundred years before Christ, Moses, who was an Egyptian, and had been initiated into the Mysteries of Isis and Osiris, prepared to lead the Israelites along their appointed path to the Promised Land. They had to be led away from all contact with the old clairvoyant wisdom and become the means for the dawn of a new epoch for the world.

What Abraham had experienced in his own person after his communion with Melchisedek, Moses had to implant into a whole people. The now decadent magical wisdom of Egypt, deeply connected with bodily passions, must be uprooted from their souls. They longed for it in the wilderness. Unattainable, it stung them to inward rebellion. The fiery serpent, symbol of that ancient way of miraculous illumination, had been mastered by their great Leader, and sacrificed on the staff of upright Sun-filled Egohood.

So they were to have no " graven images " in their religion as aids to their faith. They had to prepare, historically and morally, for the time when their inner consciousness would awake to self-dependence. Their " I " must learn to recognise a new sort of relationship to their God—to grasp Him in *thought*, and to be able to feel the reality of personal responsibility.

It necessitated a stern discipline. Long years must pass in desert wanderings, in temptations and

157

hardships, in thirst and hunger. The holy Tabernacle, carried by the labouring Priests, revealed nothing to the people. All they had was the far-off promise of a fertile land and the dim sense of a tremendous mission. The unknown impulse to develop their Egohood drove them onward. Jehovah was above them. Christ was in front of them. But without knowledge, they had to grow strong in faith.

The Sun, the Stars, and the Moon had hitherto been venerated in successive phases of human evolution, as the Sources of divine guidance. But now the " Word of the Lord " manifested Himself through the elements —in water and wind, in earthquake, in fire and cloud. Now He was nearer than the Sun, nearer than the Moon or other planets. He was close to Nature, announcing Himself through Jehovah to Moses as the " I am "; and accompanying the children of Israel as a " pillar of Cloud by day and as a pillar of Fire by night ".

And in front of Jehovah as His " countenance " went the " Angel of the Lord "—Michael, the Archangel, the Folk-spirit of the Hebrew people.

Many times in the Old Testament narratives, Michael appeared to them in their visions, pointing the way through the different crises in their history. In the latter centuries before Christ they had no lack of terrible moments of decision or terrible doubts as to their destiny. But Michael appeared, " clothed in fine linen ", as Daniel saw him—" his loins girded with fine gold of Uphaz; his body was like the beryl, and his face as the appearance of lightening, and his eyes as lamps of fire, and his arms and his feet like in colour to polished brass, and the voice of his words like the voice of a multitude." . . .

" Lord! Thou who hast closed the fiery castles of Heaven with Thy spirit-breath! Thou double-bodied one, Master of Fire, Creator and Concealer of Light, fire-breathing one, fiery-courageous one, beautiful shining one, Ruler of the Light, fiery-bodied, Light-spender, Fire-scatterer, fiery tempestuous one! Luminous living one, Fire-revolving, Light-evoking, Lightning-blazing one! Fame of the Light, Increaser of the Light, Holder of fire-gleaming Light, Master of the Stars! O reveal to me the Names that have never entered into mortal Nature! —that have never been expressed in language by any human tongue or in any sound of human voice. Names that are exalted and eternal! "

In these magnificent words an old Mithraic Liturgy invokes the God Mithra. He is Michael the Archangel of the Sun, the Prince of Heaven. For the Hebrew people he was the mediator of Jehovah's will. For us, he is the Champion of Christ.

Always he is described as clothed in Light, and as clothed in Fire. His Light is the illumination of thought. His Fire is will. Fire penetrates Light, and Light penetrates Fire. Thought and Will are the sword of the Ego. They are the " double-bodied " power that prepares the way for Christ, who comes between them, into the heart, as Love.

In Chaldea Michael was called Marduk, who with his stormy breath blasted the darkness of chaos and separated the divine world from the earthly, and to hold them balanced became the " Keeper of the Midst ".

In the East, he is the God Indra.

" Who made firm the quaking Earth, and stilled the mountains that were torn with unrest, who extended the measure of airy space, who supported the Heavens—he, O people, is Indra!

" Who slew the Dragon and made the seven Rivers to flow, who set free the cattle from the dungeon of Vala, who generated Fire between the stones, who in battle is invincible—he, O people, is Indra! . . .

" He without whom there is no victory, upon whom the warriors call for help, who shatters the unshatterable, he, O people, is Indra! . . .

" Heaven and Earth bow down before him, the mountains tremble at his impetuous approach; he, the festal Soma-drinker, who carries the thunder-bolt in his arm, the thunderbolt in his hand—he, O people, is Indra! . . ."

In the Old Testament Michael showed himself to Moses, as he was then, and as he was to become: once as the " Angel of the Lord " in the burning bush on Horeb—a revelation of the Divine will bestowed from without; and on Sinai in the lightning—the penetrating inward-working force of the light of Thinking: the promise of the in-dwelling force of human wisdom.

And as the great heavenly forerunner of Christ, Michael appeared to Balaam, when he was on his way, bribed by Balak, to curse the Israelites.

Three times the ass that Balaam is riding sees the Angel of the Lord barring the path, with his drawn sword in his hand. But Balaam sees nothing, and only beats her.

After the third time, his eyes are opened; he sees the overwhelming Presence, and knows why Israel must not be cursed but blessed:

" How shall I curse whom God hath not cursed?
Or how shall I defy whom God hath not defied?

" For from the top of the rocks I see Him, and
from the hills I behold Him. . . .

" I shall see Him, but not now: I shall behold
Him, but not near.

" There shall come a Star out of Jacob, and a
Sceptre shall rise out of Israel. . . ."

Michael cleaves a path through the spiritual
Universe for the descending Logos. Into the stream of
all the generations of Israel he thrusts ever deeper the
Sun-light of reasoned Thinking, and stirs the sleeping
Ego-consciousness into wakefulness.

Beneath him, on the Earth, is his human representative the prophet Elijah—receiving his full force, but
reflected as it were like moonlight from Jehovah. This
light makes *inward* what is outer. . . . Elijah is " very
jealous for the Lord God of Hosts "; he knows that
the Israelites must possess their Lord as an inward
self-conscious realisation, as of a God who is within the
heart. What Michael bestows, Elijah is to receive and
proclaim. He is like a burning torch; everywhere
purifying with his fire the people who have been
chosen. His mantle falls not only on Elisha, but
covers Israel like a banner.

Centuries pass. Destiny brings the children of Israel
to the place where the vision of Michael and the
Dragon—under the names of Marduk and Tiamaat—
had coloured all the Mystery teachings; to Babylon,
for the second Captivity.

At this time, a little less than six hundred years
before Christ, there lived in Babylon another Zarathas, or Zarathustra, who has generally been supposed
to be the originator of the teachings called by his name.

This Zarathas continued the old Zarathustrian Sun-wisdom, although changed and tinctured by the later age and the different country.

Is it a mere coincidence that in Babylon, under the continuing after-glow of the original Zarathustra, there began to grow up among the captives the conviction that the Messiah would soon come and free them from their bondage? Was not the shining Marduk the Preparer of His way? Zarathustra's ancient word still seems to echo there: " He will descend to Earth. He will overcome age, death, and decay. . . . He will be the victorious Saviour, sur-rounded by Apostles. . . ."

Many of the Psalms, and the later Chapters of the Book of Isaiah, were written at this time, and are ardent with the expectation of His coming. Zion, the Holy City, is yearned over and longed for, as never before, by its exiled children:

" By the rivers of Babylon, there we sat down, yea we wept,
        when we remembered thee O Zion.
    We hanged our harps upon the willows in the midst thereof.
    For, there, they that carried us away captive, required of
        us a song;
    And they that wasted us required of us mirth, saying,
    Sing us one of the songs of Zion.
    How shall we sing the Lord's song in a strange land?
    If I forget thee, O Jerusalem, let my right hand forget her
        cunning.
    If I do not remember thee, let my tongue cleave to the roof
        of my mouth;
    If I prefer not Jerusalem above my chief joy. . . ."

And the prophet cries:

" Oh that thou wouldest rend the Heavens, that thou
        wouldest come down.
    That the mountains might flow down at thy presence!
    . . . Thy holy cities are a wilderness,

Zion is a wilderness, Jerusalem a desolation.
Our holy and beautiful house, where our fathers praised
    thee, is burned up with fire;
And all our pleasant things are laid waste. . . ."

The history of the Jews, even as the history of the
world, reveals in a strange and moving way that it also
shares in the " twilight of the Gods ", and must live
through a decadence of its old esoteric wisdom if it is
to discover the dawn of any new era.

The mysterious cleavage which characterises world-
history before and after Christ, has its image in the
very structure and natural features of Jerusalem itself.

It is built on the spurs of two hills, Mount Zion and
Mount Moriah.   Many records, traditions, and
researches testify to the volcanic nature of the region.
Legends and myths, as well as modern discoveries,
point to an extraordinary prevalence of great subterranean chasms and clefts under the ancient city,
so that the rocky eminence where the Temple of
Solomon stood has been likened to " a stone freely
hovering over an abyss ".

It is as though in the creation of the Earth these
regions had remained longer than others in a state of
planetary turbulence, where fire and water struggled
for mastery over the earth.

For untold ages this site must have been a place of
prehistoric Mysteries.   The cavernous fires of Mount
Moriah were separated in past times by a deep chasm
from Mount Zion.   In the old initiations it may well
have been like a passage traversed through Hell to the
Heights of Zion where " Heaven came to meet " the
new initiate.

David chose the peaceful and kindlier Zion to be
the heart of Jerusalem. Solomon moved the centre to
the strong rocks of Mount Moriah, on whose heights

Abraham had offered Isaac as a sacrifice, and in whose depths was Melchisedek's ancient sanctuary. And thus it remained, crowned with the outer splendours of the Temple until the end of the old dispensation.

The chasm between the two places was gradually closed, artificially or naturally, and for long ages the sound of many waters could still be heard beneath it in the depths of the Earth. The healing pools of Siloam and Bethesda must have received from them their mysterious ebb and flow.

A legend tells that when the foundations of King David's palace and Temple were to be laid in Zion, men had to dig ever deeper and deeper, even down to 1,500 yards; when suddenly the diggers came upon an earthenware vessel engraved with the divine Name of Jehovah. The King, amazed, dared to lift the vessel, and immediately the primeval subterranean floods gushed upwards with tremendous force and could not be subdued. Only the magical power of Ahitophel, who knew the right commanding words, availed to save the world from destruction.

Creative Powers have stamped upon these regions the eternal mystery of the " inner " and the " outer ". . . . In Galilee the exquisite flowering fertility and sunniness of Nature; in the grim valley of the Jordan and the Dead Sea, the bitter salt and barren rocks of a landscape that lies 1,200 or 1,500 feet below sea-level. Again and again such contrasts are to be found.

Mount Moriah and the Temple picture that which calls to the mind the stern justice and righteousness of Jehovah and the Law. The loftier Zion—and its very sound wakens a sense of quiet eternity—calls up the picture of the Sun of Peace.

Melchisedek—whose name, as St. Paul says, is " by interpretation King of Righteousness, and after that

King of Salem, which is, King of Peace " Melchisedek united them in himself; he was a fore-picture of the " Righteousness and Peace that have kissed each other " in Moriah and Zion; the outgoing external Power of Righteous Goodness, and the inner healing wonder of Peace in the soul. . . .

This is the mystery of Jerusalem. It was displayed before all the world when the Sun-Spirit united Himself with the dark Earth.

The prophets who foretold Him are full of this polarity: all the darkness of sin and downfall and punishment, and all the light of salvation and the rejoicing in a return to " Zion " . . . Death, and Resurrection.*

Infinite trials, wars and ravagings, still lie before the Jews even after the end of the captivity.

During five hundred years they come under the dominion of four dynasties—of Persia, Greece, the Asmoneans, and Antipater and the Herods. Slowly the foreign influences, and most of all the Greek, began to undermine the older solidarity of the Jewish tradition, and to split it up into two camps: those who were zealous for the Mosaic Law, and those who leaned towards a rationalised Hellenistic paganism.

The crisis came about a hundred and sixty years before our era, with the heroic uprising of Mattathias and his five sons, and of the seven Maccabean brothers, against the tyrant Antiochus Epiphanes.

These twelve arise like living flames, inspired by Michael, to protect their faith and their land. It is as though the voices of all the prophets of the past embody themselves in this last proclamation of constancy.

* Hebrews, vii.

One by one the seven sons of the Maccabean mother are tortured and killed before her eyes. But each one, in his own words, points triumphantly to the victory over death and the certainty of immortality. Their fire sears the soul of the tyrant:

" Thou, like a fury, takest us out of this present life, but the King of the world shall raise us up, who have died for His laws, unto everlasting life. . . ."

But the flame lit by the Twelve flickers out in succeeding generations. The rule of the Herods begins.

In the midst of the people's decadent symptoms of pride and exclusiveness, of trivial disputes and pedantries, of opposition and exasperation, there grew up the communities of the Essenes. In secret, practising austerities and purifications, they meditated on the profound teachings imparted by Jesus Ben Pandira concerning the advent of the Messiah.

The world had gone dark. But in their hearts the Light lived.

The inner history of Israel and Judah is something entirely removed from the type of supersensible experience in which all the various Mystery Schools of other lands had been bathed. In them, there was always the " flight of the alone to the Alone "—the rising up from earthly connections to heavenly origins. Though it is true that this quest was undertaken so that light could be brought down from above into earthly knowledge. But the history of the Jews is mighty with the " words of the Earth ". It has the strength of the Rock in it. It is Sinai, it is Horeb, it is Mount Moriah. It is Zion itself, and the Temple—

ever rising anew out of its ruins. It is the story of Man, fallen, and prophesying his own salvation.

The Sun was never absent from this people. But how did they behold it? They saw it in the twelve characteristics of the Tribes; they saw it in the colours of the twelve precious stones of the breast-plate; in the twelve Gates of Jerusalem. Everywhere the Sun-light was broken into its twelve component parts—but on the *Earth*. Descriptions of heavenly things are told in terms of the Earth and its elements: likened to the rainbow; to the fire; to gold; to the " appearance " of a beryl or a jasper or an emerald; to the colour of the " terrible Crystal ". . . .

Water and rock and tempest and lightning and earthquake; the Cedar and the Rose, the mountain and plain and desert—these, for the Jews, are the signature of the Sun on the Earth. And its Word thunders in prophecy, using the words of the Earth, when the heart is stilled to listen:

Arise, shine; for thy Light is come,
And the Glory of the Lord is risen upon thee.

For behold, darkness shall cover the earth
And gross darkness the people.
But the Lord shall arise upon thee
And His Glory shall be seen upon thee.

And the Gentiles shall come to thy Light
And Kings to the brightness of thy rising.

The Sun shall be no more thy Light by day;
Neither for brightness shall the Moon give light unto thee.

For the Lord shall be unto thee
An everlasting Light,
And thy God thy Glory.

The Sun shall no more go down;
Neither shall thy Moon withdraw itself;
For the Lord shall be thine everlasting Light,
And the days of thy mourning shall be ended.

———

Sing and rejoice, O daughter of Zion!
For lo, I come, and I will dwell in the midst of thee,
Saith the Lord.
And many nations shall be joined to the Lord in that day,
    and shall be my people;
And I will dwell in the midst of thee,
And thou shalt know that the Lord of Hosts
Hath sent me unto thee.
And the Lord shall inherit Judah,
His portion in the Holy Land,
And shall choose Jerusalem again.
Be silent, O all flesh, before the Lord!
For he is raised up out of his holy habitation.
Rejoice greatly, O daughter of Zion!
Shout, O daughter of Jerusalem!
Behold thy King cometh unto thee.
He is just, and having salvation; lowly,
And riding upon an ass,
And upon a colt the foal of an ass. . . .

———

Who hath believed our report?
And to whom is the arm of the Lord revealed?
For he shall grow up before him as a tender plant,
And as a root out of dry ground;
He hath no form nor comeliness; and when we shall see
    him, there is no beauty that we should desire him.
He is despised and rejected of men;
A man of sorrows and acquainted with grief:
And we hid as it were our faces from him;
He was despised, and we esteemed him not.

Surely he hath borne our griefs and carried our sorrows;
Yet we did esteem him stricken,
Smitten of God, and afflicted.

But he was wounded for our transgressions
He was bruised for our iniquities;
The chastisement of our peace was upon him;
    And with his stripes we are healed.

———

And the Lord whom ye seek
Shall suddenly come to His temple.
He shall come, saith the Lord of Hosts.

But who may abide the day of His coming?
And who shall stand when He appeareth?
For He is like a refiner's fire. . . .

———

The voice of him that crieth in the wilderness,
Prepare ye the way of the Lord,
Make straight in the desert a highway for our God.

Every valley shall be exalted,
And every mountain and hill shall be made low:
And the crooked shall be made straight
And the rough places plain:
And the Glory of the Lord shall be revealed
And all flesh shall see it together;
For the mouth of the Lord hath spoken it.

———

And a Man shall be as an hiding-place from the wind,
And a covert from the tempest;
As rivers of water in a dry place,
As the shadow of a great rock in a weary land.

The eyes of the blind shall be opened
And the ears of the deaf shall be unstopped.
Then shall the lame man leap as an hart,
And the tongue of the dumb shall sing.

For in the wilderness shall waters break out
And streams in the desert.
And the parched ground shall become a pool
And the thirsty land springs of water. . . .

And an Highway shall be there, and a Way,
And it shall be called
　　The Way of Holiness.*

THE LIGHT IN DARKNESS

In the Beginning was the WORD
And the WORD was with God,
And the WORD was God.

The same was in the Beginning with God.

All things were made by Him;
And without Him was not anything made that was made.

In Him was LIFE,
And the LIFE was the LIGHT of men.

And the LIGHT shineth in darkness;
And the darkness comprehendeth It not.

And the WORD was made FLESH
And dwelt among us.
And we beheld His Glory.

———

I AM the Light of the world:
HE that followeth Me shall not walk in darkness
But shall have the Light of Life.

As long as I AM in the world, I AM the Light of the world.
While ye hath the Light believe in the Light,
That ye may be the children of Light.

I AM come a Light into the world
That whosoever believeth on Me
Should not abide in darkness.

GOSPEL OF ST. JOHN, viii, 12; ix, 5; xii, 36-46.

O Jerusalem, Jerusalem, Thou that killest the prophets
and stonest them that are sent unto thee!

* These quotations are from the prophets Isaiah, Zechariah and Malachi.

How often would I have gathered thy children together, even as a hen gathereth her chickens under her wings—and ye would not! . . .

And they crucified Him, and two other with Him, on either side one, and Jesus in the midst. . . .

———

And there was a darkness over all the Earth until the ninth hour. And the SUN was darkened, and the veil of the Temple was rent in the midst. . . .

. . . Then said Hell unto his wicked ministers: Shut ye hard the gates of brass, and on them the bars of iron, and withstand stoutly, lest we that hold captivity be taken captive! . . .

And there came a great voice as of thunder, saying:

Remove, O princes, your gates, and be ye lift up ye doors of Hell, and the KING OF GLORY shall come in.

And when Hell saw that they so cried out twice, he said as if he knew it not:

Who is the KING OF GLORY? . . .

And the Lord of Majesty appeared, in the form of a man, and lightened the eternal darkness and brake the bonds that could not be loosed; and the succour of His everlasting might visited us that sat in the deep darkness of our transgressions and in the shadow of the death of our sins. . . .

When Hell and Death and their wicked ministers saw that, they were stricken with fear at the sight of the Brightness of so great a Light in their own realm, seeing CHRIST of a sudden in their abode. . . .

Thou that didst lie dead in the sepulchre hast come to us living: and at Thy death all creation quaked and all the stars were shaken: and Thou has become free among the dead and dost rout our legions.

Whence art Thou, Jesus, a man so mighty and bright in majesty, so excellent, without spot and clean from sin?

Then did the KING OF GLORY in His majesty trample upon death, and laid hold of Satan the prince and delivered him into the power of Hell, and drew Adam to Him unto His own Brightness. . . .

These are the divine and holy
Mysteries. . . .

————

And behold, there had been a great earthquake.

For the Angel of the Lord descended from Heaven, and come and rolled back the stone from the door of the sepulchre and sat upon it.

His countenance was like lightning, and his raiment white as snow.

And for fear of him the keepers did shake, and became as dead men.

And the Angel said unto the women, Fear not ye; for I know that ye seek Jesus, which was crucified.

He is not here; for He is risen. . . .

————

(All the above quotations are from the Gospels, with the exception of the Descent into Hell, which is from the Apocryphal Gospel of Nicodemus.)

CHAPTER XIV

GNOSIS

" I will sing praises to thee O Light, for I desired to come to thee. I will sing thee praises O Light, for thou art my deliverer.

Leave me not in the Chaos. Save me, O Light of the Height, for it is thou that I have praised.

Thou hast sent me thy Light through thyself, and hast saved me. Thou hast led me to the higher regions of the Chaos. . . .

Because I have had faith in the Light, I shall not be afraid; and the Light is my deliverer and I shall not fear. . . .

. . . The Light hath become a wreath round my head; and I shall not depart from it, so that the emanations of Self-willed may not rob it from me.

And though all matters be shaken, yet shall I not be shaken.

And though all my matters perish and remain in the Chaos— yet shall I not perish.

For the Light is with me, and I myself am the Light."

(The Song of Pistis Sophia.)

AMONG the many early Christian writings is the Gnostic account of Christ teaching His disciples after the Resurrection and before the Ascension. This is known as the " Pistis Sophia ".* The Gnostics are so called because they based their Christianity on the foundations of the ancient Mystery wisdom, or Gnosis.

The development of philosophical thought had reached the greatest possible heights in Greece and Rome; and this really quite new achievement was naturally applied by those who were struggling to understand the profound secrets of the Resurrection and, above all, of the Incarnation. But it could not

* Translated and edited by G. R. S. Mead: published by (John M. Watkins, 1921).

grasp them fully. Because, no matter how advanced and lofty human thinking may be it is nevertheless allied fundamentally to the material world; it must have the material world as its ground. The diviner things elude its grasp.

But the Gnosis did not have its origins in the kind of thinking which had matured in Roman times. It was the aftermath of the revelations that had been received by the Initiates of old in the Mystery Temples. But only an aftermath—a method of knowledge, whose last harvest had been garnered. But it still had a mission to perform, to preserve—to re-collect as it were—those elements which pointed to the purely spiritual heights and depths of the Universe. . . . It may in a certain sense be likened to that gesture which the great painters of the Renaissance gave to the forerunner of Christ, John the Baptist: the finger pointing heavenwards, to the Sun. . . . And to his words: " I saw the Spirit descending from Heaven like a dove."

The Gnostics placed the level of human thought below the level of Sophia, the Divine Wisdom; and the divine wisdom itself they placed thirty tremendous spiritual levels below the ultimate sublimity of the primal Father of the worlds.

The thirty levels between Sophia and the Highest were called Æons; something that signifies both Worlds and Beings and Times—each one of them an individual and utterly exalted mystery. Sophia, the divine wisdom, who is so much higher than human thinking, knows that she has fallen from her original world of Light. But her holy faith reveals to her the possibility of return, if she casts out from herself all that may be imagined as " desire ".

Desire—*Achamod*—is the sphere of existence in which humanity dwells. . . . There is desire even in the purest

human thinking. But real spiritual knowledge is
" Light ". The path to this Light is the path cloven
through the Æons by Christ.

Some fragments from the *Pistis Sophia* are quoted
here. They have an entirely unearthly beauty of their
own. The whole conception of the Gnosis is certainly
difficult to grasp, and the language is often obscure and
quite foreign to our ordinary understanding; but there
exists nothing else in the world which, if one
approaches it in the right mood, can make so tremendous an impression as this picture of the Risen Christ
in His Vesture of Light, surrounded by His awe-struck
disciples.

It is a completely spiritual picture. Such experiences could not have been had if the hearers had been
listening merely with their physical ears, or looking
with their physical eyes. They were in the spirit. And
it is this which gives us, paradoxically, so intense a
feeling of the reality of this intercourse. And it lends
also a poignant reality to the simple words in the first
chapter of the *Acts*, where we are told that He was
taken up into Heaven, and that Clouds received Him.

The following is an extract from the Pistis Sophia:

And it came to pass then, on the fifteenth day of the
Moon in the month Tybi, which is the day on which
the Moon is full, on that day then, when the Sun had
come forth in his going, that there came forth behind
the Sun a great light-power shining most exceedingly,
and there was no measure to the light conjoined with
it.

For it came out of the Light of Lights, and it came
out of the last Mystery. . . .

And that light-power came down over Jesus and
surrounded Him entirely, while He was seated

removed from His disciples, and He shone most exceedingly, and there was no measure for the light that was on Him.

And the disciples had not seen Jesus because of the great light in which He was, or which was about Him; for their eyes were darkened because of the great light in which He was. But they saw only the Light, which shot forth many light-rays.

And the light-rays were not like one another, but the light was of divers kind, and it was of divers type, from below upwards, one ray more excellent than the other . . . in one great immeasurable glory of light, it stretched from under the Earth right up to Heaven. And when the disciples saw that light, they fell into great fear and great agitation.

It came to pass then, when that light-power had come down over Jesus, that it gradually surrounded Him entirely. Then Jesus ascended, or soared, into the height, shining most exceedingly in an immeasurable light. And the disciples gazed after Him and none of them spake, until He had reached into Heaven; but they all kept in deep silence. . . .

Then, on the ninth hour of the morrow, the Heavens opened, and they saw Jesus descend, shining most exceedingly, and there was no measure for His light in which He was. . . .

The light was of a threefold kind, and the one kind was more excellent than the other. . . .

And it came to pass, when the disciples saw this, that they feared exceedingly, and were in agitation. Then Jesus, the compassionate and tender-hearted, when He saw His disciples that they were in great agitation, spake with them, saying " Take courage. It is I, be not afraid."

It came to pass then, when the disciples had heard this word, that they said: " Lord, if it be Thou, withdraw Thy light-glory into Thyself that we may be able to stand; otherwise our eyes are darkened, and we are agitated, and the whole world also is in agitation because of the great light that is about Thee."

Then Jesus drew to Himself the glory of His light." . . .

(Jesus explains to His disciples that He had ascended for a brief space in order to receive his Vesture; that now He was clothed in it, and would stay for a while with them and teach them the Mystery of the Universe. He further describes His ascent, and the nature of His Vesture and its light. He tells how He reached the highest sphere.)

". . . There was no measure for the light that was round about Me, forty-and-nine times more than the light with which I had shone in the houses of the Fate.

And all the Angels of the Æons and their Archangels and their rulers and their gods and their lords and their authorities and their tyrants and their powers and their light-sparks and their light-givers and their unpaired and their invisibles and their forefathers and their triplepowers, saw Me, shining most exceedingly, and there was no measure for the light that was about Me. And they were thrown into agitation the one over against the other, and great fear fell upon them when they saw the great light that was about Me. . . .

And they agitated all their Æons together and all their spheres and all their orders, fearing and being greatly agitated because of the great light that was about Me—a light not of the former quality that was about Me when I was on the Earth of mankind, when the light-vesture came over Me—for the world could

not bear the light such as it was in its truth, else
would the world at once be destroyed and all upon it—
but the light which was about Me in the twelve Æons
was eight-thousand-and-seven-hundred times greater
than that which was about Me in the world among
you."

. . . It came to pass then, when Jesus had finished
speaking these words unto his disciples, that they fell
down all together, adored Him, and said to Him:
" Blessed are we before all men, for unto us Thou hast
revealed these great exploits."

In the Acts of the Apostles it is told how Fire
descended at Pentecost. This is the direct continuation of the Easter experience and the Ascension. One
could compare it to a sudden illumination of the
memory. . . . How much of the intercourse between
Jesus and His disciples must have been pure inner
clairvoyant understanding and insight, often taking
place quite apart from His actual physical presence!

How much of the three years must have seemed to
the disciples like a dream when they looked back upon
them and the Last Supper and the betrayal, and all
that followed, like something scarcely yet realised at
all. And then, suddenly everything becomes clear. All
is now so full of " Light " that every word that springs
to the disciples' lips is true; they are bathed in truth
and enlightened memory; each one's own illumined
Ego stands forth in shining equality with Spirit, so
that there are no barriers between their speech and the
understanding of the people who hear them. . . .
Think of the Sun! There is no Light like the heart of
the Sun, and no Fire like the flame of its Love. . . .

Surely Jerusalem, in that moment, shone out into
the darkness of cosmic space like a faint Star, where the

order of a God's radiant Vesture touched it, and began to kindle the dust of the Earth into life.

The drama of these first days continues:

Saul—afterwards St. Paul—was still "breathing out threatenings" against the Christians and was on his way to persecute those who were at Damascus. We will let him tell it in his own words:

... "Whereupon, as I went to Damascus with authority and commission from the chief priests, at midday, O king, I saw in the way a light from Heaven, above the brightness of the Sun, shining round about me and them which journeyed with me.

"And when we were all fallen to the Earth, I heard a voice speaking unto me, and saying in the Hebrew tongue: Saul, Saul, why persecutest thou Me? It is hard for thee to kick against the pricks.

"And I said: Who art thou, Lord?

"And he said: I am Jesus, whom thou persecutest. But rise, and stand upon thy feet: for I have appeared unto thee for this purpose, to make thee a minister and a witness both of these things which thou hast seen, and of those things in which I will appear unto thee, delivering thee from the people, and from the Gentiles, unto whom I now send thee,

"To open their eyes, and to turn them from darkness to light."

PART II

TOWARDS FULFILMENT

" I have come, and I have ploughed for thee the fields."

CHAPTER XV

" HE MUST INCREASE "

WE have tried to trace the universal premonitions and expectations of an end of the old world when the Sun had been the central distributor of spiritual power. The realisation that this end could be but a new beginning was slow to ripen.

Gradually, as the centuries of our era passed, experience of the spiritual reality and livingness of the Universe lost its old awe-inspiring and all-embracing majesty. The power of the Divinity of the Sun has to be discovered elsewhere—invisibly working in history, in the thoughts and deeds of men. In a certain sense the Heavens empty themselves. They are, for human consciousness, spread out over Infinity as a " finished work ". . . .

If in the following pages of this book the influences developing in Christendom are given sole prominence, it is because the central impulse of the present world-age of civilisation is European and Western, and *has been raised upon a directly Christian foundation.*

What happens to this civilisation in the near future will determine the trend of events throughout world-history: just because this age, and the Western and Central world, have begun to recognise the principle of a universal human striving in an undivided Earth. *And this is the Christ-principle.*

It is now so deeply rooted in mankind, whether consciously or unconsciously, whether among professed Christians or not, that as a principle it has developed ahead of the representative Christian Churches. And because it now has this strength, it is attacked by adversary powers from every conceivable point.

When this is understood, Christianity is seen to possess something peculiar to itself, namely, that all ancient religious conceptions prepared the way for it, and, so far as their initiated leaders were concerned, *consciously;* since all recognised equally the same fundamental beginnings of evolution—the " ALPHA " of the world. The " OMEGA ", the ending, cannot spring from any element foreign to the " ALPHA ". They must belong together.

No other world-teacher has proclaimed this so clearly as Christ, the Representative of the " I AM ". This does not make Christ into a possession of the Christians only, but hints at His universality from the Beginning to the End, whether He is everywhere called by the name of Christ, or not.

Neither is Mohammed the exclusive possession of the Mohammedans, nor Buddha of the Buddhists, nor Confucius of the Confucians. For lack of any one of them other religions, including the Christian, would be the poorer, and all humanity would be infinitely the poorer.

There is, and always will be, a certain interchange between all. And this living movement is brought about because mankind wanders from land to land and from faith to faith, in the course of time and through many incarnations, until the " OMEGA " is reached.

It is not a question of any theory of " comparative religions " seeking some abstract points of agreement.

Nor is Christianity to be regarded as a synthesis of all religions. The simplest way to conceive of it is that the great world-teachers are " brothers ", but among them is One who is the Elder Brother and the Leader of humanity, whose evolution is *His* evolution too. . . . " I ascend to My Father and to your Father."

If one really studies the contents of the previous chapters without prejudice, one will not be able to avoid recognising the fact that they really do represent, spread over many hundreds and even thousands of years, a kind of world-prophecy. But it would of course require a much more detailed presentation to substantiate what can only be indicated in a single volume, namely, that the esoteric content of the ancient Mystery-religions pointed to the same transcendent Being, as the highest they could conceive. He made Himself known in the infinite Universe; then in the Sun; then in the planets; then in the elements. . . . His gradual approach was not imaginary, and not the *result* of a diminution of the higher spiritual consciousness of the initiated seers; rather was His approach the *cause* of it.

This is something which it is hard to understand or to accept. Yet this approach is at last concentrated in the memorable words that echoed in the wilderness: *The Kingdom of Heaven is at hand!*

The enormous preparation was now ended. It had reached the first stage of its fulfilment. St. John the Baptist was inspired to gather the whole great past together and to point to the future: " I must decrease; He must increase."

John himself represented the entire world-prophecy, which had now become silent. While He, whom the ancient Orient had called Vishvakarman, the Persians

Ahura-Mazdao, the Egyptians Osiris, the Greeks Apollo, and had identified Him in one way and another with the spiritual Essence of the Sun—His power must *increase*.

But how? As the inner force bestowed upon the awakening human Ego! As the power of Ascension poured out upon the Earth and mankind.

Personal responsibility, personal recognition of what is right for each world-age, or each race, or nation— this is the task laid upon the " I am ".

The two vast world-phases are comprehended in two words: the first is *Wisdom*. Not strictly speaking a human wisdom; for it had to be discovered in the higher levels of consciousness by the few, brought down, and translated for the people through parable and myth and the many elements which went to build the foundations of civilisation.

The second world-phase, in which we now live, is comprehended in the word *Love*. If the phase of proclamation comprises thousands of years, the phase of fulfilment will also last thousands of years.

But this strikes into our thoughts as a terrific question: *What of to-day?* Is it progress? or is it defeat and downfall of the cosmic plan?

If we are to try and answer this question it will now be necessary to follow, in outline, the development of human thought up to the present time. Such a review will have to be as brief as possible for it could easily weary the reader. The history of the last two thousand years is a very different thing from the history of earlier times, because it is so packed with known details that tend to obscure its basic realities.

How can we summarise the story of our own era and the trend of this second great world-phase? Only with the words: *He must increase.* The Light of the World must increase. But at first in the darkness, like a germinating seed. . . .

After the birth of Christianity man's thoughts no longer look as before to the Spiritual Sun for their inspirations of wisdom. They begin to look into themselves to find the " kingdom of Heaven ". They recognise their humanity as the expression of self-awareness and self-dependence. They feel the strength of personality; and within, or in a certain sense above this personality, a higher self-sense which inculcates in the lower the urge towards some kind of perfection, some kind of ideal. This ideal is no longer something which reposes in the sublime minds of the Gods alone, but is within man's own capacities of will.

We shall see how this works itself out.

History becomes an affair of individual initiative and individual genius. Destiny, of course, plays its part in it; because, though gradually forgotten, the laws of reincarnation have not ceased. There is such a thing as the " resurrection of ideas "—reborn in those who first conceived them. Causes are always followed by effects, though the intervals between may be a hundred or a thousand years.

And here once more it must be emphasised that what has been called the " solar myth "—which is no myth but a grand reality—should not be forgotten wherever there are peoples that have pledged themselves to the Christian conception of the world. Because they have thus pledged themselves, and yet to-day find their faith seemingly on the brink of an abyss, only a new vision of its cosmic meaning will build the bridge of light whereby to cross over the dark valley of doubt.

If the Being of the Sun has descended through Life

and Light to Love, so the " Sun " in man—his Self—
has surely to ascend from Love and through Love to
Light and Life, and at last to know what is meant by
the Creative Word. And because the beginning, in
our time, has to be made with love, St. Paul calls it
the " greatest of the three ".

THE TURNING POINT

The soul of the Greek age of culture shed the after-
glow of its prime everywhere, and all Europe
received something from its rays. Alexander the Great,
in his short life, had made every effort to foster it.
But, like everything else, it had already fallen from its
original purity.

The cultural life of Rome, at the time of Christ,
represented an extravagant display of the treasure and
gifts of a once magnificent spiritual climax, whose fruits
were found in the incomparable beauties of the Arts.

Philosophy—a word that came to be used in the
first centuries of our era to cover many different symbols of thought—became, so to say, the hall-mark of
superiority in the social life, but the Mysteries by that
time were decadent and possessed but a shadow of
their former spiritual insight. Nevertheless, the original impulse behind the pure Greek culture was still
vital, and did not fade until the fifteenth century.

But deeply hidden in the innermost heart of the
Græco-Roman life of thought was the threefold
conception of the nature of the Sun: the " ground "
of the Universe; its creative Soul, or Logos; and its
physical appearance and qualities.

In a certain sense the Mysteries retained their
power in the first century or two after Christ. Italy
and Greece were still literally sown with Temples. All
cultivated lands had their little Temple with its statue

of a God. The most perfect art was expended in the building of the greater Temples in the cities, with their paintings and sculptures, their marbles and ivory and gold.

The principle of initiation—that is, the fact that the spiritual causes of the world could be known and communion could be held with the real Beings who were called by the names of the planetary Gods—this principle, in spite of its decadence, still carried with it enormous authority; so that the Cæsars, claiming initiation as their right, whether they were worthy or not, felt themselves as equal to the Gods. This was the sin of Rome.

One tremendous idea, or rather certainty, glimmered through the shadowy enlightenments of this strange epoch: it was, that a decisive turning-point had actually arrived in the whole history of the world. For the Roman Cæsars it was embodied in the presentiment, so emphasised by the oracular sayings of the Sibyls, that the fall of Rome was predestined and imminent.

Into this civilisation entered the " revolution " of Christianity.

Two most remarkable figures stand out in the fourth century A.D.: St. John of Chrysostom, and Julian the Apostate, who for a short time was crowned Cæsar.

In this book it is not intended to present " history " in the ordinary sense of the word, but rather to present pictures. Let us begin with Julian. . . .

He was a youth of royal blood with the great Roman traditions behind him, brought up as a child to be a Christian; endowed with a passionate love of knowledge and truth; in danger of his life again and again, even in his childhood, because he was a victim of others' political intrigues and ambitions. His destiny enabled him to go to Athens where he was initiated—not, in this case, by virtue of his position in life, but because of the ardour and cleanness of his soul—into the Mysteries of Eleusis.

These revealed to him the divine origin of the world and the real nature of the Gods; above all, he learnt about the threefold Mystery of the Sun. Profoundly moved by these experiences, he could not reconcile them in his heart with the claims of the Roman Christianity as he then found it, already tending towards formalism and exotericism. Through his initiation he was aware that there must of necessity be a real continuity between the old Mysteries and the new world—between the Sun Spirit and a World-Saviour.

But, wherever possible, the traces of such continuity were being ruthlessly obliterated; temples were now being pulled down, statues of the old Gods discarded and broken—not all at once, but gradually, for political reasons. But Julian dreamed of a universal restoration of the great Hellenic wisdom. Would it be possible to find, by such restoration, final proof of the truth of Christianity?

He believed that man was destined to evolve, and to transform the Earth, by co-operation with the divine Beings; he found, in the Christianity that he knew, and that he outwardly confessed, the operation of *human* resolve and sacrifice and reason, full of soul— but lacking the magical spiritual power of the old initiation knowledge. He believed in a self-dedication to the higher powers of the world that would be strong enough to be more than human, able to take hold of Nature's laws and work with them. The " world's end "—the climax that was prophesied—could then be transformed into a world reborn.

Since he knew that in Persia an initiation could be undergone that would enhance what he had already learnt, he decided that his expedition against the Persians might possibly be brought to such a conclusion that he could be admitted into their Mysteries. . . . But on the way there he was murdered by one of his own soldiers, who was, it is said, a Christian convert.

Such was Julian the Apostate—a man condemned and reviled on the one hand, venerated and beloved on the other; persecuted by political intrigues; magnanimous and truth-loving; but the light in his soul not comprehending itself.

Against this background, we can quote a few short passages from his lengthy and famous address on the " Sovereign Sun ". It was written at Antioch on the day of the festival *Natali Solis Invicti*—25th December, A.D. 363. . . . " I feel how difficult it is for the human mind even to form a conception of *that Sun* who is not visible to the sense, if our notion of Him is to be derived from the Sun that is visible; but to *express* the same in language, however inadequately, is, perhaps, beyond the capacity of man! To fitly explain *His* glory, I am very well aware, is a thing impossible. . . .

" That divine and all-beauteous World, which from the highest vault of Heaven down to the lowest Earth is held together by the immutable providence of God, and which has existed from all eternity, without creation, and shall be *eternal for all time to come*, and which is not regulated by anything, except approximately by the *Fifth Body* (of which the principle is the solar light), placed, as it were, on the second step below the world of *Intelligence*, and finally by the means of the ' Sovereign of all things, around whom all things stand ': this Being, whether properly to be called ' that which is above comprehension ' or the ' type of things existing ', or ' the Good ' as Plato regularly designates Him: *this* then is the Single Principle of all things, and which serves to the universe as a model of indescribable beauty, perfection, and power.

" And, after the pattern of the primary substance that dwells within the Principle, He hath sent forth *out* of Himself, and like in all things *unto* Himself, the Sun—a mighty God, made up of equal parts of intelligible and creative causes. . . .

" And in the third place, the visible disk of the Sun is, in an equal degree, the source of life and preservation to things visible, the objects of sense; and everything which we have said flows down from the Great Deity upon the *intelligible* gods,* the same doth this other visible deity communicate to the objects of sense.

" Of this there are clear proofs, if you choose to investigate things non-apparent by the means of things that are visible. . . ."

This, in a first outline, presents the idea of the threefold Sun: the primary divine Being, that rules in all Intelligence—the Good; then that which issues as His Substance; and, as Julian tells later, takes the " middle position ", partaking both of divine Intelligence, and ruling among the surrounding planetary Intelligencies on the one hand; and on the other, having in Himself also " creative causes ". And thirdly, the visible disk of the Sun with its physical life and light permeating the world of sense.

He goes on to speak of Light itself as an " incorporeal and divine image of what is transparent in its action ". It has a most perfect part—a " flower " of Light; a diffused radiance, called by the Phoenicians

---

* " Intelligible " is here used in the sense of " supersensible ".

the " Soul of the Stars ". This seems to be the same as what Julian calls the " Fifth Body "—the *quintessence* among the elements: the quintessential Light.

This middle Being of the Sun represents the element of Soul in the Universe.

To continue with Julian:

". . . These two essences (the Intelligible—or divine—and the Sensible) which are the causes of mutual attraction does the Sun concentrate into one. . . .

" *One* indeed is the Creator of all things, but *many* are the creative powers revolving in the heavens; we must therefore place the influence of the Sun as *intermediate* with respect to each single operation affecting the Earth.

". . . It must . . . be laid down that the Sovereign Sun *proceeded from the One God*—one out of the one Intelligible World; he is stationed in the middle of the Intelligible Powers . . . bringing the last with the first into a union both harmonious and loving, and which fastens together the things which were divided: containing within Himself the means of perfecting, of cementing together, of generative life, and of the uniform existence; and to the world of Sense, the author of all kinds of good; not merely adorning and cheering it with the radiance wherewith He Himself illumines the same, but also by making subordinate to Himself the existence of the Solar Angels, and containing within Himself the unbegotten *Cause* of things begotten; and moreover, prior to this, the unfading, unchanging source of things eternal."

About ten years before Julian was writing his *Sovereign Sun,* there was born in Antioch, John, called

Chrysostomos, the " golden-mouthed "—the greatest orator of the ancient Christian Church.

Innumerable legends surround his life's story; but as he was a person of supreme importance for the spiritual life both of his own time and for the future, this is not to be wondered at.

As we have seen, Julian was one of those who believed in the approaching end of the Roman world, and indeed in a downfall and end of *all* the world as it was then known unless it could be saved by a restoration of the ancient wisdom. The Emperor Constantine, who died in 337, had been certain that at least that part of the Sibylline phophecy was true which said that in Rome " foxes and wolves would have their habitation and become mighty ". And so he had removed the capital of the Empire to Constantinople (Byzantium), and had taken the Palladium—sacred symbol of the ancient wisdom upon which it was believed the power of Rome had rested—and buried it there.

The Christians, on the other hand (for Constantine was not converted till the very end of his life) believed in the continuity of Rome, but as a spiritual force in history. Christianity had already developed its two main tendencies: the one more external, formal, and powerful; and the other esoteric, spiritual, and retaining the elements of the pre-Christian Mysteries (or Gnosis) to a certain extent.

We need not go into any details of all the various nuances of these latter tendencies, except in connection, at present, with St. John Chrysostom. He was in fact a representative of that Christian esotericism which finds its origin in the " beloved disciple ", John, whose Gospel is, even for the present time, the most profound and the most sublime. From the followers of St. John Chrysostom arose the sect called Johannites, or by some the " John Christians ", who took their title from the Evangelist.

The Irish Christianity, itself based upon the same spiritual foundations of the ancient Gnosis, recognised its affinity with the " John Christians ".

Those who were followers of the John Christians knew that an initiation, or " awakening of the Higher Self "—as an experience bringing with it the attainment of knowledge of the true nature of Christ—was possible. Of course, such a thing entailed a long and arduous preparation. But, with this awakening once accomplished, everything that had pertained to the lower self was, so to speak, destroyed. This was understood as the apocalypse of the soul. Therefore the John Christians always believed in the possibility of new revelations, occurring perhaps at long intervals of time, concerning the meaning of the Gospels. The exoteric teachings, however, tended to regard this attitude as heretical.

Centuries later, within the continuing stream of this Johannine Christianity, we find the symbol of the Holy Grail.

The Knights of the Order of the Holy Grail are not mere legendary persons. They are followers of the stream of the esoteric Christianity of the Johannites. All knights of the Grail, in all countries, had to suffer misunderstanding and persecution.*

On the other hand the more external Roman form of Christianity was, in every sense, the means for the widest possible extension of Christian teaching over the Earth. It had to be the rain and sunshine necessary for the first harvests. The more hidden elements were

* See *Weltgeschichte im Lichte des heiligen Gral* (9th century), by Dr. W. J. Stein.

like " deep cultivation " . . . they could not appear on the surface.

St. John Crysostom takes St. John the Evangelist as his inspirer. Indeed the actual writing of the Apocalypse* has been attributed to him. In his lifetime, however, he was accused of having stolen or appropriated an original script, or part of it, of the *Revelation* and of having published it as his own. He, like others, interpreted the expected " end of the world " in the fourth century in terms of the Apocalypse. An actual date was announced by him as the date of the final catastrophe: 13th March, 399.

A Russian writer, Nikolaus Morosow,† claims to have proved that the Apocalypse was actually written by St. John Chrysostom, who, like the other John, was exiled in Patmos. Morosow details every event in the Apocalypse as a tremendous vision, vouchsafed to John of Chrysostom, of the atronomical heavens during the night of 30th September, 395. Immense research and calculation have gone to the making of Morosow's book; and since there has always been some uncertainty with regard to the authorship of the Apocalypse —as well as its meaning—his views are of great interest.

On the other hand, Rudolf Steiner, in a course of lectures on the Apocalypse, shows how this great vision is substantially a profound experience of *every* soul who is able to attain a high degree of Christian initiation. One can say it is part of the " Mystery school " of the disciples of Christ. . . . " If you could go back ", he says, " into the Mysteries of ancient Greece, the Orphic and Eleusinian Mysteries, or

* The *Revelation* of St. John the Evangelist.

† *Die Offenbarung Johannes.* By Nikolaus Morosow. Spemann, Stuttgart. 1912. With introduction by Prof. A. Drews.

those of Egypt, ancient Chaldea, Persia, and India,
you would find the Apocalypse everywhere. It existed;
it was there. It was not written, but it passed from one
generation of priests to another, through generations
of Initiators, the memory being so vivid in those days
that it could master this abundant material. . . . Thus
the Apocalypse was nothing new, but its application to
the event of Golgotha was something new. . . . It is an
ancient sacred ' book ' of humanity, and has only been
presented externally (in writing) by the disciple whom
the Lord loved and to whom He bequeathed the task
of announcing His true nature. . . ."

All this explains how the accusation of " stealing "
the Book of Revelation levelled against John Chrysostom, goes to prove that he was, to a certain degree, a
Christian Initiate, and therefore familiar with the real
meaning of the visions and symbols. Only, he was not
able to understand, or did not wish to reveal, that they
covered a vast period of human evolution.

The edition of the Apocalypse attributed to St.
John Chrysostom spread rapidly over Asia Minor.
Moreover, a year or so previously, the entire population had been smitten with terror by a total eclipse of
the Sun. And in this period originates the following
legend:

One night, when all slept, two men came silently
into John Chrysostom's room. One of them handed
to him a roll of papyrus and said: " Receive this roll
from my hand! I am John, who lay on the breast of
the Lord at the Last Supper. There I received the
Divine Revelation. God bestows upon thee, there-
with, the power to know the whole Truth, so that thou
mayest nourish men with this imperishable language
and with wisdom, and stop the mouths of heretics and
Jews, who speak unlawfully of God. . . ."

There is no question but that John of Chrysostom
knew the apocalyptic book himself, as a personal
mystical experience, and entered the ranks of those
who fought against the decadent and vainglorious
elements in the Church, and fanned the flame in the
hearts of those who expected immediately the " end of
the world " and the second Advent of the Saviour.

But reading between the lines, we see at the same
time that he had always in mind also the " apocalypse
of the soul " as an eternal reality: the winged splendours of the divine wrath coming down into the
kingdoms of the lower Ego, and establishing there at
last the realm of inward peace.

These two figures—Julian the Apostate and John of
the Golden Mouth—stand as tremendous symbols at
the turning-point of the evolution of mankind.

The one seeking to restore the threefold cosmic
Mystery of the Sun, and to regenerate the ancient and
dying wisdom; the other pointing to the Mystery of
the threefold Word: Life, and Light, and Love, and
their one-ness in Christ; thus to the end of the old
world, and its rebirth in the Spirit.

   " This Table takes the place of the manger, for
here too the Body of the Lord will rest, not, as of
yore, clad in swaddling clothes, but bright with
the radiance of the Holy Spirit.
   " Picture to yourselves what it means to behold
the SUN that has come down from Heaven to dwell
on Earth, letting His radiance shine out from this
place over *all* men!
   " But if the Light that is *visible* cannot shine
without arousing wonder in the hearts of all who
behold it, only consider what it signifies to see the
brightness of the SUN of RIGHTEOUSNESS streaming

forth from our own flesh, and sending Light into the soul."*

And now let us turn to the West, and see two other figures who point to the beginning of a new world, and the end of the old.

The expectancy of the end of the world had been very widespread. It is not to be wondered at; for actual vision of the spiritual powers working in Nature had become dim and nearly altogether obscured.

Nature is something which everyone knows. She never absents herself. The stars are constant, the seasons are constant; bodily needs and satisfactions through Nature are constant. But if she changes the appearance that men are wont to see, then there must be fear and consternation.

But time heals. Slowly, as the message of Christianity spread, Nature could be seen in a new light. And as this light of " natural philosophy " began to dawn, the long-past visions seemed like a deep shadow of ignorance and superstition which was drifting away. And it was so. For only a very few people had access to the still more ancient wisdom which had been full of clarity and power and creative certainty. It was its decadence that lay nearest to the early centuries of our era.

Two main streams that were to flow into the new world were both of them Christian. The one had its great representative in Saint Augustine, and the other in Saint Patrick. The one was to build up the Church; the other to preserve—for some centuries at least—the spiritual fruits of mystic experience, as the foundation stone of Christian community.

* St. John of Chrysostom, Christmas Sermon.

With the after-glow of Hibernia behind it, every-thing that is called " Irish " or " Celtic " Christianity springs from a kind of soul-quality that has something in it of the deep wisdom of childhood, and awakens in others a spirit of warmth and tenderness. On the other hand its will to sacrifice is unbreakable, because it has as its " aura " the capacity of pure vision. In this stream there remains for a long time the concep-tion of Light and Darkness in conflict, and especially in Nature.

In the other stream, martyrdom is a kingly crown; the struggle of the soul centres round the lightning-flashes of pure thought. Thunder is the language of its teachers. The Church is the stronghold of faith.

Then there is a third stream. And this is hidden in the Mysteries and Order of the Grail, which in the eighth or ninth century was united, through individ-uals, with the Irish Christianity. Below the surface it lives on, and it cannot die.

But it is a complicated process, this beginning of the Earth's transformation—as it is conceived individually within the three main trends of its development. They represent man's search for the Sun which has " wandered upon the Earth ".

For sheer power, and for its glorying in the might of the Trinity and the universality of Christ, there is perhaps nothing at this time in the West to equal the " Lorica ", or " breast-plate " of St. Patrick.

I arise to-day:
  in vast might, invocation of the Trinity;
  belief in a threeness;
  confession of Oneness;
  meeting in the Creator.

I arise to-day:
  in the might of Christ's Birth and His Baptism;
  in the might of His Crucifixion and Burial;
  in the might of His Resurrection and Ascension;
  in the might of His Descent to the Judgment of Doom.

I arise to-day:
  in the might of the Cherubim;
  in obedience of Angels;
  in ministration of Archangels;
  in hope of resurrection through merit;
  in prayers of Patriarchs;
  in predictions of Prophets;
  in preaching of Apostles;
  in faiths of Confessors;
  in innocence of holy Virgins;
  in deeds of good men.

I arise to-day:
  in the might of Heaven;
  Splendour of the Sun;
  whiteness of Snow;
  irresistibleness of Fire;
  the swiftness of Lightning;
  the speed of Wind;
  Absoluteness of the Deep;
  Earth's stability;
  Rock's durability.

I arise to-day:

in the might of God	for my piloting;
Power of God	for my stability;
Wisdom of God	for my guidance;
Eye of God	for my foresight;
Ear of God	for my hearing;
Word of God	for my word;
Hand of God	for my guard;
Path of God	for my prevention;
Shield of God	for my protection;
Host of God	for my salvation.

    against every demon's snare;
    against all vices' lure;
    against concupiscence;
    against ill-wishes far and near.

I invoke all these forces:
    between me and every savage force that may come upon
        me, body and soul;
    against incantations of false prophets;
    against black laws of paganism;
    against false laws of heresy;
    against idolatry;
    against spells of women and smiths and druids;
    against all knowledge that should not be known.

Christ for my guard to-day;
      against poison, against burning;
      against drowning, against wounding,
      that there may come to me merit.
Christ with me, Christ before me,
Christ behind me, Christ in me,
Christ under me, Christ over me,
Christ to right of me, Christ to left of me,
Christ in lying down, Christ in sitting, Christ in rising up,
Christ in all who may think of me!
Christ in the mouth of all who may speak to me!
Christ in the eye that may look on me!
Christ in the ear that may hear me!

I arise to-day:
      in vast might, of the Trinity prayed to:
      believing in a Threeness;
      confessing a Oneness;
      meeting in the Creator;
Domini est salus, Domini est salus, Christi est salus;
Salus tua, Domine, sit semper nobiscum.

Fairly near to the date of St. Patrick, about a century earlier, lived the blind bard Ossian. His poems like a last monument, and a tremendous one, to the memory of the old ancestral second-sight. The whole of Nature is in them, not as the background for the Light of Christ, but for the dying heroic age. The Sun is shrouded in the mists that encompass the dead. The living are the banner-bearers of the invincibility

of human courage. Courage, transmuted in the Sun,
is the same as Love. The standard of Fingal was called
the *Sunbeam*.

" We sat that night in Selma, round the strength
of the shell. The wind was abroad in the oaks. The
spirit of the mountain roared. The blast came
rustling through the hall, and gently touched my
harp. The sound was mournful and low, like the
song of the tomb.

" Fingal heard it first. The crowded sighs of his
bosom rose. ' Some of my heroes are low ', said the
grey-haired King of Morven. '' I hear the sound of
death on the harp. Ossian, touch the trembling
string. Bid the sorrow rise; that their spirits may
fly with joy to Morven's woody hills! '

" I touched the harp before the King; the sound
was mournful and low.

" ' Bend forward from your clouds ', I said,
' ghosts of my fathers! bend. Lay by the red terror
of your course. Receive the falling chief; whether
he comes from a distant land, or rises from the
rolling sea. Let his robe of mist be near; his spear
that is formed of a cloud. Place an half-extinguished
meteor by his side, in the form of the hero's sword.

" ' And oh! let his countenance be lovely, that
his friends may delight in his presence. Bend from
your clouds! ' I said, ' ghosts of my fathers!
bend '."

And this:

" Green thorn of the hill of ghosts, that shakest
thy head to nightly winds! I hear no sound in thee;
is there no spirit's windy skirt now rustling in thy

leaves? Often are the steps of the dead, in the dark-eddying blasts; when the moon, a dun shield from the east, is rolled along the sky.

" Ullin, Carril, and Ryno, voices of the days of old! Let me hear you, while it is yet dark, to please and awake my soul. I hear you not, ye sons of song; in what hall of the clouds is your rest? Do you touch the shadowy harp, robed with morning mist, where the rustling sun comes forth from his green-headed waves? . . ."

Magical and majestic is one of his descriptions of Fingal coming in the dawn to his massed and waiting warriors. Through the dense mist there gleams for a moment his sword, then his shield moving to and fro, then his whole figure " greatly dim in all his arms "; and behind him, caught in the rising sun, the hill glitters in the light. . . . Immortality is in every line of the poem.

Patrick's world of Nature is the whole universe, visible and invisible, founded on the Rock of Christ. Ossian's is all the elements—the earth, the water, the air and the fire—melted together into the sun-and-moon-filled mists of another world; a fleeting shadowy world, but so near that it echoes to the clang of smitten shields, and stirs a fiery courage great enough to love death, even when it is a friend who falls.

These fragments from Ossian are introduced by way of contrast and emphasis. For it is so necessary to grasp—at least in the imagination—the change of consciousness that is taking place in these early centuries.

Somewhat later—in the sixth century—Christian interest turns to St. Columba, spiritual successor of St. Patrick in the West. Around him are other heroic

souls that shine like stars in the half-light of the
Western Isles. These are they from whom Europe
received enthusiasm for the tidings of Christ. St.
Columbanus, contemporary of St. Columba of Iona,
left, with his Irish monks, a trail of monasteries across
European lands whose influence will never be forgotten.

Celtic hymns, invocations, charms, poems, customs
—contain the most pure evidence of how the spirit
of a people could experience the Light of the World
as a cosmic Being who penetrated all Nature. Deep
wisdom lies concealed in many of their simplest songs.

The " nine rays of the Sun "—which are the nine
Orders of the spiritual Hierarchies—are a reality
to these people; Angels and Archangels, and the
whole company of Heaven, are always present in their
consciousness. The " Three-One " is " with us day
and night ". Scarcely a single poem, whether
connected with religion, labour, the seasons, the
common intimacies of homely life, but has its reference
to the " Holy Three "—Father, Son and Spirit; or to
the golden-shining St. Michael, the " king of the
Angels "; or to Christ as the " King of the Sun ", the
" king of the elements ".

But one could perhaps say too that the Celtic
people, quite recognising that the end of the world
had really taken place, kept their love for the old
world that was still there, hidden under the mountains
and the lakes and the seas. It was a world asleep, that
would assuredly wake up again one day. In the meantime it had its dreams, which rose up unbidden out of
the twilights, and caught men unawares in a silvery
net of longing, and drew them into the " hollow
hills "—or to Tir-nan-og, the heart of the mysterious
West.

Knowest though what thou art
In the hour of sleep—
A mere body—a mere soul—
Or a secret retreat of the Light?

SIXTH CENTURY—BARDIC.

CHAPTER XVI

THE MIDDLE AGES

THE conception of the universe which prevailed from the third century up to the fifteenth was the astronomical system of Ptolemy.

To-day we regard the Sun as the central physical power of our planetary system; but according to Ptolemy, and continuing up to the time of Copernicus, it was the Earth that was regarded as the centre.

Before the Greek age of culture, observations of the stars were not yet based on reasoned calculations but on inspiration and clairvoyant perception. In Grecian times, however, calculated astronomy became not only possible but a deep necessity for the next stage of the evolution of thought. The Greeks were really quite shocked by the astronomical wisdom of the past, which had been able to observe with a wonderful accuracy many of the apparent irregularities of the planetary motions; but such " staggerings " of the planets appeared to the cultured Greeks as most unseemly for the majesty of the Gods! Plato desired his pupils to discover if possible the existence of more uniform circular movements in the planetary system.

Ptolemy, who lived in the second century after Christ, succeeded in creating such a system, showing the Earth as a central focus; it contains many intricacies of its own, far removed from present-day thought, and cannot be described here. This idea prevailed up to the fifteenth century.

Although this system is a " thought-out " one, it is at the same time definitely an after-echo of the wisdom taught in the old Mysteries, when the Earth had been regarded as the field of work of the Gods, and thus a spiritual centre. But for our later science, it is a mechanical impossibility that planets should be able to revolve round any focus that is only " spiritual " and has nothing to do with the laws of gravitation and attraction!

Copernicus (born 1473) conceived a system with the Sun in the centre and the Earth revolving on its axis round it. Both these thinkers gave the heavenly bodies uniformity of circular movements. Kepler (born 1571) began to set aside this uniformity. Newton (1643) applied terrestrial laws to the whole Universe. This was the real beginning of our mechanical idea of it.

Our modern age calls the Middle Ages, when the Ptolemaic system still prevailed, *dark*, although they still retained, to a great extent, a spiritual view of the world. There were people who believed that the planets were not only inwardly organised but also that their visible movements were guided by divine Beings, whom they called the Intelligencies of the stars. And there were also other Beings who opposed these Intelligencies, the Star-demons.

It was also believed that before the Fall, it was Man who had been destined to rule the planet Earth, and, in ruling, to direct its divinely appointed motion within the whole harmony of the spheres. But because of the Fall he had lost the power to accomplish this task. . . . The Fall was therefore regarded as something utterly and even cosmically catastrophic; it was the *sin of the world*.

Having such a background then, the Christians of

the early Middle Ages were able to immerse themselves
with the utmost intensity of feeling into the idea of
salvation from the effects of this sin through Christ:
the only cosmic Being, the highest Spirit of the Sun,
who through Love, was able to take upon Himself the
" sin of the world ".   The general mood among
Christians was often one of deep sadness because of
this apparent failure of man to establish himself as one
of the spiritual Hierarchies—" a little lower than the
Angels, but crowned with mercy and honour ".

Read only this fragment from Cynewulf's poem
Christ, written in the eighth century:

" Verily in distress we utter these words, we entreat Him who
    created man that He may not elect to declare the doom of
    hapless man, of us, who sit in prison sorrowing for the Sun's
    joyous journey, until the Lord of Life reveal Light to us,
    become a Guardian of our soul, and gird the feeble mind
    with glory. . . .
" O rising Sun, most radiant of Angels sent to men upon the
    earth, and true beam of the Sun bright beyond the stars—
    out of Thyself Thou dost ever enlighten all seasons. As
    Thou, God verily begotten of God, Son of the true Father,
    wast ever without beginning in the glory of Heaven, so
    now Thine own handiwork, in its distress, beseeches Thee
    boldly to send us the bright Sun, to come Thyself, that
    Thou mayest bring Light to those who long erstwhile have
    sat here covered with darkness and in gloom, enfolded by
    sins in eternal night, and who have had to endure the dark
    shadow of death! "

Or this, from the *Diatesseron* of an Alsatian monk,
Otfried, written in the ninth century:

" We are in sorrow and are suffering want for much that
    was dear to us, and our heritage is a time of bitterness.
    Sorrowfully we grieve in this land here below, being held
    in many bonds by our sins.
" Care and sorrow are here our lot; bereft of all knowledge
    of our home. Orphans, all forsaken, our plaints rise up to

Heaven. Alas! How hard thou art, thou strange country; how hard a mother do I find thee. Forsaken and full of care we wander.

" Within myself can I find nothing of thee that is dear; no other good, but cause for lamentation, and a heart full of pain and care, most great and manifold. . . ."

Such words do not spring from personal moods of depression; they are great, even cosmic, lamentations for man's fall and the loss of the vision of the spiritual Light in Nature. The belief in One who had come to the Earth from the Sun as a Saviour aroused a quite special kind of mood, particularly in Northern and Western countries. That the world had needed salvation indicated the startling fact that Man's Fall had brought all Nature with it.

Among those still able to experience such feelings the thought of the Sun was filled with sorrows because once it had illuminated the purity of Nature and made visible the secret and heavenly chemistry of all the elements and the bright fleeting colours of their super-natural agents. Now, all this had vanished from sight and the material world alone revealed itself.

Nevertheless, the Sun was an undying reminder of what had happened. It had been the home of Christ; He had brought the Light of this home with Him into the Earth, where it still appeared as though engulfed in the darkness of human sin. So to look up to the Sun could be, as well as a source of grief, an ineffable experience. For man lived by it, animals lived by it, plants lived by it, minerals glowed with transparent colours because of it.

But gradually in these centuries its spiritual power came to be experienced in the awakening of a new consciousness; it shone in the soul as pure intellect, guided by the Ego.

All this makes the Middle Ages appear so strange a combination of light and darkness.   Outside—a confusion of values, turmoil, bloodshed, huge contrasts;   inwardly, after the tenth century, an indescribable passion for the miracle of human thinking, intelligence, and creative discovery.   Now it was possible to understand the meaning of *man*—" Manas " —the thinking soul redeemed. . . .   And what of Nature? Here, one could at last feel Love; the selfless Mother of human life.

In the tenth and eleventh centuries, the primitive worship of the Virgin first began. She was the Queen of Heaven, the star-spangled, the crowned, the Mother of the Sun. . . .

Sun, Crystal, Water—faith can surely trace
the Virgin-birth as proven by their hints:
the Stone, if wetted in some Sunny place
gushes intact and scatters golden glints.

In this conjunction there is subtly shown
The Ghost, the Word, the Virgin, and the Son.
The Sun's the Word that dews the Virgin Stone,
the Child's produced by penetrating Sun.

The priestly Water washes her. The Word
is entering but unviolating Light.
The Stone's the bearing Maid. The Son's interred
in Flame, a lantern on our fleshly night.

Through Water comes the pure-conceiving Breath
and grows a Virgin, God and Flesh in one.
Nature's reshaped, and lends a life to death:
new harmonies of spirit are begun.*

The Virgin-worship took its rise in Chartres, where long before the Druids had adored the " Virgin who was to bear a Child ". Fulbert, Bishop of Chartres at

* Hildebert the Venerable.   Eleventh century.   From *Medieval Latin Poets.*

the close of the tenth century, by his hymns of praise to the Virgin, wrought her diadem and her awakening. And for the science of that day, there reigned the Goddess Natura, accompanied by the Seven Liberal Arts: Grammar, Rhetoric, Dialectic; Music, Geometry, Arithmetic, and Astronomy.

To study the Art of Grammar in those times was to study the wisdom of the eternal Word; to live with Dialectic was to expand one's thought into the twelvefold circle of the stars and seek in the whole Universe for the heart of Truth. All the seven Arts were as though handmaidens to the Mother of God. Platonism was Christianised in the Schools of Learning.

Platonic thought carries the thinker into a world of pre-existence, in the search for a wisdom that is virgin.

But this pure world of thought had to develop further, to take a deeper hold of physical life; and the Schools found the way in the passage from Platonic to Aristotelian thought. Its strong clear logic shone with brilliance in the soul of Thomas Aquinas, the " doctor angelicus ".

The principal centre where first Platonism and then Aristotelianism were cultivated, influencing the whole of Europe, was the School of *Chartres*. Immortal names surround the memory of it: Bernard of Chartres, Alan de Lille, Bernardus Sylvestris, John of Salisbury, Thomas Aquinas, and many, many others. They were the great bridge-builders—from the time ending about the tenth and eleventh centuries, when the last vestiges of the former actual experiences of the spiritual world gave final place to the dawn of the modern intellect.

Even up to the eighth and ninth centuries the identity of Christ with the Sun-Spirit had not been wholly lost—as is clearly to be seen in the poem by Cynewulf. But this conception grew more and more clouded. Christ was still revered as a divine Being; but thinking, though a spiritual capacity, is bound to the Earth, and as such could not sustain, in terms of thought alone, the cosmic secret of His Being.

Yet another factor, coming from an entirely different direction, had to give this change a materialistic trend. And we find this element pouring itself into European culture from the Arabs. The first to bring a mingled Mohammedanism and Aristotelianism, *via* Spain, to the School of Chartres, was Gerbert, the teacher of Fulbert, at the close of the tenth century.

This influence was the early forerunner of that method of thinking and research which laid the foundations of pure materialistic reasoning. It was the temporary destiny of civilised mankind to develop so that all attention would ultimately become centred, not upon that which as a " cosmic intelligence " was irradiated by the Sun, but upon that which reflected it only: the crescent Moon is the symbol of Arabian wisdom. Gerbert thus brought into the learning of the Middle Ages the seed of modern natural science. But for a long time the balance was held between the two tendencies.

At the very close of the thirteenth century, a hundred years or so before the beginning of the new age, one of the greatest of all its forerunners left behind him a sign which, like all such signs, was too near the Spirit to be carried on intact into this new enthusiasm for earthly knowledge, to keep steadfast within it the memory of what man is in his real being. . . . It is Dante; who *sees in the threefold Sun " our image painted "*.

The Divine Comedy, perhaps the greatest poem
ever written, still towers over the world like a beacon
out of the past. It reveals many of the shadows of the
past age beneath its beams, but makes them clear and
transparent in the last lines of the last Canto of the
Paradiso:

> . . . " In that abyss
> Of radiance, clear and lofty, seem'd, methought,
> Three orbs of triple hue, clipt in one bound:
> And, from another, one reflected seem'd,
> As rainbow is from rainbow: and the third
> Seem'd fire, breathed equally from both. O speech!
> How feeble and how faint art thou, to give
> Conception birth. Yet this to what I saw
> Is less than little. O eternal light!
> Sole in thyself that dwell'st; and of thyself
> Sole understood, past, present, or to come;
> Thou smiledst, on that circling, which in thee
> Seemed as reflected splendour, while I mused;
> For I therein, methought, in its own hue
> Beheld our image painted: steadfastly
> I pored upon the view. As one
> Who, versed in geometric lore, would fain
> Measure the circle; and, though pondering long
> And deeply, that beginning, which he needs,
> Finds not: e'en such was I, intent to scan
> The novel wonder, and trace out the form,
> How to the circle fitted, and therein
> How placed: but the flight was not for my wing;
> Had not a flash darted athwart my mind,
> And, in the spleen, unfolded what it sought.
> Here vigour failed the towering fantasy:
> But yet the will roll'd onward, like a wheel,
> In even motion, by the love impelled
> That moves the Sun in heaven and all the stars."*

In these centuries one stage of experience overlaps
another. Dante sees the Sun as the revealer of the
great indescribable secret of man's spiritual origin.

* Rev. H. F. Cary's translation. (Fred. Warne and Co., 1844.)

The divine archetypal Man shows Himself in the pure
and primal light of the *threefold Sun.*

The early medieval poets, even long before Dante,
feel the Sun rather as a symbol of the goal of their
longing. For them sunrise and sunset are the diurnal
revelation of birth and death.

It is the Divine *Will* which circles in the spheres of
Dante's *Inferno, Purgatorio,* and *Paradiso.*

The Divine *Thought,* and human Feeling, bathes the
lesser souls of the medieval poets in gleams of Nature's
beauty.

Not yet has Day
  cleared in the East a shining way,
though here are drawn
  the twilight curtains of the Dawn.
The watchman cries
  to all the sleeping folk, Arise!
Over the dark sea now the Sun has passed.
Dawn on the hill-tops. Ah, the Sun at last.

But look, the foe
  are climbing stealthily below,
onwards they creep
  to take the unguarded in their sleep,
and still there cries
  the warning herald-voice, Arise!
Over the dark sea now the Sun has passed.
Dawn on the hill-tops. Ah, the Sun at last.

The North Wind blows
  from where Arcturus glimmering shows,
in morning's haze
  the stars have shorn away their rays,
and nearer now
  towards the Sunrise moves the Plough.
Over the dark sea now the Sun has passed.
Dawn on the hill-tops. Ah, the Sun at last. *

  * Anonymous. Tenth century. From *Medieval Latin Poets.*

CHAPTER XVII

GENIUS

The sun doth rouse the all, and maketh stars to dance.
Then if thou art not moved, in the Whole thou hast no part.

Since the wise man shineth like the Sun
God will be full of Suns, when Time is done.

I too must be a sun, and with my rays I'll paint
Th'unclouded sea of God's Entirety.

The way to the Light where God dwells, breaks off. He who
does not himself become that Light, will not see Him in all
eternity.

ANGELUS SILESIUS, 1624-1677.

IN spring-time the tiny buds on tree and bush
hesitate so long in showing signs of growth, and
then seem suddenly in a single night to have gained
confidence, throwing aside their enclosing sheaths and
unfolding their innumerable varieties of green.

So in Europe, beginning in the fifteenth century,
the spirit of man triumphs and shines forth in the
Genius of personalities. Threefold is this shining in
Europe: in mysticism, art, and knowledge of the
Earth.

The great geniuses of the Renaissance time can
really be said to have had a special mission, not only
for a generation or two, but for a whole epoch of
culture. The earlier ones among them had to be great
enough to forge an unbreakable link between the
spiritual and the material conceptions of the world; to
preserve somehow a force (which has reappeared

again and again up to our own time) that would not be entirely lost in the approaching darkness: a force whereby the inner Light continues.

The astonishing growth arises alongside the stream of orthodox religion, rather than out of it. Whence has it come? One might say from ancient Greece— from Rome; it is a rebirth. But how? Can such things arise of themselves, apart from the conscious co-operation of beings? Who are these who come to their birth with such an eagerness for creative deeds, like many small Suns from heaven? . . .

For three centuries they lavish their gifts upon the world. All that they give comes from the passionate urge to discover the material nature of the Earth. It is there, under their feet. It responds to the light of their thinking and opens its secret doors to them.

The three powers of the Soul are roused to master three realms of life: the will urges to the great voyages of discovery; the heart urges to mystical contemplation, to religious reform, and to noble art; thought urges to lay the foundations of natural science and invention. In the midst of the black deeds of the Inquisition these suns of genius rise, like mirrors reflecting the great Sun itself, creating the new and destroying the old.

A world was required where the genius of this new age could unfold itself. In the Middle Ages Europe was still a chaos of overlapping and conflicting interests. England was involved in the destinies of France in such a way that it was not yet possible for the former to concentrate itself and lay the seeds of a future Empire; but a severence would enable it to prepare for this preordained development; and an impetus would arise for the future shaping of European countries.

The Maid of Orleans, Jeanne d'Arc, was the instrument chosen to create this severance and set in motion the rise of the post-medieval age; and in a few brief years she accomplished her mission.

Alone, with her inspiring Voices to sustain her, she defied all the terrors and the powers that rose against her indomitable will. She was utterly and flawlessly certain of the reality of her task and the divine source of the instructions she received. She was like a force of Nature; and, indeed, she helped to shape the world.

The world's life of thought begins at this time to assume two tendencies: in the East, there is a vast residue of the ancient cosmic wisdom, which, involved in the universal descending of human consciousness, becomes vitiated by impurities that darken the moral effects of spiritual vision. The knowledge of a Universe, once seen as a pleroma, a fullness, of many different spiritual beings, could become, in the East, a temptation to gain egoistic powers. A kind of decadent magic was really possible there.

To the West, the love of earthly knowledge had to grow slowly in the direction of dominion of another kind, to be won through the brilliance of its science of the physical world. In the midst, a certain protection is at first present; central Europe is the soil in which genius germinates; also a pure mystical aspiration, which recognises the limits that have now been set to spiritual knowledge, but recognises no limits to the experience of human aspirations.

Thus the old " way between the two extremes " becomes, at this time, as though incarnated in space in East and West; but the balance is held at first by the sacrifices and the ardours of the great mystics, of the astronomers, the painters, the mathematicians and

scientists.   They unite themselves with the Earth's
destiny and shine, as Angelus Silesius says, like Suns.

Leonardo da Vinci, Raphael, Michelangelo, Titian,
Tintoretto, Rembrandt, Van Dyck, Velasquez, El
Greco, Holbein, Dürer—and innumerable others—in
the realm of art.   In philosophy and in science,
Copernicus, Galileo, Bacon, Giordano Bruno, Tycho
de Brahe, Kepler, Newton—and later Wren—there is
no end to them; writers and reformers like Luther and
Erasmus and Zwingli and Calvin; there are Shakespeare and Milton and Spencer and Thomas More in
England; and all the great discoverers and voyagers
among the Dutch and the Portuguese and the English;
Boehme and Tauler, the great German mystics; and
there are notable rulers too, and great statesmen. . . .
The very names alone of all of those who in those
centuries " found themselves " as citizens of the Earth,
would cover pages of this book. . . .

What is it that stamps these men with a quality
which we have lost?   It is really their discovery of
manhood, of selfhood, and at the same time of the
continents and oceans of the Earth itself.   The old
unearthy wisdom that once raised its eyes heavenward
to the Sun, now looks down and finds as it were a
miracle in every phenomenon of the physical world.

And in the moment that man first begins to concentrate his whole attention upon it, in that moment the
astronomers remove the Earth from her central place
in the planetary system, and set the Sun in the midst.
If one imagines oneself as possessing the older belief—
that the Earth was the Star towards which the Gods
looked with interest as the very heart of their labours—
and then finds that man " thinks it " into a position
where it is a mere attendant upon the Sun; such a
change would have a tremendous effect upon the soul.

It must at long last generate endless doubts as to the real meaning of human existence.

Yet, even if the Sun seems then to have become only the bestower of physical light and life and nothing more, still there is the search for its divinely spiritual reality. If this cannot be found in the heavens, is it not perhaps in man's own powers of understanding and creation? . . . And the physical world *is* beautiful! Lyrical poets, of the early part of the period especially, touch heights of exquisite tenderness in their love of the Earth, in its nights and days and the entrancing events of its seasons.

We can speak of this period as one that is at first really filled with spirituality; not as it once had been: not, except in rare cases, able to soar into realms that had been still open to early Christian seers; but a spirituality whose gaze, as with the saints and mystics, turns inward into the soul; or, with others, seeks from horizon to horizon of the physical world for the hidden signature of God in Nature.

" Our whole teaching ", says Jacob Boehme, " is nothing else than how a man should kindle *in himself* God's light-world. . . . When thou beholdest the deep, the stars, the elements, and the Earth, then thou comprehendest not with thine eyes the bright and clear Deity, though indeed He is there and in them; but thou seest and comprehendest, with thine eyes, first death, and then the wrath of God. . . .

" Christ saith: I am the Light of the World; he that followeth Me shall have the Light of eternal Life. . . . With the inward eyes we must see in His Light: so shall we see Him, for He is the Light; and when we see Him then we walk in the Light. He is the Morning Star and is generated in us and riseth in us, and shineth in our bodily darkness. . . . In a similitude we liken the Sun to the creature of Christ, which is indeed a body; and we liken the whole deep of this world to the eternal Word in the Father." . . .

On the other hand, there are those great ones who seek the light in the outer world; and one is endlessly astonished at the range of their genius, which is so often not limited to a single talent, but kindles itself through its own brightness in many different ones. Each stood alone in his individuality, and found little or no protection against the tyranny of the orthodox faith which had become hardened in dogma and lustful for power; and the shadow of the Inquisition would brook nothing that was likely to shake the Church's established conception of the world. . . . The geniuses towered over all; many went to their death or into lonely poverty as payment for their devotion to the truths they had revealed.

Giordano Bruno (1548–1600), a philosopher who took astronomy and other sciences " in his stride " like so many others of his time, was perhaps one of the last to uphold the belief that the movements of heavenly bodies were not ruled by laws, but by souls. Every star has its own soul, he says, which may be compared to the souls of animals that do not " deliberate " as man does, but know, through the higher Divine Intelligence which rules in each of them, what they have to accomplish.

According to the same principle the souls of the worlds think and act. Bruno says: " These divine Animals, the stars, move freely in their orbits by the force of that soul which is much more certainly present in these higher, perfect, divine bodies than in us, who are of more ignoble condition, and who draw from them spirit and body, come forth living out of their bosom, are nourished by them, and at length are dissolved back into them." . . .

" You may say if you will that the worlds change and decay in old age, or that the Earth seems to grow grey with years, and that all the great Animals of the universe perish like the small, for they change, decay, dissolve. Matter, weary of old forms, eagerly snatches after new, for it desires to become all things and to resemble, as far as possible, all being."

For Bruno, and for others too, it was not possible to reach a definite conception of the Divine Cause of existence, but only to learn of Him through the revealed Universe and through all the observable world of Nature; not as direct knowledge, but as God immanent, reflecting Himself in all; too transcendent to be reached otherwise than by the vision of His " image ", visible everywhere, that " shows forth and preaches the majesty of his first Principle and Cause ".

Bruno is an ardent admirer and supporter of Copernicus and his system, though he finds him too much of a student of mathematics and not enough of a student of Nature to reach the highest results, whereby he might " liberate both himself and others from so many vain inquiries, and fix their contemplation on things abiding and sure ".

Looking as it were both ways—to the spiritual and to the material conceptions of the world—he balances the past and the future; and has in him, one feels, the already germinating seed of what must come at long last, when our modern science too will one day see itself as " not enough of a student of Nature ".

For to be a student of Nature in Bruno's sense is to study the metamorphoses of the *living*, and not the anatomy and chemistry of the " dead ".

It is impossible, in reading the life of Giordano

Bruno, or passages from his many literary works, not to feel that here is a soul who is light in Light.

But after seven or eight years' imprisonment, he was burned at the stake, a spectacle for a Roman holiday. Just one of many such; an arch-heretic; hardly to be noticed except to be despised.

And in the lines which follow he is addressing his own spirit:

E' ja age sublimes tentat natura recessus!
Nam tangente Deo fervidus ignis eris!

Resting, rooted, entwined, in the Earth thou growest, O mountain,
Turned to the Stars on high, towering thy brows are uplifted.
Spirit from Cosmic Heights ordains thy impassable limits,
Severs thee, interrelated, from kingdoms of Zeus and of Hades,
Guards thee from losing thy right, engulfed in the sloth of the Nether,
Sinking laden with dust down into Acheron's flood!
Nay!—but Heavenward wend thee! There thou findest thy dwelling!
Touch thee but God, thou wilt break into flame-crested Fire.*

The men of genius who really transformed the world at that time were those who created the instruments of scientific research. In remoter ages, the human being himself sufficed as the instrument for gaining knowledge, training himself in the Mysteries to receive inspiration and revelation. For these men of the sixteenth, seventeenth, and eighteenth centuries certainly it is still inspiration; but now it approaches them through the observation of physical facts, enabling them to *invent*—to " come upon " as the dictionary has it.

* Translation from a German rendering by E. C. M.

Then the intellect seizes hold; the telescope is created; the microscope; the eye and later others of the senses become gigantic in their powers through these things that are " come upon ". A whole principle of science flashes out like lightning when Galileo watches the swinging lamp in Pisa Cathedral. . . .

And it is Galileo who first discovers the spots on the Sun—dread symptoms, so we are told to-day, of its ineffable and inescapable dying.

Astronomy is one of the wonders of these centuries. It seems as though the stars press towards the Earth asking to be known, looking down at this pure and spiritual enthusiasm which is lit in the souls of men; but which is destined at last to lead their successors to banish these same stars into infinities of millions of light-years, and to forget the Spirit of the Universe.

For the Copernican system took hold of the world. Other great men developed it further, and it rules our present epoch. It was Newton (seventeenth century) who, in discovering the law of gravitation and applying this purely terrestrial fact of knowledge universally, created a caricature of truth which time will certainly erase.

" Physical astronomy " (as distinct from the practical and the theoretical)—says a modern Encyclopaedia —" applies the sciences of terrestrial nature, by proper instruments, to the heavenly bodies, and has come to be really the great welding science of the Universe."

It is even possible to write such a sentence and yet not be aware of what it discloses! People are fond enough of saying that what is one man's meat is another man's poison; but it occurs to no one that what is meat for the Earth may indeed be a poison for the Heavens. For their laws *cannot be identical*.

During the sixteenth and seventeenth centuries the art of portrait painting rises to astonishing heights. This again shows how the power of personality is asserting itself. Landscape painting still retains a delicate spirituality, expressing itself in the love of detail, in a half-dreaming astonishment at the beauty of the world. It is painted for itself—even if it serves as a background for more important figures; there is nothing of sympathy or antipathy flowing through the painter's impressions of Nature. She is accepted as the greatest of all artists herself.

If one has the opportunity to visit some representative collection of portraits, such as the National Portrait Gallery in London, certain stages of the development of Egohood are clearly to be discerned; for the earliest portraits are those of a still half-spiritual people, but in the fifteenth, sixteenth and seventeenth centuries extraordinary powerful personalities appear. It is a new world; the faces reveal in a subtle way the importance of what it is to be human. Men have become masters of their humanity.

Later, this seems to fade away, to give place to a kind of smugness—perhaps a self-satisfied consent to all the limitations which have arisen within the once illimitable possibilities of spirit. And lastly there is the cool completeness of modern faces that are intellectual and detached. But one feels them as though without fire. Without—perhaps—the future. Because everything has become important for the present. Human experience and opportunities are felt to be enclosed between physical birth and the enigmatic ending of life. . . . Nothing is left but a phantom imagination of

man—the " image "—conceived not as Dante conceived it, but as entirely earthly.

It was the fifteenth century that had marked the
beginning of the period when the Ego was felt as the
bearer of the bright light of reason, thrown outwards
upon the physical creation. And at first—though
gradually diminishing during the next centuries—
there remained united with this, and balancing it, a
dim awareness of those " clouds of glory " which the
descending Egohood still trailed after it. So that all
the now illumined world of matter had not yet quite
ceased, as it were, to melt into the horizons of the
spiritual and divine.

Such a combination is the very stuff of which Genius
is made. It lives where no fixed barrier is set up between
the two worlds. This is the cause of its suffering; for
neither world is then wholly real.

In those centuries the problem of " know thyself "
was not solved; because the time was not, and is not
yet, wholly ripe. But as it could not be solved it grew.
The more intense the development of material knowledge, the more the understanding of the spiritual
weakened.

Certainly the philosophers of those days would not
have described the progress of reason and intellect in
these terms. But the fact that such a development of
consciousness existed is testified to in a thousand ways.
Everyone knows for instance the famous saying of
Descartes the Frenchman: " I think; therefore I
am." Trends of experience are to arise which crystallise later into two (and more) different ways of feeling
the " I am ". In middle Europe especially was felt the
need to *struggle* for knowledge; because in this battle
the Ego could realise itself.

But it is characteristic of the English that they do not want to find themselves through inner struggle, but through outer experiences and contacts.

Shakespeare, for example, makes all his characters alive through the realism of their destinies. . . . For him the Ego is really the *person*, and the person acts and thinks: " I am; therefore I think and do." It is the opposite of Descartes.

One pictures Hamlet, for instance, in whom this quality wakes: he sees the grave-digger casting up old skulls with his spade as he digs. Hamlet takes them in his hands, thinks first of the living flesh that once covered them, then of the words, deeds, character, profession, of which these dry bones were once the scaffolding. . . . What the Ego has done is linked with all the *other* things—tongue, lips, cheeks, laughter, and songs—that were built upon the bones. . . . " That skull had a tongue in it, and could sing once; how the knave jowls it to the ground, as if it were Cain's jaw-bone, that did the first murder! This might be the pate of a politician . . . or of a courtier, which could say ' Good morrow, sweet lord! How dost thou, good lord ? . . .'

" There's another; why may not that one be the skull of a lawyer? Where be his quiddities now, his quillets, his cases, his tenures, and his tricks? Why does he suffer this rude knave to knock him about the sconce with a dirty shovel, and will not tell him of his action of battery? "

And with Yorick's skull:

" Alas, poor Yorick! I knew him, Horatio; a fellow of infinite jest, of most excellent fancy. . . . Here hung those lips that I have kissed I know not how oft. Where be your gibes now? Your gambols?

Your songs? Your flashes of merriment that were
wont to set the table on a roar? Not one now, to
mock your own grinning? Quite chapfallen? Now
get you to my lady's chamber and tell her, let
her paint an inch thick, to this favour must she
come." . . .

In the end the bones remain: last witness of a man.
Not the impalpable part of the dead hovering over
these bones is important: but Hamlet's own thinking;
which, when he sees them, is swift to seize upon them
as the very ground of personality. *This*—these bones—
are the witness of the Ego the physical body! It comes
first and goes last. Even Alexander's when it is dust,
and turns into loam, may still stop a crevice in a
wall. . . .

Shakespeare presents us here with the picture (and
elsewhere other such pictures) of a definite type of
Ego-realisation. It is not the *meaning* of man that is
sought for. Instead the Ego accepts facts about him.
And so with all the drama of destiny, as Shakespeare
saw it, which is nothing else than human.

Speaking generally, this is all still chaotic in the
fifteenth and sixteenth centuries. But the ferment calls
forth the Reformation; and has produced the whole
movement which we call Humanism.

Descartes, all the philosophical thinkers, greet the
Ego as it were through the soul of the moment. They
stand before the thought-trend of the day, rising out of
yesterday, as it mirrors itself in them, and struggle
against it.

Giordano Bruno is different; he is one of the
beacons whose light comes from the past but goes on as
light, inspiring many generations, because it was
kindled in him from the Universal. And the painters—

they, too, are timeless. These receive the Ego into the heart.

The great scientists and discoverers must seek it through the Earth, and the senses. It is found by them as something present, new, and youthful—but rushing into the future.

Shakespeare discovers it in the totality of man: in his past, his present, and his future, but entirely human. It is the creator of destiny.

Such a period as this must be outstanding. Heaven and Earth are really confronting one another in the soul of man. But the pendulum is swinging earthwards. Time will produce the " dark Satanic mills " . . . and gold will take the place of the Sun.

Sonnet.

Full many a glorious morning have I seen
Flatter the mountain-tops with sovereign eye,
Kissing with golden face the meadows green,
Gilding pale streams with heavenly alchemy;
Anon permit the basest clouds to ride
With ugly rack on his celestial face,
And from the forlorn world his visage hide,
Stealing unseen to west with this disgrace:
Even so my sun one early morn did shine,
With all-triumphant splendour on my brow;
But, out! alack! he was but one hour mine,
The region cloud hath mask'd him from me now.
      Yet him for this my love no whit disdaineth;
      Suns of the world may stain when heaven's sun
                 staineth.
                        SHAKESPEARE.

Easter.

From *Resurrection.*

Sleep, sleep, old Sun, thou canst not have repast
As yet, the wound thou took'st on Friday last;
Sleep then, and rest; the world may beare thy stay,
A better Sun rose before thee to-day,

Who, not content to enlighten all that dwell
On the earth's face, as thou, enlightened hell,
And made the dark fires languish in that vale,
As, at thy presence here, our fires grow pale.
Whose body having walk'd on earth, and now
Hasting to Heaven, would, that he might allow
Himself unto all stations, and fill all,
For these three days become a minerall;
Hee was all gold when he lay downe, but rose
All tincture, and doth not alone dispose
Leaden and iron will to good, but is
Of power to make even sinfull flesh like his. . . .

JOHN DONNE, sixteenth to seventeenth century.

From *The Nativity.*

. . . A stable was Thy court, and when
Men turn'd to beasts, beasts would be men:
They were Thy courtiers; others none;
And their poor manger was Thy throne.
No swaddling silks Thy limbs did fold,
Though Thou couldst turn Thy rays to gold.
No rockers waited on Thy birth,
No cradles stirr'd, nor songs of mirth;
But her chaste lap, and sacred breast,
Which lodg'd Thee first, did give Thee rest.

But stay: what light is that doth stream
And drop here in a gilded beam?
It is Thy star runs page, and brings
Thy tributary Eastern kings.
Lord! grant some light to us, that we
May with them find the way to Thee!
Behold what mists eclipse the day!
How dark it is! Shed down one ray,
To guide us out of this dark night,
And say once more, " Let there be Light! "

HENRY VAUGHAN, 1656.

CHAPTER XVIII

THE LAST PAGEANT

THE continuous flow of scientific knowledge that began so rapidly to transform man's conception of the world, did not lack its contrasts in idealistic philosophy, romanticism, and even in a kind of rationalistic mysticism. As at every turning-point, some things lingered from the past, and others were premature children of the future.

With the light of thought directed towards the outer world it might seem that everything had at last reached its appointed goal. But this impression would be only partly correct. It would be quite correct, however, if we could see that this development has to undergo a much further transformation. For man, in realising his individual independence and his apparent dominion over Nature, gradually forgets that his real task is to redeem her by discovering that matter is spiritual.

He begins, as he must, by finding in himself the source of a certain power, but no longer recognises himself as the instrument for diviner powers who have bestowed his self-conscious Ego upon him. So the heaven-sent sunlight of his genius begins to suffer an eclipse. He drags it down into the darkness.

With the coming of the nineteenth century—about the middle of it—there are thinkers who are able to put into words what is living in the subconscious part of countless human souls. This is fear. The shadow of fear; that is like a presentiment; fear of that Threshold which marks the boundary between the physical and the spiritual worlds, and which modern science has built up as a vast barrier against which even the most advanced intellects throw themselves in vain.

Physically unheard, but nevertheless present and resounding in the depths, words echo from this Threshold:

" Wherever you may look, O man—into every realm of Nature—into all artistic inspiration—into all history as you yourself have conceived it out of your brilliant theories—nowhere can you find Yourself. For you are Spirit. Through and through both you and Nature are permeated by cosmic spirituality—a spirituality of many exalted Beings. It is They who seek to think in your spirit, and to touch the Earth as its Healers, through you. Never, so long as you believe that it is the grey matter of your physical brain that creates your thoughts and impels you to deeds, will you cross this Threshold that you yourself have set up. Change your thoughts! Only then shall you be led over the abyss! "

The fear engendered by the deeply subconscious knowledge that an eventual crossing of this Threshold lies unavoidably before mankind, was expressed in a most curious and impressive way in a work by Ludwig Feuerbach, who lived about the middle of the nineteenth century.

The philosophy of Fichte, Hegel, and Schelling represented the highest and purest level of human thinking at that time. It prepared the last step of the way for a type of thinking which, if it were to mature, could come naturally to a true conception of the spiritual world. Not to a vague " mist " of spirituality, but to awareness of the great Hierarchies of Beings Themselves: to the Angels, Archangels, Archai, and all the other greater Hosts recognised by St. Paul—up to Cherubim and Seraphim. . . .

This step was not taken. It still remains to be taken in the twentieth century.

Ludwig Feuerbach set himself to combat this tendency to spiritual awakening with all his might—because he felt the hidden fear.

. . ." The man who is active and concerns himself with the facts of human life, has no time to think about death, and hence no desire for immortality. If he thinks about death at all it is because he sees it as a warning to adjust himself as wisely as possible to the fragment of life which has fallen to his lot; not to squander his precious time on worthless things, but only to devote himself to the accomplishment of his chosen task." . . .

. . . " If man were only destined to find his perfection outside the Earth in Heaven, upon Uranus or Saturn or wherever you like, there would be no such thing as philosophy, and no such thing as science or any kind of knowledge.

" Instead of abstract general truths and entities being the objects which our spirit seeks to grasp—instead of thoughts, knowledges, concepts—which are now the spiritual inhabitants of our heads—these inhabitants would be our heavenly brethren from Saturn and Uranus. Instead of mathematics, logic, or metaphysics, we should possess exact replicas of members of these heavenly populations. They would thrust themselves between us and the objects of our

research, shutting us off from them, and creating in us
an everlasting solar eclipse. . . .

" They would be closer to us than our thoughts and
our ideas and conceptions, for they are not purely
spiritual and abstract entities like the former, but are
concrete spiritual Beings of sense, expressing only
imaginative force. Our whole spirit would then be
nothing but a dream, a vision of some more perfect
future. Thus he who by the weight of his reasoning is
prevented from floating on the surface of this illimitable ocean of imagination, will surely know that in the
depths of his being, as in an asphyxiating air, the light
of the Angels, and of all the Hierarchies, must
inevitably be extinguished." . . .

So for Feuerbach human intellect and reason is the
" Sun "; and this inner self-conscious and intelligent
light would, it seemed to him, suffer an eternal darkening in the presence of anything " concretely " spiritual.

Nevertheless, if such ideas—such dread of the
immortal perfections—find their way into human
heads at all, it can prove but one thing: that beings
higher than man exist in very truth, and have the
power to obtrude their reality even into the thoughts
of those who utterly oppose them. What Feuerbach
conceived as a darkening of his humanity is Light.
What he felt as illumination—abstract reasoning—
was destined in a hundred years to eclipse the true
light of the whole Earth.

Again expressive of this fearful premonition, but in
another fashion, is an extraordinary poem written
about 1830 by Friedrich Viktor Strauss.

He sees the tortured sleep of humanity in the modern
age: men murmuring and thirsting in anguish at the
approach of a dreadful dawn; aware of the failure of
human reason to save the world; yet given up to it,

caught in its sinister toils, while hearing the hammer-blows of destiny in the shaking of the Earth under the footsteps of a coming Redeemer.

In the eighteenth century it was still possible to have what one might call " threshold experience "; that is, to sense spiritual truths and spiritual beings, but reflected in the human mind as in a cloudy mirror, and generally stimulating the search for reality by " the primitive earthy strength of human reason alone ". The mirrored images of the Spirit beckoned to the past; human reason to the future. Logic, by itself had revealed itself barren for creative purposes; mathematics seemed a surer way. . . .

Of the former, the real mirrored spirituality, perhaps the supreme example is William Blake. For though he desired to build Jerusalem anew, in " England's green and pleasant land ", he could not see clearly the predestined way that man's conscious-ness would first have to take: through the darkness. Without realising it perhaps, he wanted to build upon the foundations of a type of consciousness that belonged to the past, but which could not be revived. He himself possessed an extraordinary clairvoyance. So far as it went, it was true and pure. But in a blind world it is terrible to possess this gift. With it, all that the soul loses when the Spirit is lost can be clearly seen; all that is dark and ugly in human life, and all that is beautiful and patient in the spiritual soul of Nature; all that in thought is false and true, living side by side in conflict and confusion. And no way out into practical reform if others cannot also *see*.

The suffering compels to poetry, or to art. Soul must cry to soul, not body to body. The dull minds whose attention is fixed upon physical utilities and expediences look upon the visionary Blake as a mad-man.

" I assert for myself ", he cries, " that I do not behold the outward Creation, and that to me it is a hindrance and not Action; it is dirt upon my feet, no part of me.

" ' What ', it will be questioned. ' When the Sun rises, do you not see a round disk of fire somewhat like a Guinea ? '

" O no, no, I see an immeasurable company of the Heavenly Host, crying, ' Holy, Holy, Holy is the Lord God Almighty '.

" I question not my Corporeal or Vegetative Eye any more than I would question a Window concerning a Sight. I look through it, and not with it."

This passionate certainty of the presence of a visible spiritual world, intermingled with the physical, entirely dominates Blake's life, his art, and his writings. His symbolic Epics are unique in their visionary imagination:

> . . . " I rest not from my great task!
> To open the Eternal Worlds, to open the immortal Eyes
> Of man inwards into the Worlds of Thought, into Eternity
> Ever expanding in the Bosom of God, the Human
>   Imagination.
> O Saviour! pour upon me Thy Spirit of meekness and love!
> Annihilate the selfhood in me: be Thou all my life! "

> " I see the Fourfold Man, the Humanity in deadly sleep
>   And its fallen Emanation, the Spectre and its cruel
>   Shadow.
> I see the Past, Present, and Future existing all at once
> Before me. O Divine Spirit, sustain me on Thy wings,
> That I may awake Albion from his long and cold repose;
>   For Bacon and Newton, sheath'd in dismal steel, their
>   terrors hang

Like iron scourges over Albion: Reasonings like vast
    Serpents
Infold around my limbs, bruising my minute articulations.

" I turn my eyes to the Schools and Universities of Europe
    And there behold the Loom of Locke, where Woof rages
        dire,
    Washed by the Water-wheels of Newton; black the cloth
    In heavy wreaths folds over every Nation: cruel Works
    Of many Wheels I view, wheel without wheel, with cogs
        tyrannic
    Moving by compulsion each other, not as those in Eden,
        which
    Wheel within Wheel, in freedom revolve in harmony and
        peace."

O impotent voice, drowned by the approaching
thunder-tread of the Giants of materialism!

But Blake's Sun of genius could also shine exquisitely
and tenderly from a clear-washed sky, in his *Songs of
Innocence*, and poems of Nature. . . .

" Did you ever see a fairy's funeral, madam? " he
once asked an acquaintance. " I have. . . . I was
walking alone in my garden, there was great stillness
among the branches and flowers and more than
common sweetness in the air; I heard a low and
pleasant sound, and I knew not whence it came. At
last I saw the broad leaf of a flower move, and under-
neath I saw a procession of creatures of the size and
colour of green and grey grasshoppers, bearing a body
laid out on a rose-leaf, which they buried with songs,
and then disappeared. It was a fairy funeral."* . . .

And is not this entirely beautiful? . . .

Thou hearest the Nightingale begin the Song of Spring.
The Lark sitting upon his earthy bed, just as the morn
Appears, listens silent; then springing from the waving
    Cornfield, loud

* From *The Life of William Blake*, by Mona Wilson. (Peter Davies, Ltd.,
London.)

He leads the Choir of Day: trill, trill, trill, trill,
Mounting upon the wings of light into the great Expanse,
Re-echoing against the lovely blue and shining heavenly
    Shell.
His little throat labours with inspiration; every feather
On throat and breast and wings vibrates with the effluence
    Divine.
All Nature listens silent to him, and the awful Sun
Stands still upon the Mountain, looking on this little Bird
With eyes of soft humility and wonder, love and awe.
Then loud from their green covert all the Birds begin their
    Song;
The Thrust, the Linnet and the Goldfinch, Robin and the
    Wren
Awake the Sun from his sweet reverie upon the Mountain.
The Nightingale again assays his Song, and thro' the day
And thro' the night warbles luxuriant, every Bird of Song
Attending his loud harmony with admiration and love.*

It was an age of brilliant literary achievement. But Science was the supreme adventure. It held out hopes of " the greatest happiness for the greatest number " —famous and most fallacious of all phrases!—coined by Priestley, the discoverer of oxygen; while ugliness and poverty and misery and oppression were to be found festering in the rising industrial life . . . No wonder that Blake, with his visions of another world, was an enigma to everyone; an impossibility; demanding the recognition and acceptance of inspiration and vision from a world shaken by revolutions and cries for social reform.

Blake is an entirely solitary figure standing there on the shores of change. All around him is a seething ferment where the broken waves of the Renaissance are sucked back into the onrush of new waves, resist them, are mingled with them, spurt up into flying foam, and are engulfed. And each new oncoming

* From Blake's *Milton*.

wave wins another fragment of the shore. Towering
above the turmoil Blake sees the great poets of the past,
" majestic shadows, grey but luminous ". But he cries
to them as to admonishers against reliance upon
ancient memories, and needed them but as revealers
of a new Inspiration pointing to the future. They
could not really help him; for paradoxically, all that
he achieved was born out of an old heroic and
inherited clairvoyance, sleeping and waking in the
blood. . . .

In his day there was the American rebellion, the
industrial revolution, and the revolution in France.
Everywhere was a struggle for freedom.

If we look towards Germany we see also an intensification of the search and longing for freedom—but
in the realm of thought: the struggle to discover the
real nature and power of the human Ego, from which
the true seed of the inspiration of the future could arise.
One might even regard Blake's passionate appeal to
the higher nature of mankind as a prayer that was not,
after all, left unanswered there.

Through Bacon and his successors the impulse had
been given towards a science dealing only with the
facts of the material world, and leaving out, as it were,
the problem of Man—the human being. At the turn
of the eighteenth and nineteenth centuries, in
Germany, it was the human problem above all that
cried out for solution; for what conception of the
world can have ultimate value if the being who creates
it does not know *himself?*

In 1772, when Blake was fifteen years old, there was
born in Germany Friedrich Hardenberg, who is known
to us best as the poet, Novalis. He, too, is an enigma.

In his delicate body lived a soul too great to show forth
in his short life more than a hint of those high achievements that are possible when a man can really make
fruitful the spirit that is within him. His was a soul
really capable of the transformation of earthly into
heavenly love.

It is at first difficult for us to understand Novalis's
worship of the young girl, Sophie, and the effects of
her death upon him. She was a mystery—the child
whose eyes were like light itself. . . . And a mystery,
too, is the spiritual ardour of this love's transformation.
Sophie, at her death, was the door through which
Novalis entered into his true human maturity—
spiritual certainty.

Naturally, he cannot be compared to Blake; for in
every sense he is Blake's opposite. Blake's love was for
mankind—for the vision of mankind's spiritual destiny.
Novalis's love for mankind was a second birth,
springing from the innermost of himself, from the
Temple wherein Sophie was the heavenly visitant.
Blake's inspiration was an unbroken thread spun from
primeval stars; Novalis's inspiration was the child of
immortal love.

Neither could be accounted as very great men in the
eyes of the world at that time. But they are there;
when the majestic pageant of nineteenth-century
idealist philosophers and natural philosophers comes
forth from the " embowered gates " of the world-soul.

Schiller was living then; and Goethe, and Fichte—
of whom Schelling said that his philosophy was like
lightning and " kindled a fire that will burn for ever ".
And it was through the influence of Fichte that
Novalis realised the profound meaning of Egohood.
He wrote:

" ' I am ' is the result of the Universe. In order
to pronounce ' I am ', I must presuppose the whole
Universe; vice versa, the absolute statement of the
' I am ' is at the same time the statement of the
Universe."

To Novalis, this was no mere cold intellectual
conception, but an awakening Light.   Through
morality, which is absolute creative power, " generative freedom "—even as the Universe is both moral
and creative—through this, the " infinite personality,
the singular divinity within us " can be realised. This
meant for him the destruction of all barriers between
the physical world and the spiritual world.

If man creates a conception of the Universe that in
itself has no place for the mystery of *Man*, then his
knowledge is only one-half of what it should be.

The realisation of this truth awoke in Novalis. He
knew that it was entirely possible, not theoretically but
actually, for mankind some day to accomplish the
resurrection of the Spirit of the Universe, together
with that of the spirit of man, which is part of it. It is
the essence of true knowledge that it should in no wise
remain at the stage of theory, even if it is supported by
a number of facts; it must be actual spiritual experience: " wisdom, reborn in the Ego ". Then it is the
same as Love. Then the *whole* is known.

Novalis was no mere poetical dreamer; for that
would have belied his very nature; he wanted to
gather into himself all possible scientific knowledge,
and permeate it with the ardours of his soul of love.

" All is seed ", he said. He planned great works . . .
knowing that each of them would assuredly be a seed
whose essence could not die.

While Blake would have destroyed the present so

that the future might be born, Novalis guessed that the future is already here—the conscious Ego, child of the Sun—that has the power to warm the seeds of a *spiritualised* science with Life and Love.

In the *Fragments* he says:

" Each step of development begins with childhood. That is why the greatest and most evolved men are so childlike."

It is his constant pointing to the " home " of things that makes Novalis so unforgettable. He " commends himself to the Beginnings ". He knows that the Beginnings are always reborn, but transformed in every real achievement.

His biographer (Friedemann) says: " Even in his most daring abstractions there lies a profound amazement, the secret shame of the intellect that it should offer the ' offence ' of knowledge to things that are wonderful; the homesickness of reason, that yearns for its primal origin. . . . Novalis understood the deepest pain of the human spirit: the bitterness of knowledge, that inimical quality of the reason that throws a baleful light on things, the vague fear of progress; he understood that every fresh triumph of the intellect is won at the cost of an increasing poverty, and creates a fresh estrangement between man and the external world. Because Novalis cannot endure this estrangement, he gives all things admission into himself, and becomes a mystic. At the end of all development he finds the beginning again. If a man has broken down the barriers between his soul and matter, and has made Nature the instrument of his will, he is also at one with her—as unconscious and Ego-less as the childlike Saviour, the Child-God, whom Novalis dreamed of as the final perfection of his being."*

But in all this indrawing of the outer world, there is at the same time the expansion of the human into the superhuman:

" Man is the higher Sense of our planet, the Star which connects it with the upper world, the eye which it turns towards Heaven." . . . Or again: " Man is a Sun: his senses are the planets." . . .

" The perfect man must live as it were in many places and in many other human beings simultaneously.

" He must continually inhabit a wide sphere and be present in manifold events.

" The sublime presence of that Spirit will gradually appear, which makes each human being into a citizen of the whole world; and which, through many beneficient associations, stimulates and strengthens him in every moment of his life, and sheds upon him the brightness born from actions that are illumined by the Sun."

In contrast to the more natural acceptance of the consciousness of Egohood which prevailed in England, its development in Middle Europe was the focus of an intense struggle to understand the *meaning* of life; a problem only to be solved within the Ego itself. Hence, in Germany, the continual stress, the unavoidable conflict, between the " either—or ", which hovers perpetually over the abyss, the very depths of being.

It we try to picture the whole situation from the eighteenth on into the nineteenth century we cannot but be astonished at the terrific ferment of ideas—a

---

* The egolessness of the Saviour was in reality its perfection of *selfless* and and cosmic Egohood.

veritable storm of thinking—that prevailed over central Europe. For western science, the question of whether the criterion of knowledge is the existence or non-existence of the Ego and its relation to the world, is not so important; rather is interest centred round the physical body of man and physical facts of Nature. The separation of the inner life of man from the objective discoveries he has made grows wider and wider in the West.

Small wonder that it becomes more and more difficult in middle Europe to create any clear conception of a self-conscious Ego, which is able to bear the weight and complexity of all this experience of the outer world, and to recognise its true relation to it! There remained a possible idealistic philosophy, or all the varieties of speculation which only served to intensify the feeling: *Ignorabimus*.

The last years of the eighteenth and the first part of the nineteenth centuries saw the blossoming in Germany of the greatest philosophical idealism. And it coincided with the most magnificent achievements in music.

The great geniuses Schelling and Hegel stand out in the first half of the nineteenth century, filling the surrounding space where Goethe not only sets the crown upon poetry, but also conjures out of heaven the inspiration for the true spiritualised science of the future.

Schelling was certain that a real and sound conception of the universe and man could only be arrived at through so much inner enthusiasm as would create in man an entirely new kind of perception—by awakening in him " spiritual senses ". Since the ordinary man does not possess this kind of perception he must

endeavour to create it. . . . " Nature is visible Spirit,
the Spirit is invisible Nature. . . . Thus here, in the
absolute identity of the Spirit in us " (which has
spiritual senses) " and in Nature outside of us, the
problem can be solved as to how it is possible for a
Nature that is external to us, to exist."

According to Schelling human science is like a
memory of the original archetypal creations before
they appeared in the visible world. A divine Spirit
has created the universe; and at last created man also,
so that He could build into the human soul just as
many avenues through which He could remind himself of His own manifold creations. That is, that when
a man says " I know ", it is as if the World-Spirit is
remembering His own creative acts. And if a work of
art is produced it is as though the World-Spirit is
repeating in miniature what was accomplished in the
production of all Nature.

And of the Ego, he says: " The Self is not a possession, it is not a capacity, or anything else of that kind;
the Self does not know, but *is* knowledge; is not good,
but *is* goodness; is not beautiful—though the body
may be so—but she *is* Beauty itself."

This was Schelling's view of the Godhead and of the
world as its revelation; but the view of its opposite,
evil, had also to be there. And here he finds the whole
world-process as the continuous overcoming of the
evil by the good. And in this process, there is Christ:
" Only what is personal can heal what is personal;
and God must become man so that man can return
again to God."

In this so-called philosophy of identity, it is not that
Schelling seeks to content himself with a " merging "
of the creative Spirit of Nature or of the Godhead with
the human spirit; but that he actually realises that the

Macrocosmic Being sees Itself in the microcosmic being, and vice versa. There are still two, not one, although one in essential likeness.*

We make a mistake if we think that this love of thinking and philosophising about things—which has so often been described as " ponderous "—was in Germany intellectual, as we understand the word. It was just because the Ego could *not* find its relation to the intellectual part of the soul that we hear so much about " plunging " into things that are " deep " or " profound " or " heart-felt ". . . . One could imagine that among the French, where the Ego is fully awake in the intellect, with brilliance and imagination, a real longing could be felt to be able to touch these deeper waters of the spirit.†

The French philosopher Victor Cousin went several times to Germany to make first-hand acquaintance with the leading German idealistic thinkers. He was enormously impressed by Hegel and Goethe. And by his vivid and brilliant lecturing in France he carried their influence with him there.

He showed that he had learned that it was through the observation of the human spirit rather than through the observation of Nature that one could arrive at a satisfying world-conception. From Hegel he had learnt that Spirit, Idea, and Thought are not existent in man alone but are also in Nature, and rule in the historical progress of mankind. Reason is not in the human mind only but is everywhere a reality.

---

* See *Rätsel der Philosophie*, Rudolf Steiner.

† The three parts of the soul are here understood as the Intellectual, the Sentient, and the self conscious. The ego should be able to relate itself in a balanced way with these three through the capacities of Thought, Feeling, and Will. For example, in Britain it is the self-conscious soul (will) which predominates; in France, the intellectual soul; in Italy, the sentient (feeling and emotional) soul. If the Ego (as in Germany) feels itself unrelated in a specific way to these, it desires them. This fact should throw some light on present world-conditions.

Hegel taught that the character of a whole people, or of a whole age, is not subject to " blind chance " or to any arbitrary proceeding, but that some predestined thought speaks through a nation's single individuals. That great men are in the world as messengers of some lofty idea, that one or another nation has to contribute to earthly history.*

But there is a great cleavage between the ideas of Victor Cousin and those of the French philosopher Comte, whose influence was destined to flow so strongly into the general stream of modern events. He turned away from the idealistic trend of thought, and maintained that a true picture of man and the world could only be gained by strictly scientific knowledge and scientific " behaviour ". No human thought could be considered ripe that did not reach this standpoint. Physics, chemistry, biology, mathematics—all these sciences from which thought builds up its pictures of the outer world—the whole structure of scientific principles and method—could at the same time build up the state, family life, civil laws and rights; in short, the complete order of society.

This is the philosophy of Positivism.

Then there is a host of thinkers, in various countries, who are unable to accept any world-conception that reaches out into a sphere of transcendental experience. The idea of a purpose in evolution, based on the assumption that everything begins and ends with what is physical alone, tends more and more to the conclusion that such a purpose is only reasonable if it is utilitarian; otherwise, if one *must* adhere to a speculative philosophy, then it is more convenient to say, in the end, " we do not know ".

In religion, it becomes even more comfortable to

* See *Rätsel der Philosophie*, Rudolf Steiner.

assume " we are not meant to know ". Though this has an air of humility, it is perhaps more arrogant than assuming " we *are* meant to know the meaning of life and what man is, but we have not yet found the key to it ". For in the latter case we place ourselves in the position of aspiring and endeavouring, which is at least a confession of insufficiency.

With a few exceptions, it is as though a very real impotence comes over mankind in the first half of the nineteenth century, to discover any satisfying solution of all these things. No matter how magnificent are the achievements in scientific discovery and experiment, and in mathematics, there is still no answer to the riddle of man himself. The ingenuity of thought is, however, entirely amazing. It constructs a huge world-labyrinth of thinking. In such a labyrinth one can be utterly lost—even if the building of it has been done with mathematical precision.

At a certain moment in the middle of the nineteenth century the spirituality of the past seems as though really lost. The riddle of life assumes gigantic and amorphous form, rising out of old mists, that are shot through with gleams of superstition . . . old fantastic tales and myths. . . . There are no longer the spiritual instruments in man with which to comprehend the greatness of all that has vanished. Moreover, Copernicus and Newton and their countless followers had long since made broad the highway leading to the notion of the Earth as a speck of dust in the illimitable universe. Joule establishes the principle of the conservation of energy. The science of thermodynamics begins to make itself ready to pronounce the prophecy of a universal heat-death of the worlds.

Darwinism, when it comes, establishes a reasonable

physical past, in spite of the " missing link ". One can imagine it must have been rather comforting to the unprejudiced.

Nevertheless, through all this a steady light is shining; but there are not so very many who allow its rays to fall upon them in their full strength. We will leave this light aside for the moment, and presently go back again to the end of the eighteenth century where we shall find its source in Goethe. Meanwhile, among the trends of thought that are still unquiet towards the end of the nineteenth century, we will look at three examples:

The philosophy known as Pragmatism suggests that there is no faculty or principle in man which gives him the possibility of deciding whether one thing is true and another false. There are no means of finding any self-existing unit of comparison or judgment. We can, of course, make certain judgments—for instance, that the Sun will rise to-morrow. But there is no guarantee that such a judgment is true in itself. All we can do therefore is to judge of things *usefully*. That which furthers life is true; that which hinders life is untrue.

Such ideas suggest that the dominion which the outer world exerts upon mankind has grown too powerful; while the belief that it is possible to find light through one's own life of thought has sunk to its lowest ebb. Science can do no more than shed a pale gleam on that " dark continent we call the Universe ".
. . . " So we shall act rightly if we can create such thoughts as correspond to our nature; which make it possible for us to work, to hope, and to live."

Man himself is the only creation which can be his own evidence of reality. But his thought is not strong enough to penetrate himself with light. " Thought remains rooted in the upper levels of the soul directly the Ego attempts to plunge into its own depths."*

Then there is the philosophy of the " As if " . . . created by Professor Vaihinger.† He believes that man is unable to create either *true* or *false* ideas, but merely ideas. They are in reality Fictions. (Such as the theory of the atom.) Hence we must view the world " as if " the ideas were true. But these fictions have nevertheless a purpose. " Truth is the most complete kind of error, for in reality there is nothing else but errors. Only, there are errors which are either more, or less, comfortable. We call the more comfortable ones ' Truth '."

For some thinkers there is no other way than to regard the outer world as illusion. Take, for instance, this sentence:

" The rose has no perfume until somebody smells it." . . .

For the man who fully accepts such an idea, the whole outer world must become an illusion. But it throws him back with a certain violence into his own being. He will feel a kind of dread, of *himself*. Who is he—what is he—if a perfume can arise just because he connects his sensation with the rose? For then nothing has any attributes—neither shape, colour, perfume, nor anything else, except through him. He gives it all. . . .

But he who does not accept this thought, but approaches the rose in freedom, feels that the rose becomes " alive "; it speaks; and it says: " I am waiting for you. Feel and experience me, and I will disclose my being to you."

* Willaim James.

† *Rätsel der Philosophie*, Rudolf Steiner.

Here is a hint of the answer to the riddle of our existence.

If we separate ourselves from the outer world in order to investigate it physically—which is the modern all-pervading scientific attitude—then we cannot by this means explain the real being of man. On the other hand, if we investigate *ourselves*—and still with the ordinary physical knowledge (for even psychology is based upon physical science)—we find only such answers as are contained in pragmatism, or positivism, or " As if ". . . .

Either way, only one-half of reality comes before us. . . .

But the roses await us. Let us look at them once more. We perceive them with sight, smell, and touch; and these senses grow warm within us through the pulsing life in them of our own Ego's reactions. And more; they call forth still subtler sensations— memories or hopes, sadness or joy. So we have left the simple realm of our senses, and feel that what they perceive is even *one* with our inmost soul. So here there is no one-sided activity; we have not merely approached the roses, but the roses have come to us.

Then we sink a little deeper into our own self—yes, into a region which for the most part has lain fallow and neglected; for we feel then the dawn of *creative imagination;* the rose is a living being, even as we are. From a world hitherto invisible the living being of the rose discloses itself, once we greet it with our own innermost self.

Then we have stepped from the sensible to the fringes of the super-sensible. Now there are no barriers. Every subtle delineation of form and colour is a truth; because they are the outer expression of inner realities—that can meet the inner reality of our own experience of them.

This is what Novalis knew; what Schelling knew; and Fichte; and many other single individuals have discovered it. But above all, Goethe.

Goethe carried his living thoughts, in freedom from the thraldom of the body, from step to step until he was able to announce the discovery of what he called the " primal phenomena " of Nature. That was the work of an Ego that could be self-knowing, and therefore free, in dynamic equilibrium with body and soul.

But he had first to know the nature of this Ego. He realised such knowledge could never be attained by the reason. For it is a *supersensible* experience.

One must not confuse this with a mystical over-flowing of feeling. It is the real key to a real philosophy. Only, " one must educate oneself to attain it ", said Goethe. " No human art can bestow it upon us." . . .

" I myself, and my necessary goal, are super-sensible."

Goethe was one of the greatest poets that have ever lived.

And some day his scientific writings will be understood also. For they were based upon that very secret for which future generations will begin tirelessly to search—*metamorphosis*. It is a law, not only operating everywhere in Nature, but in man likewise. Even thinking can be transformed:

Thinking sees the rose in the world which is perceptible to the senses, in a certain form and colour, and can analyse it and study it in the physical world and with physical means.

But change the thinking to creative imagination, and the rose will be found to have changed too; it shows itself as part of the world of Life, whose laws determine its essences and potencies. If it has healing properties, the relation of its root, blossoms, and leaves to the organs and processes of the body can be discovered through this higher imagination.

In this sense " imagination " is the fruit of the ability to question all things that are perceived, as to their true nature. It arises through being able to feel an all-absorbing interest in and love for them. Examining them with the critical and intelligent eye of scientific research seldom allows one to reach imagination, unless it is accompanied by a conviction that there is something " behind " the object which cannot be arrived at by thought alone, but which can be perceived in a mental image, or picture. But one must first start with the physical tangible facts.

Goethe could not conceive that there could be any ultimate truth in examining a single phenomenon of Nature if it was cut off, for such examination, from the universal life in which it was embedded.

Schiller said to Goethe: " You gather together the whole of Nature in order to gain light on a single detail; where the forms of the phenomena merge into the universal, there you seek the explanation and the reason for the individual." . . .

To place something one observes into the *whole*— as one might, for instance, think of a plant as it lives and grows in its surroundings—in cold and warmth and rain and sunshine and moonlight; follow, as though with spiritual fingers, its every living detail of form and texture in relation to these surroundings; this is to discover that the plant is the image of something greater. For it embodies all Nature's laws. This is then the gateway to imaginative insight.

The next step is Inspiration. Inspiration is nearer

to hearing than to seeing. It is far removed from mere thought, and lifts itself out of imagination as waking lifts itself out of dreams. It is the swift irrefutable *knowing*, that sets one's feet upon the way, through all the changing phenomena of the world's " becoming ", to that which is final and immutable: the archetype. To reach actual knowledge of this " primal pheno- menon " needs the silencing of every personal prejudice and the renunciation of all intellectual struggle. It is Intuition, and Intuition is Love.

Goethe, poet and artist, learned to discipline his heart and brain so that he found these steps to higher knowledge. He could be a scientist too, because the discipline enabled him to retrace his steps again from the primal phenomena to the visible world, recognis- ing, on the way, all the separate subsidiary phenomena and their significance for a total comprehension of the object of his research. He did not remain, so to say, on the mountain-top with the primal phenomenon, but in experimentation demonstrated its existence.

This is the lesson which science could have learnt from him. It pointed out the path by which the knowledge of the material world could be illumined by purely spiritual experience. But the fascination of Newtonian and Darwinian thought became too strong in the world. Darwinism poured over Germany like an exhilarating flood.

Nevertheless, the law of metamorphosis in thinking reveals the operation of this law in all natural science.

In its ultimate manifestation in man, metamorphosis is reincarnation. In the Universe, the rebirth of Worlds.

Goethe reveals the law of metamorphosis also in the drama of *Faust*. He gives there the picture of the man who, by his own effort, ascends from stage, between the ever-present "opposites" that dominate the world. What awaits him at the end? The "Mothers of Existence"—the Eternal Feminine. Pure Love.

But the darkness of the end of the nineteenth century, and of the twentieth, had to come.

Goethe stood at its threshold—the "Man with the Lamp".

Raphael

The Sun-orb sings, in emulation,
'Mid brother-spheres, his ancient round:
His path predestined through Creation
He ends with step of thunder-sound,
The angels from his visage splendid
Draw power; whose measure none can say;
Thy lofty works, uncomprehended,
Are bright as on the earliest day.

Gabriel

And swift, and swift beyond conceiving,
The splendour of the world goes round,
Day's Eden-brightness still relieving
The awful Night's intense profound:
The ocean-tides in foam are breaking,
Against the rocks' deep bases hurled,
And both the spheric race partaking,
Eternal, swift, are onward whirled!

Michael

And rival storms abroad are surging
From sea to land, from land to sea,
A chain of deepest action forging
Round all, in wrathful energy.
There flames a desolation, blazing
Before the Thunder's crashing way;
Yet, Lord, Thy messengers are praising
The gentle movement of Thy Day.

The Three

Though still by them uncomprehended,
From these the angels draw their power,
And all Thy works, sublime and splendid,
Are bright as in Creation's hour.

(From Goethe's Faust. Prologue in Heaven.)

From Goethe's Fairy-tale,

The Green Snake and the Beautiful Lily.

. . . When the Snake found that she had reached the place she looked about her with curiosity;   and although her brightness did not fully illumine the circular chamber she could see the nearer objects very clearly. Looking up, she saw, with awe and astonishment, a gleaming niche where stood the statue of a noble King, made entirely of gold. Its size was larger than life, but the figure represented a small, rather than a large, man. His well-proportioned form was clothed in a simple mantle, and a wreath of oak-leaves bound his hair.

Scarcely had the Snake perceived this splendid figure, than the King began to speak, and asked:

" Whence comest thou? "

" Out of the clefts of the rocks ", replied the Snake, "where the Gold lives ".

" What is more beautiful than Gold? " asked the King.

" Light ", answered the Snake.

" What is more living than Light? " asked the other.

" Speech ", said the Snake.

During this conversation the Snake had looked stealthily round about, and observed another statue in an adjoining niche. A silver King was enthroned there—a tall and slender figure;   his limbs were enveloped in an embroidered mantle, his crown and sceptre were adorned with precious stones; his countenance was serene and dignified, and he seemed about to speak, when a dark-coloured vein which ran through the marble of the wall suddenly became brilliant, and caused a soft light to glow throughout the Temple. By this illumination the Snake could see the third King—a mighty seated figure of brass, leaning upon his club, wearing a crown of laurel, and looking more like a rock than the figure of a man. The Snake wanted to glance round at the fourth King who was furthest away from her, but the wall opened of itself, as the illuminated vein in it suddenly flashed like lightning, and was as suddenly extinguished.

A man of medium height now drew near, and attracted the attention of the Snake. He was dressed like a peasant and carried a little lamp in his hand, into whose motionless flame it was delightful to look. In a wonderful way, and without throwing any shadows, it lit up the whole of the vault.

" Since we already have light, why dost thou come hither ? " asked the golden King.

" Thou knowest that I may not illumine that which is dark ", replied the old man.

" Will my kingdom end ? " asked the silver King.

" Late, or never ", answered the other.

The brazen King then asked in a voice of thunder, " When shall I arise ? "

" Soon ", was the reply.

" With whom shall I be united ? "

" With thine elder brother."

" And what will become of the youngest ? "

" He will rest."

" I am not tired ", exclaimed the fourth King, in a deep but trembling voice.

During this conversation the Snake had wound her way softly through the Temple, looking at everything which it contained, and approached the niche where the fourth King stood. He leaned against a pillar, and his face was sad.   It was difficult to distinguish the metal of which the statue was made. It resembled a mixture of the three metals of which his brothers were formed;   but it seemed as if they were not properly blended, for the veins of gold and silver crossed each other irregularly throughout the brazen mass and destroyed the effect of the whole.

Then the golden King asked, " How many secrets dost thou know? "

" Three ", was the answer.

" And which is the most important? " inquired the silver King.

" The open one ", replied the old man.

" Wilt thou reveal it to us? " asked the brazen King.

" When I have learned the fourth ", was the reply.

" What does it matter to me? " muttered the composite King.

" I know the fourth! " cried the Snake. Drawing near to the old man she whispered in his ear.

" The time has come! " cried he in a tremendous voice. The Temple re-echoed to it;   the metallic statues rang;   and in the same moment the old man plunged towards the West and the Snake towards the East, and both passed with great rapidity through the clefts in the rock.

Every passage through which the old man went filled itself up behind him with gold; for his lamp had the wonderful property that it could turn all stones into gold, all wood into silver, dead animals into precious stones, and it could destroy all metals.

But, in order to do this, it had to shine alone.

If any other light was near, it could only glow with a beautiful clear radiance, which gave joy to every living thing." . . .

What is the " fourth secret " whispered by the Snake?

It is the admission of the human spirit—the Snake herself—that all the sparkling brilliance of modern intellectual knowledge at last recognises the necessity of sacrificing itself.

So the Green Snake makes herself ready to throw her gleaming body across the abyss that separates man's knowledge of the physical world from his knowledge of the spiritual world and its divinely beautiful " Lily "—the higher wisdom of insight wedded to Love.

When this admission is made, the " time has come ". . . .

The three first Kings are the unalloyed powers of the human soul—Thinking, Feeling, and Willing. The " mixed King " is their amalgamation in the lower Ego. His destiny is to fall asunder, releasing the pure and unmixed powers. But in his disintegration he rises to the heavens, and unites with the Divine. Transformed and transfigured he will rule invisibly over his brothers in freedom. The bright winding coils of the intellect will lay themselves under the feet of countless thousands, in humility, and they will pass over her body to the Temple, which will have risen from the depths.

But after Goethe—Darwin.

It is as though we hear the clang of iron doors that shut against the Man with the Lamp.

Physical science, mechanised science, reddened with Sunset splendours, comes at the end of the Pageant.

It is a long and close procession; so long, that night falls before the end of it draws near.

As it moves onward, we hear some voices. . . .

Their words remain in the memory. . . .

Darwin wrote in his Autobiography:

" With respect to immortality, nothing shows me so clearly how strong and almost instinctive a belief it is, as the consideration of the view now held by most physicists, namely, that the sun and all the planets will in time grow too cold for life, unless indeed some great body dashes into the sun and thus gives it fresh life. Believing as I do that man in the distant future will be a far more perfect creature than he now is, it is an intolerable thought that he and all other sentient beings are doomed to complete annihilation after such long-continued progress. To those who fully admit the immortality of the soul, the destruction of the world will not appear so dreadful.

" Another source of conviction in the existence of God, connected with the reason and not with the feelings, impresses me as having much more weight. This follows from the extreme difficulty or rather impossibility of conceiving this immense and wonderful universe, including man with his capacity of looking backwards and far into futurity, as the result of blind chance or necessity. When thus reflecting, I feel compelled to look to a first Cause having an intelligent mind, in some degree analogous to that of man; and I deserve to be called a Theist. This conclusion was strong in my mind about the time, as far as I remember, when I wrote the *Origin of Species*, and it is since that time that it has very gradually, with many fluctuations, become weaker.

" But then arises the doubt—can the mind of man, which has, as I fully believe, been developed from a mind as low as that possessed by the lowest animals, be trusted when it draws such grand conclusions? "

Not long before, Wordsworth had written his Ode on *Intimations of Immortality*:

" There was a time when meadow, grove and stream,
  The earth and every common sight,
    To me did seem
  Appareled in celestial light,
The glory and the freshness of a dream.
It is not now as it hath been of yore;
    Turn wheresoe'er I may,
    By night or day,
The things which I have seen I now can see no more.

Whither is fled the visionary gleam?
Where is it now, the glory and the dream?

        . . . Those shadowy recollections,
    Which, be they what they may,
Are yet the fountain-light of all our day,
Are yet a master-light of all our seeing;
    Uphold us, cherish, and have power to make
Our noisy years seem moments in the being
Of the eternal Silence. . . ."

Wordsworth feels the oncoming shadow of the great era of Doubt; he interprets it through the image of childhood and adolescence and maturity; but knows that the link with childhood—and this could apply equally to the human race—is the guarantee of immortality.

Unlike Darwin, who so mistrusts the attainments of minds that he believes have sprung from the lowliest possible origins—it is just this link with the past that Wordsworth feels is so important and so glorious. If this is lost, all is lost. And this thread, spun from the inner light of many souls, runs through the whole fabric of the nineteenth century—gleaming like gold among the deepening shadows of materialism.

They are splendid shadows, nevertheless. They are like dark buttresses built by the indomitable courage of science, to support the stupendous edifice it is destined to erect.

The investigation of absolute matter, absolute weight, number, and measure, is a task for gods who have Magic as their servant. Technical science *is* magic. . . . Nature remains quiescent; and allows everything. . . But she is an abyss; which at any moment may engulf the intrepid discoverer. Or she may darken his soul with veil upon veil of doubt, and cause him to deny her inmost Spirit, and his own.

What could be grander than this description of the physical Sun?—whose distance from us, we are told, is 92,900,000 miles, and diameter 866,000 miles; and from whose body enormous flaming masses can be seen under certain conditions, some of them 80,000 miles high streaming out into space:

" Majestic indeed are the proportions of those mighty prominences which leap from the luminous surface; yet they flicker, as do our terrestrial flames, when we allow them time comparable to their gigantic dimensions. . . . The magnitude of the displacements that have been noticed sometimes attains many thousands of miles, and the actual velocity with which such masses move frequently exceeds 100 miles a second. Still more violent are the convulsions when, from the surface of the chromosphere, as from a mighty furnace, vast incandescent masses of gas are projected upwards. . . .

". . . In all directions the Sun pours forth, with the most prodigal liberality, its torrents of light and heat. The Earth can only grasp the merest fraction, less than the 2,000,000,000th part of the whole. Our fellow planets and the Moon also intercept a trifle; but how small is the portion of the mighty flood which they can utilise! The sip that a flying swallow takes from a river is as far from exhausting the water in the river as are the planets from using all the heat which streams from the Sun. . . ."*

And what could be more full of courage than this overwhelming question?

" The Sun, having no extraneous supply of heat, must necessarily emit ever less and less of its life-giving radiation, and as it does so, the temperate zone of space, within which alone life can exist, must close in around it.

" To remain a possible abode of life, our Earth would need to move in ever nearer and nearer to the dying Sun. Yet, science tells us that, so far from its moving inwards, inexorable dynamical laws are even now driving it further away from the Sun into the outer cold and darkness. And so far as we can see, they must continue to do so until life is frozen off the Earth, unless indeed some celestial collision or cataclysm intervenes to destroy life even earlier by a more speedy death. This prospective fate is not peculiar to our Earth; other Suns must die like our own, and any life there may be on other planets must meet the same inglorious end. . . .

" Is this, then, all that life amounts to? To stumble,

* *Story of the Heavens.* Sir Robert Ball.

almost by mistake, into a universe which was clearly not designed for life and which, to all appearances, is either totally indifferent or definitely hostile to it, to stay clinging on to a fragment of a grain of sand until we are frozen off, to strut our tiny hour on our tiny stage with the knowledge that our aspirations are all doomed to final frustration, and that our achievements must perish with our race, leaving the universe as though we had never been? "*

" Whatever you may say ", said the Green Snake, " the Temple is built ".

" But it does not yet stand upon the river ", said the Beautiful Lily.

" It still rests in the bowels of the Earth ", continued the Snake. " I have seen the Kings, and spoken to them."

" And when will they awake? " inquired the Lily.

The Snake answered, " I heard the mighty voice resound through the Temple, announcing that the hour had come."

METAMORPHOSIS

In the Acts of the Apostles the Ascension of Christ is described. " Clouds received Him out of their sight." And then " men in white apparel " told the disciples how He would come again " in the Clouds ".

In the Gospels (Mark xiii, Matthew xxiv, and Luke xvii) His future coming is also described, but as a tremendous and overwhelming event, affecting every human being and every nation and the whole Cosmos. There are signs in the Heavens, a darkening of Sun and Moon, wars and rumours of wars, nation rising against nation, false Christs and false prophets, universal destruction, flight, fear, famine, and

* Sir James Jeans, *The Mysterious Universe*.　(Cambridge University Press.)

weeping. . . . And the Son of Man's coming like the lightning shining " from the east even unto the west ". " Behold, He cometh with clouds."

It is supposed that these events are an allusion to the wars and devastation so soon to follow the birth of Christianity. " This generation shall not pass till all these things be fulfilled."

But they point to our own time. Mankind is of a generation of the Spirit, and not limited to a particular century.

Deeply veiled are the mysteries of the language of the Gospels! . . . Where death is, where the corpse of the old world now reveals itself, killed by man's faithlessness, come the eagles—the far-seeing ones, the royal birds of Heaven; just as the evil vultures gather round a dying man.

It is Christ who comes when something dies, and brings a new birth; and with Him come those who knew Him before, those of the eagle eyes who can soar into the Clouds and see Him; and all others who understand that these cherubinic Clouds are another world, perceptible by a higher consciousness alone. He comes into man's spiritual vision, and not in a human physical form.

The second coming is to be understood only in this way. It is the sublime signature placed at the foot of the first page of the history of the Ascent of Man.

Paul, in his vision on the road to Damascus, thirty-three years after the birth of Christ, was the great forerunner of those who, after the twentieth century has passed its thirty-third year, will begin to have the vision of Christ " in the Clouds "; not a physically seen appearance in the sky only, but a clear perception of His presence—as clear as any physical reality is to the senses, but not consisting of material substance.

Locked in the hearts of countless people to-day are experiences that they feel as something strange and unaccountable, which at some particular moment have shattered their old complacency and filled them with a sense of the profound mystery of human existence. Many are apt to call such experiences " fancy ". Often they are dismissed from the conscious mind as evidence of ill-health. But they continue to work, nevertheless, in the subconsciousness; and sooner or later—perhaps after decades—some other event calls them to life and endows them with reality.

Such experiences are greatly on *the increase to-day* and their character is infinitely varied. Sometimes it may be no more than the sudden vision of a future scene or event, the outcome of a present undertaking; or of some long-forgotten past happening which is now reaping an unforeseen harvest.

Certainly in past centuries innumerable saints and mystics have seen Christ and other spiritual beings in visions. But the seeing that is destined to begin in the twentieth century will be far more real than vision. It will be *experience*. It will not be possible to doubt its reality. Not only in moments of physical or spiritual anguish, or at the point of death, or in selfless deeds of heroism do a few begin already to see Him; but also in the stress of great decisions, and in the hours when problems seem utterly insoluble and hope destroyed. Sometimes He may inspire human speech —but only if a man's spirit speaks in freedom from personal wish or longing, sincerely seeking the way to universal equity of judgment.

Again and again in the stress of battle and danger to-day men tell in halting words of angelic presences that protect or warn them. If all the thousands of such experiences which have arisen in these latter years all over the globe could be gathered together and told to the world, there would be no occasion for psychological explanations or intellectual criticisms of them. What is hinted in the pages of this book would be abundantly confirmed.

That the Clouds will open is not a Christian tradition only, is shown by the fact that it is known, even to the date of its commencement, by some of the greatest teachers in other religions and races also. It is one of the profound mysteries of human existence.

The secret of this impending change has been guarded for long ages. But when the time drew near it was finally quite openly taught and fully explained in Europe by one man—the Austrian philosopher and seer Rudolf Steiner. The time had come when these deeper aspects of Christianity had to be told.

In order to make such things comprehensible for the modern attitude of thought, such a teacher had to be fully acquainted with every branch of modern knowledge. His extraordinary and completely conscious seership enabled him to reveal the spiritual background and content of all material history, science, and of all the arts. Not as something mystical and insubstantial, but in every detail capable of practical application. It was said of him that he had created the framework of a new era of civilisation. The foundation necessary for the coming expansion of human consciousness was laid in his important work *The Philosophy of Spiritual Activity*, formerly called *The Philosophy of Freedom*, which dealt with this great problem from the standpoint of pure thought.

Spiritual progress always meets with opposition. The greater the possibilities of enlightenment, the greater the onslaughts of demonic darkness. That the world is plunged into chaos comes from the immanence of a divinely-appointed crisis in human development. The most impressive words ever recorded in connection with this world-change stand out in letters of flame:

> " Behold, I have told you before. . . . I have foretold you all things. . . . Watch ye therefore. . . ."

The divine Powers guiding the advent of the new age seek to establish among men a recognition of the value of individuality as the guarantee of man's spiritual nature and its legitimate freedoms.

Every human being is in reality destined to growth, expansion, and enlightenment. But this cannot be so long as man denies spirituality to the Universe. If the Universe continues to live on in men's thoughts as something based on physical laws alone, darkness must dwell in the soul and the Light of the world will not shine there. Materialistic science, if developed to its uttermost, means permanent unfreedom. Then the past will devour the future and engulf it in the shadow of evil.

Nevertheless, during the last few centuries the progress of mankind really depended upon his coming to grips with the material world in every respect. But the moment has been reached when what may be called sub-Nature, and the subhuman, dazzles the eyes and entices man to form judgments which, if applied to human life as a whole, are the very reverse of what he imagines.

The Earth is a creation; and like all things created in matter, has the tendency to perish; that is, to form within itself that which must eventually be cast off as dross, if the living part is to rise to higher conditions of being. This process, where it leads on the one hand to the subnatural, is, in a sense, as difficult to grasp as what is supernatural. The subnatural also calls for effort and self-sacrifice, for new formulae, new experiments, a new language. When these are found it seems as if a whole new glorious world were being discovered. But it is a world of death. Out of its elements arise the synthetic discoveries, and the robot; and a false mirror-picture of humanity—a " double "—which is allied only to the perishing and the illusory, the calculated and the classified and the mechanistic. In such a world there is no room for the soul of man. It calls into being a lower " threshold ", which, if the spiritual outlook on the other side is lost, can only be crossed as a way that leads eventually into an abyss.

For a long time we have been very certain that two and two make four. But the Cosmos has its own divine incalculability, and may at any moment announce in a voice of thunder that it is not so. This men call " apocalypse "—when the divine Light comes and is inescapable; when the mountains will no longer cover us, nor the shadows of the hills hide us.

The problem what to do and think about Good and Evil has become so tremendous that it profoundly stirs many hearts with a longing for a renewal of the spiritual life. The latter cannot become really fruitful unless the deeper significance of the new age is understood, at least by a few: *it is that the intensification of materialism coincides with the coming of a new Christ-vision.*

Yet how small and insignificant is the general picture of Him that lives in men's thoughts to-day! He, whose slightest gesture could command Nature's every manifestation; whose word could have brought all Heaven's legions to His aid; whose sufferings darkened the Sun and shook the Earth; who said

" All power is given to Me in Earth and Heaven ";
before whom the demons trembled and cried, " We
know Thee who Thou art, the Holy One of God! "

But not only did He possess all power; He was all
wisdom and all love.

He is not an imaginary Being; not an abstract
" principle "—not a mere " representative " of something; but a Being from another realm, who lived
three years in the human body of Jesus of Nazareth.
Having supreme command of life, He " could lay it
down and take it again "—in another form. And in
this other *spiritual* form He is waiting to reveal Himself
visibly to men in the twentieth century.

If this long-expected revelation is fundamentally
rejected, man's physical senses will become more and
more abstract in their perceiving. It will seem to them
that to be able to reduce every phenomenon whether
in man or Nature to a mathematical or chemical
formula, is a magnificent achievement. All is then
" abstracted ", even from Truth. . . . There are two
Mayas, or Great Illusions, not one. The one which the
philosophers and sages of old knew, was the ordinary
world as perceived by the five physical senses; they
called it an illusion because they understood the
spiritual senses, and with them perceived the spiritual
and not the earthly world as the great Reality.

The second *Maya*, which we have now reached, is the
world of calculated abstractions. This lies, not above,
but far below, what is called materialism; and the
climb out of it will be harder, and the suffering greater.

And as for Christianity itself: we have been able
to reach this point in the study of it only because we
have conjured before our eyes so many pictures out of
past ages. Such a review, sincerely and sympa-
thetically undertaken, can give the modern man a

firm assurance that Christianity is not a comparatively recent creation, but the oldest. It rules from the beginning to the end of earthly evolution. Christ was always known by the great seers and teachers, but differently named and differently conceived. The seeds of every religion germinated in His Light.

It is in fact an overwhelming experience in the moment that this becomes clear to anyone. It reveals the reason for the past descent of the spirit of man and the inevitable direction of the future as an ascent. Transubstantiation—the transformation of matter to spirit—is the task of mankind.

But the ascent, like the descent, is a gradual process. No one need feel sceptical about it because it is not patently obvious two thousand years after the beginning of the so-called Christian era. The impetus of the Fall is not even yet arrested; it overruns the turning-point. Ascending and descending impulses are battling with one another still.

Moreover, with the awakening of a new spiritual consciousness, dangers increase. "False Christs and false prophets will arise." But the true Christ will not again be clothed in physical flesh. It is the false Christs who will proclaim themselves in the body. But it is now the eyes of the spirit that have to learn to perceive the risen Christ in the aura of the Earth as St. Paul saw Him. That is the forward step.

Long ages will still pass in denial and doubt and scornful disbelief before mankind as a whole will grasp the true nature of this new human faculty.

What will be there to begin with will be the restless striving towards a new conception of man and the universe; a striving that will be more urgent, more intense, more fraught with contradictions and para-doxes—infinitely vital, inspired or darkened, more merciful and compassionate, yet perhaps more bitter and cruel in personal antagonisms. For the Ego is a two-edged sword! . . . The true and perfect " Ego-ism " is when we make the interests of all other Egos *our own* interests. *This is the only way to all the Freedoms.*

So the near future will undoubtedly present a far greater enigma than the past. A deepening and heightening of consciousness means an increase of human responsibility. And it is utterly essential that we make ourselves capable of recognising, and even remembering, the spiritual currents of history, and to perceive its hitherto hidden processes as the fiery seed of the future.

" The great impulse given by Christ ", says Rudolf Steiner, " which was first foretold and then entered the world, is only now at the beginning of its work; and an even deeper understanding of it must arise. For Christ is so great that each successive epoch must find new methods by which to know and understand Him." . . .

And I saw a new Heaven and a new Earth,
For the first Heaven and the first Earth were passed away.

And the City had no need of the Sun, neither of the Moon
    to shine in it;
For the Glory of the Lord did lighten it
And the Lamb is the LIGHT thereof.

His Countenance was as the Sun shineth in his strength.
And when I saw Him I fell at His feet as dead.
And He laid His right hand upon me, saying unto me:
Fear not.
I am the first and the last.
I am He that liveth and was dead;
And behold, I am alive for evermore. Amen.
And I have the keys of hell and of death.

I am Alpha and Omega, the Beginning and the End.
(From the Revelation of St. John.)

INDEX